FEMININE LAW

FEMININE LAW
Freud, Free Speech, and the Voice of Desire

Jill Gentile
with
Michael Macrone

KARNAC

First published in 2016 by
Karnac Books Ltd
118 Finchley Road
London NW3 5HT

British Library Cataloguing in Publication Data

A C.I.P. for this book is available from the British Library

ISBN-13: 978-1-78220-277-6

Typeset by Medlar Publishing Solutions Pvt Ltd, India

www.karnacbooks.com

For
my parents,
Emile and Helen Gentile:
Between all that was said and all that
remains unsaid, my love and gratitude.

Censor the body and you censor breath and speech at the same time.
Write yourself. Your body must be heard.

—*Hélène Cixous*
The Laugh of the Medusa.
In: Signs. *Vol. 1, No. 4 (Summer 1976),*
pp. 875–893, p. 880.

For millions of years, mankind lived just like the animals. Then some-
thing happened which unleashed the power of our imagination. We
learned to talk and we learned to listen. Speech has allowed the com-
munication of ideas, enabling human beings to work together to build
the impossible. ... All we need to do is make sure we keep talking.

—*Stephen Hawking*
British Telecom television
advertisement, 1993

CONTENTS

ACKNOWLEDGEMENTS

My journey to chart free speech's story, took me (and my fellow traveler, Michael Macrone) to many homes away from home. Seeking to create a space for thought and for writing meant freeing ourselves from the conventions and distractions of our actual homes. And so the book carries (for us) an otherwise unacknowledged sense of place: from Frenchtown, New Jersey to Santa Barbara, California; from Newport to Greenport, from the mountains of Keene and Lake Placid, New York, to the beaches of Sanibel and Shelter Islands; from the mystical magic of Woodstock to the different mystical magic of Big Sur, bookended in a place called "Heaven" in Fire Island. Each granted us serenity and a space to glimpse freedom's home.

But this book's odyssey also led me to spend many solitary weekends in my actual home. Though I welcomed these as offering me the chance to dig deeply into an amazing whirlwind of ideas, I did feel the deprivation that such focus required. Along the way, my friends and family sustained me, honoring that space, distracting me with reminders of the very world I was hoping to speak to. So love buoyed me, as have colleagues who supported me and this project in a variety of ways.

Many thanks to my colleagues in the New York University Postdoctoral Program in Psychotherapy and Psychoanalysis, especially to those in the Independent Track, and to my colleagues at the Institute for the Psychoanalytic Study of Subjectivity in New York City and at the incubating DreamTank. *Das Unbehagen* and its listserv came along, or I found my way to it, at just the right time when I needed an Other, offering an array of voices, Lacanian spins, and unfamiliar thinkers that helped me to deepen and expand this book's narrative. Another voice from farther afield became an increasingly familiar Other, providing unexpected companionship and inspiration: Kevin Stroud's *History of English* podcast instigated our pursuit of etymological links to freedom's speech and free association's story.

My patients too, though they remain unnamed, insinuated their way into this book; their stories and quests helped me to glimpse a common text and to intuit desire's law. I am deeply grateful.

My intellectual homes also house a community of friends who offered enthusiastic support and encouragement that helped me to endure. Among this wide group to whom I give my thanks, several need to be named:

My early mentors, George Atwood and the late Mannie Ghent and Steve Mitchell.

Of my friends and colleagues, all of whom, in various ways, sustained me—directly and indirectly—as the ideas that animate this book evolved, my particular thanks to Michael Guy Thompson, Beatrice Beebe, Jennifer Shortell, Anita Pecorara, Zan Jacobus, Mimi Spiro, Stephanie Manes, Mark Singer, Sarah Mendelsohn, Amy Joelson, Arthur Gray, George Makari, Miki Rahmani, Steven Reisner, Martin Stone, Mari Ruti, Phil Ringstrom, Jim Fosshage, Heather Ferguson, Galit Atlas, Lew Aron, Mark Gerald, Barbra Locker, Jamieson Webster, Seth Warren, Katie Gentile, Steven Knoblauch, and members, past and present, of my study groups. Great thanks also to Mal Slavin for his abiding friendship and for joining me in my psychoanalytic journey. Deirdre Day's and David Klugman's paintings transformed distracted Googling into revitalizing excursions. I felt that David's "In Hiding" was meant for this book. Sydney Hyman offered visual inspirations for the book's cover, while Angie Riley's vision of agency guided me. Also invaluable were my siblings, Laurie Gentile, Patty Coutu, and Vin Gentile, and friendships with Susan Buchanan, Seth Jacobson, Toby Knobel, Holly Kowitt, Pia Garcia, and Rosemary Smith, who, along with my loving family, tolerated my prolonged absences, rooted for me to sustain my fidelity to this project but also compelled me to occasionally come up for air. Mary Ryan and Joe Cohn provided not only the welcome flicker of conversation—philosophical, mundane, and silly—but also many shared cups of tea. Pasquale Pasquino and John Ferejohn inspired me with sparkling conversation over equally inspiring food and wine, and introduced me to authors and ideas that found their way onto these pages.

Michael Cader and David Levin offered generous guidance through the labyrinth of finding a publisher. Thanks to Karnac Books who became that publisher, taking a chance and providing a home for this book and its ambitious scope, quirkily situated between psychoanalysis and a panoply of other discourses. Constance Govindin, Rod Tweedy, and Cecily Blench helped each step of the way, with graciousness and grace. Thorina Rose's illustration graced the book's cover design, both capturing and freeing my vision with her own unique aesthetic.

My heartfelt thanks to Steve Botticelli for his exceptional friendship during this process, and, along with my dear friends Mike Britton, Diane Coutu, Deirdre Day, David Lichtenstein, Tracy Morgan, Rebecca Coffey, Laurie Gentile, Mort Milder, Esther Sperber, and Evan Malater, for providing generous and insightful readings and editorial guidance. Jonathan Shedler offered resources, insights, and humor into psychoanalysis's contemporary ontological condition. I am very grateful that my writing of this book has been supported by a grant from the Psychoanalytic Society of the Postdoctoral Program, Inc.

My thanks to editors, friends, and colleagues, Bill Coburn, Jay Greenberg, Don Greif, Ruth Livingston, Elliot Jurist, David Lichtenstein, Sally Bjorkland, and Steve Kuchuck who helped me improve essays submitted for journal publication. Specific thanks to the publishers of *The Psychoanalytic Quarterly; Psychoanalytic Perspectives, Contemporary Psychoanalysis, Psychoanalytic Psychology,* and *Division/ Review* for granting permission to use prior publications (listed below) in this volume.

Evan Malater's contributions belong in a category of their own. Evan's passionate and acrobatic thinking on free association, a topic of his own compelling, original scholarship, insinuated itself into these pages, as did some of his poetic turns of phrase.

Jonathan Slavin, though he will not recognize the fact, long ago inspired my thoughts about "Having No Thoughts"—the title he gave a talk in response to my own protestations of muteness. That talk spawned, these many years later, what would become a chapter in this book. That chapter, along with Jonathan's sustaining deep, incomparable friendship and shared interest in theorizing agency, provided the early kindling for this book.

Jeff Pusar has been through it all, shining light with a lantern of compassion and fortitude to my quest for words. I'd be in the woods forever otherwise. Words remain inadequate to express my deep gratitude.

Jane Ackerman and I, years ago, together found our way to an early love of psychoanalysis and rediscovered each other in the course of her profound gift in reading and editing this manuscript. Committed to my hopes, and to my journey, Jane copyedited the smallest details and helped me to elucidate its biggest ideas, all on a tight budget of time. I am deeply grateful for her generosity, grace, and perceptive intelligence.

Above all, Michael Macrone found a way to lure this book from its inchoate place in my mind, to a real, genuine "space between." His intellectual agility and gift with words and ideas are unsurpassed. Michael's endurance, imagination, compassion, and commitment made it possible for me to carry this book from conception to fruition. If there is a labor of love, this book is a reflection every bit as much of his labor as his love. My heartfelt appreciation and love.

Permissions acknowledgements

Gentile, J. (2016). What is special about speech? *Psychoanalytic Psychology, 33*: 73–88. Copyright American Psychological Association. Adapted with permission.

Gentile, J. (2016). Naming the vagina, naming the woman. *Division/Review,* no. 13 (Winter 2016). Copyright American Psychological Association. Adapted with permission.

Gentile, J. (2015). Parrhesia, Phaedra, and the polis: Anticipating psychoanalytic free association as democratic practice. *Psychoanalytic Quarterly, 84*: 589–624. Copyright The Psychoanalytic Quarterly, Wiley.

Gentile, J. (2015). On having no thoughts: Freedom and feminine space. *Psychoanalytic Perspectives, 12*: 3, 227–251. Copyright Taylor and Francis.

Gentile, J. (2016). On spatial metaphors and free association: Phallic fantasy and vaginal primacy. *Contemporary Psychoanalysis, 52* DOI: 10.1080/0010 7530.2016.1101563. Copyright Taylor and Francis.

Excerpt from HÉLÈNE CIXOUS: "COMING TO WRITING" AND OTHER ESSAYS, edited by Deborah Jenson, with an Introductory Essay by Susan Rubin Suleiman, translated by Sarah Cornell, Deborah Jenson, Ann

Jill Gentile is on the faculty of the NYU Postdoctoral Program in Psychotherapy and Psychoanalysis, and a training and supervising analyst at the Institute for the Psychoanalytic Study of Subjectivity in New York. She is a corresponding editor of *Contemporary Psychoanalysis* and on the editorial board of the *International Journal of Psychoanalytic Self Psychology*. Her essays, describing a semiotic and phenomenological trajectory of agency, desire, and symbolic life, have been published in many psychoanalytic journals. A founding member of the DreamTank collective, dedicated to the application of psychoanalysis to democracy and to the public sphere, she is a practicing psychoanalyst and clinical psychologist in Highland Park, New Jersey and in Manhattan, New York. She attended Brown University and earned her PhD at the University of Rochester.

Michael Macrone, currently the Chief Technology Officer at Publishers-Marketplace.com, has authored nine books on language, literature, and ideas, including *Brush Up Your Shakespeare!* and *Eureka! (a.k.a. A Little Knowledge)*. He has bachelor's degrees from Brown University in

Semiotics and Mathematics, and a PhD in English from the University of California, Berkeley. He has taught Web Design at the California College of Art, and his work as an interactive designer has earned numerous awards.

PREFACE

This book began as a project to open new pathways, new spaces between—between fields, between subjects, between discourses. It also began as the expression of a symptom, a symptom of psychoanalysis's solipsistic confinement and, to my mind, of the world's seeming desperation to find its way to the analyst's metaphoric couch.

But the book also began, as all symptoms may begin, with my need to speak in a space that extends beyond mere solipsism and beyond the body's closed loop of symptoms, and also beyond the microcultures of clinical practice and of professional conversation. But these microcultures are not just confining. Their discourse delves deeply into crevices ordinarily unexposed in conventional conversation. We psychoanalysts practice at the margins of culture and society, in the crevices between conscious and obscured, even unconscious, knowledge. Psychoanalysis has always dwelt in these crevices, these cracks. Perhaps it has to.

Yet over the past several years I've become convinced that psychoanalysis is central to our political and cultural life. Beyond that, and perhaps improbably (given its aristocratic and, to some degree, authoritarian image), psychoanalysis has much to contribute to a theory of democracy. In these pages, I try to justify that grand notion by focusing on what I believe are the core ideas and core practices of psychoanalysis and democracy: free association and free speech, which occupy a shared space, an insecure place of possibility.

I believe this is a newly emerging—and as such, a rarely explored—idea, and one likely to be met with some skepticism. But psychoanalysis's recently renewed, sometimes exuberant if also cautionary, engagement with the world beyond the consulting room has positioned it to build new bridges between disciplines and discourses. I've wondered what might emerge as I try, as we try, to speak to a new audience, one that may not yet exist, as it only might emerge as we meet, as we come into being, meeting anew, from similarly frustrated conversations and intellectual cul de sacs. I hope this project contributes to that mission.

A few chapters herein, plus sections of others, are devoted to how the United States Constitution and its First Amendment has been interpreted and applied over the centuries. I approach this topic not as a trained historian, legal scholar, or political scientist, but as someone compelled to grapple with it as my own ideas about free speech and democratic transition incubated in the clinic. Small revelations accumulated over the countless hours of clinical listening and interaction that mark the course of my career. These grew into larger revelations and recognizable patterns of how psychoanalysis illuminates democratic empowerment. It became clear to me that this empowerment hinges on the growth of personal agency and the claiming of free speech. As my patients and I struggle toward this goal in our sessions, stomping together through the challenging terrain of bruised egos and mutual longings, we endure matters of heart and mind, suffering and despair, defeat, and even (eventual) victories. This endurance inspires me to begin speaking in these pages, close to home and far, of free speech.

One thing you'll discover as you follow my argument is that as psychoanalysis has evolved, its ideas have diversified, and its core tenets are sometimes disputed. When I speak of contemporary psychoanalysis I will often favor what is known as the "relational" paradigm. However, many relational analysts won't recognize as theirs my amalgam of theory and practice, because my influences (like theirs) span a diverse range of spectacular voices in our field. My work finds its home in some space among Freud and Jacques Lacan, D. W. Winnicott, Wilfred Bion, Julia Kristeva, Heinz Kohut, Thomas Ogden, and Jessica Benjamin, among many others. My particular relationships to these thinkers, as well as my clinical experiences, have resulted in a personal psychoanalytic "idiom," to borrow from Christopher Bollas. The idioms of other schools and disciplines, especially attachment theory, developmental semiotics and phenomenology, critical feminist theory, and recent currents in speculative realism, also find their way into my description of psychoanalysis, mirroring how my clinical experience led me into forays that created new alliances and new conversations.

And so my portrait of psychoanalysis is ultimately and inevitably also a personal composite, responsible to its history and its literature but also inflected by my own vision of its potential. When I tell stories of my clinical work, I will describe choices and rationales that will in some ways resemble, but in other ways vary, perhaps unsettlingly, from the stories a different analyst would tell. Sigmund Freud makes regular appearances in these pages, as do a number of other theorists, better and less known, historical and contemporary. I try to situate their ideas in what I call a *space between*: a space for dialogue, a *third* space.

The space between is the heroine of this story. However variously psychoanalysts have come to describe it, most of us intend to signify a space that lies between the patient and analyst. But we also mean a space that lies beyond their shared construction and thus which belongs, paradoxically, to each and to both, that is, all, of us. To my way of thinking, it also has its own transcendent—material and (energetic) spiritual—status. This third space is one that you'll be hearing a lot about in the pages to follow.

Some of you are probably wondering at this point what I mean by the "feminine law" of my title. Just as feminine law at first told me its story almost inaudibly, in murmurs, before speaking to me with increased intensity as this text evolved, this book will tell that tale, though it won't do so immediately or obviously. If psychoanalysis offers us any truth, that truth was founded upon the obscured voices and bodies of women and so finding the most revealing and generative form for that truth will take some time and thought. I hope that if you sustain the odyssey traced by this book, the conclusions I reach will repay your investment.

You may read the book in its intended sequence or otherwise; follow my lead or your own meandering desires and interests. For me, this journey began with personal (and idiosyncratic!) fascinations and questions, but it quickly came to include author Michael Macrone, who soon became my de facto editor. Michael stepped into the fray in such an immersive way that the book became a far more collaborative venture. He has helped me enormously to harness my meandering ideas, by challenging them and helping me to create narrative coherence and momentum, and engaging and doing battle with me through a staggering number of visions and revisions, and by endowing the book with his own grace, style, and inflections, be they etymological, editorial, or otherwise.

My wish is that you, our reader, make it your own encounter as much as it has been one between us and a set of ideas and the panoply of rich thinkers who have espoused these ideas. The book, after all, is a story of free association and free speech. It is a story of the ever-elusive quest to claim that freedom, and one's own singularity of desire and agency, in our paradoxically free and conditioned encounters with you, with the Other. It is the story of a space, essential and yet intangible, that conditions our listening and speaking. And it is the story of Desire's voice and democratizing telos as she finds movement and freedom in that space. Let's gather in whatever fashion we do, as we together contemplate free speech and free assembly as a matter—and therapeutic action—priceless to both psychoanalytic and democratic pursuit. Perhaps we will find each other on and between these pages.

INTRODUCTION

Psychoanalysis and democracy have at least one thing in common: a signature commitment to freedom of thought and speech. This book aims to describe how the psychological discipline and the political system aim at common goals, from angles that sometimes converge and sometimes diverge. I will explore how free speech, in democratic society, and free association, in psychoanalysis, share much beyond that essential if aspirational adjective, "free." Their origins are strikingly similar, and they share a particular intellectual DNA. Ultimately, we will find that both psychoanalysis and democracy locate freedom in a particular "space," that is, in a metaphorical territory for open encounter. I call this the "space between."

This fundamental space is governed by what I will call a "feminine law." In psychoanalysis, the story that links gender and speech begins with Sigmund Freud's relationship to his female patients and extends to current conflicts over sexual roles and gender identity. Perhaps surprisingly, democracy has always, from its origins to the present, grappled with how to handle female speech and female desire. Though my conscious intent in writing this book had been to illuminate the mutual resonances between psychoanalytic free association and democratic free speech, another story emerged: The story of how the space of speech, its silent, receptive, and ultimately feminine foundation, gives rise to desire's voice and to the voice of democratic desire.

Let's begin telling this story by introducing the two basic terms that shall appear throughout: *free association* and *free speech*.

In psychoanalysis, "free association" is the name for a patient's unguided and uncensored thoughts, or rather for the *articulation* of those thoughts. Freud, who founded psychoanalysis, came to regard it as "the science of unconscious mental processes" (Freud, 1925d, p. 70). He discovered free association as the pathway by which people, in surrendering to their unconscious (thoughts not necessarily of their own choosing), can claim agency for their own minds and bodies, creating the possibility for self-determination. It is the pathway by which we question and deconstruct the tyranny of imposed meanings in favor of expressive freedom. Its practice sets in motion, as the French psychoanalyst and theorist Julia Kristeva (2007, p. 431) puts it, an "infinitesimal revolution."

When I discuss "free speech" in this book, I sometimes refer to any unconstrained discourse, sometimes to what's regarded as the natural human right to express (political or personal) beliefs and desires. However, what I mean by "free speech" also refers particular right to freedom of thought and expression as envisioned by the Founding Fathers of American democracy, and to how that right has evolved to be understood over the course of U.S. Constitutional history. By "Founding Fathers" I refer to those men who emerged from the American Revolution to form the first United States government. Many of these same men would contribute to the U.S. Constitution; in that role, I sometimes more precisely call them "Framers" of the Constitution and, specifically, of the Bill of Rights. To these men, perhaps especially to James Madison, free speech, the right to voice one's views without fear of government reprisal, was at the heart of democracy and essential to the viability of the new government. It was valued not only as a basic human right, but as assurance that individual expression, particularly political and religious expression, would be a matter of self-determination and not be subject to governmental incursion or tyranny. Although I mainly refer to how free speech protections have evolved in the context of the U.S. Constitution and its First Amendment, I aspire to define what is essential for the flourishing of free speech across human (and geopolitical) contexts.

These are the basic and original understandings of psychoanalysis's and democracy's fundamental principles or "rules." So what is the analogy between them, historical or contemporary? Where do they stand today, and how may we assess their records on freedom?

Psychoanalysis and its rivals

The story of psychoanalysis may, from the broadest perspective, be seen as one of rise and fall. It may have taken a few decades to emerge from obscurity and surmount opprobrium, but then Freud's new science was on a roll, at least for a short while. Following Freud's visit to Clark University in 1909, psychoanalysis achieved widespread visibility in North America. Hungarian analyst Sándor Ferenczi was full of optimism as he wrote Freud a hubristic letter in 1914, boasting that "it will be easy for us … to disable our antagonists (who are certainly not even oriented to [its] elements …)" (Falzeder & Brabant, 1993, pp. 551–552). And it is true that psychoanalysis gained in prestige and credibility after the Great War, and again after World War II—within and outside academia, within and outside mental health disciplines. In the United States, organized psychiatry claimed the mantle of psychoanalysis for physician-psychoanalysts (under the auspices of the American Psychoanalytic Association, until a landmark lawsuit in 1988 opened the doors to non-physicians). An influx of immigrant analysts from Europe, fleeing Nazi persecution, further swelled the ranks, as did the graduates of new training institutes and programs. Psychoanalytic research (largely conducted by psychologists) was hitting its stride in the 1940s and 1950s (Bornstein, 2001, p. 5). As early as 1953, the growing numbers of practicing psychoanalysts caused concern that the supply of analysts might outstrip the population's demands (Knight, 1953, p. 206).

That preoccupation is remarkable from a contemporary vantage point whence, as I shall discuss below, psychoanalysis is often devalued and deemed irrelevant to the culture. But it also signaled a growing institutional orthodoxy that had begun to characterize the field. Arguments over who was eligible for training and over what qualified as officially sanctioned doctrine led a number of members who espoused unconventional views to resign. The unbecoming nature of the field's ever-present insularity and schisms prompted this lament by Robert Knight in his 1953 address to the American Psychoanalytic Association:

> The spectacle of a national association of physicians and scientists feuding with each other over training standards and practices, and calling each other orthodox and conservative or deviant and

dissident, is not an attractive one, to say the least. Such terms belong
to religions, or to fanatical political movements, and not to science
and medicine. Psychoanalysis should be neither a "doctrine" nor a
"party line." Perhaps we are still standing too much in the shadow
of that giant, Sigmund Freud, to permit ourselves to view psychoanalysis as a science of the mind rather than as the doctrine of a
founder. (Knight, 1953, p. 210)

By the 1960s and 1970s, as Robert Bornstein (2001, p. 4) dramatically
puts it, "without warning, it all fell apart. As the behavioral, biological, and cognitive perspectives grew … the influence of psychoanalysis
waned." Ferenczi's assessment was wrong: clearly not all antagonists
would be bested, nor all resistance overcome. Resistance and ridicule
have in fact been a constant in the field's history—with respect to its
professional practices and legitimacy, its scientific validity, its claims to
knowledge. Freud himself would not have been surprised: He foresaw
that psychoanalysis, insofar as it would both animate and threaten society, would inevitably be shunted from the mainstream and would have
to struggle for its very survival. In George Makari's words,

Since it destroyed sicknesses that society in part created, psychoanalysis would be seen as the public's enemy. "Because we destroy
illusions, we are accused of endangering ideals," Freud warned. Psychoanalysts, it seemed, were fated to be gadflies and outcasts, carry-
ing out a message no one wanted to hear. (Makari, 2008, p. 245)

And yet Freud's psychoanalysis might, perhaps more radically, one day
garner social acceptability. As Makari goes on to say, "It was a liberal's
dream: increasing rational control over unreason and furthering
individual emancipation. And it called for nothing more than the
practice of psychoanalysis: it would be a revolution from the couch"
(ibid., p. 245).

It was a revolution that would meet its counter-revolution, several
times over. Today there are scattered markers that augur a renewed
vibrancy and engagement with the public (e.g. the *New York Times* has
launched a popular series, "Couch," dedicated to stories from within
the consulting room). If this is the case, it would counter a longstand-
ing reversal of fortune. Beginning in the 1970s, the narrative of rise
had given way to a narrative of fall, one that has often been measured

against Freud's attempt to position psychoanalysis as a natural science (a move that spawned a prodigious and ongoing debate). In the mid–1980s, to take a fairly well-known example, Adolf Grunbaum (1984) challenged psychoanalysis's empirical claims and its validity as a science. While Grunbaum's critics denounced his critiques as extremely reductive of Freud's thought, some damage was done. The damage would be amplified by Jeffrey Moussaieff Masson's contemporaneous assault on Freud, whom he claimed had assaulted the truth by suppressing evidence of childhood sexual abuse in order to promote his own theories. The challenges of Grunbaum, Masson, and others would, after about a decade, culminate in a *Time* magazine cover story questioning the theories and practical benefits of psychoanalysis: "Is Freud Dead?" (*Time*, 1993).

Doubts about psychoanalysis gained traction, even among those wary of the Freud-bashers' motives. The question, for example, of whether psychoanalysis is a "real" science had been a point of controversy long before Grunbaum, even and perhaps especially to Freud himself. Much hinges on matters of definition—of reality, of science, of unconscious elements—and on matters of epistemology. The debate centers on whether the field is best classified as an interpretive or hermeneutic enterprise, with its home among the humanities rather than among the physical sciences, or vice versa. Others, myself included, believe this is a false dichotomy and that psychoanalysis is best understood as situated in a space between the arts and the sciences. In any event, as Harold Blum reflects, "the present state of theoretical competition, confusion, internal contradiction, and occasional internecine family feuds has likely contributed to the major decline in academic and public regard and respect for psychoanalysis" (Blum, 2011, p. 597).

Psychologist Jonathan Shedler has done much to rebut the skeptics and to advance psychoanalytic claims to legitimacy. Using meta-analytic techniques to align disparate findings with a common metric, Shedler (2010) has demonstrated that the treatment efficacy of "psychodynamic therapy" certainly compares favorably with that of treatments touted as "empirically supported" or "evidence based." In fact, empirical support for psychoanalysis as a valid treatment model had existed for some time prior to Shedler's revelations. Yet critics have long challenged these studies, disputing what they actually demonstrate. This is not a battle psychoanalysis seems destined to win any time soon despite continued uphill traction. In this day and age, as the British analyst Peter Fonagy sums it up,

> In observational studies there are great limitations, because everything is effective. Psychoanalytic psychotherapy is effective, Cognitive-Behavioral Therapy (CBT) is effective, swimming with dolphins is effective, and all of these are effective treatments. What you can't tell from this is what is actually working. (Jurist, 2010, p. 4)

Nonetheless, psychoanalysis is often compared invidiously to cognitive behavioral therapy (CBT) and pharmaceutical interventions. Both emerge as psychoanalysis's chief rivals, and both shine with the luster of so-called empirical validity and scientific credentialing, including those touted by a pharmaceutical industry propped up by its massive economic infusions into ostensibly valid, but often deceptively framed, drug treatment efficacy studies (see Kirsh, 2010). In the battles over scientific turf, state funding, and private sponsorship, a host of various fashionable and initially endowed variants (Electromagnetic field therapy (EMFT); Dialectical Behavior Therapy (DBT); Eye Movement Desensitization and Reprocessing therapy (EMDR)), emerge as allies of CBT. That these models also draw inspiration from psychoanalytic insights and use techniques compatible with many psychoanalytic assumptions (Shedler, 2010, p. 107) is a fact often glossed over in a media and professional culture that favors quick fixes and that seeks to distance itself from a practice "tainted" by its associations with psychoanalysis. And psychoanalysis has a hard time marketing itself, given its labor-intensive practices, its often qualitative ("soft") data, and its frequently high cost, in terms of both time and money. It has been rather unsuccessful (thus far) at publicizing results such as those of Shedler, who concludes that "the benefits of psychodynamic treatment are lasting and not just transitory and appear to extend well beyond symptom remission. For many people, psychodynamic therapy may foster inner resources and capacities that allow richer, freer, and more fulfilling lives" (2010, p. 107).

Meanwhile, serious mental illness costs America $193.2 billion in lost earnings per year (National Alliance on Mental Illness, 2013). To a culture in crisis—a culture marked by disturbingly high and rising tides of depression, anxiety, post-traumatic stress, insomnia, sleep disturbances, and a host of other symptoms[1]—there is an undoubted allure to pharmaceutical solutions for emotional maladies. But our increasing reliance on pills seems to spell the demise of psychoanalysis and of its signature practice of talking. Paul Stepansky, editor until it closed of *The Analytic Press,* one of the last publishing houses dedicated to psychoanalytic writing, has called psychoanalysts to account for the field's "self-encapsulating nature"—arguing that this insularity contributes to its marginalization (Strenger, 2010). Compounding this insularity is the disenfranchisement (in the U.S.) of psychoanalysis from academic departments of psychology, which (to a large degree) have rejected training in clinical psychoanalysis (Masling, 2000).

By contrast, psychoanalysis remains vibrant in exile, having found itself courted by departments of literature, media studies, anthropology, critical studies, gender studies, history, linguistics, and more. It is my impression, that—while and perhaps because psychoanalysis inevitably poses a provocative challenge to the culture—a curiosity and desire to learn about it will always prosper, wherever its seeds are planted. Furthermore, from a global perspective, especially outside the Anglo-American world (for example, in France and South America), the field appears healthy, even prosperous.[2] Doug Kirsner (2000), surveying the persistent appeal of psychoanalysis in these countries, shows that psychoanalysis is not only firmly rooted in academic departments of psychology, but broadly disseminated, knitted into the fabric of cultural and intellectual life and public debate. In these cultures, psychoanalysis isn't merely a technique; it's a philosophical approach to human nature. But its popularity abroad is scant comfort at home.

Many psychoanalysts in the U.S. are chastened and dispirited by the current climate, and they struggle to speak (and be heard) in a healthcare economy in which the very idea that healing requires the cultivation of a sharing and trusting relationship is dismissed in favor of algorithms and manualized treatment models. Little credit accrues from data showing that investments in mental health care and prevention offset medical costs, as well as the social costs of untreated depression and the attendant economic costs (by way of lost productivity—see Langlieb & Kahn, 2005). Some practice from what psychoanalyst Christopher Bollas (2013) describes as a position of defensive retreat a cautious, apologetic psychoanalysis.

And so psychoanalysis finds itself at the margins. It speaks from the margins. But—as this book aims to show—that is the source of its power. What it leverages, through human relationship, is remarkably accessible and would be available to nearly everyone were it not for real problems of unequal distribution of speech opportunities. Psychoanalysis achieves its results through a remarkably human, non-technological practice of talking freely, of *free association*.

Indeed, from the vantage point of those who trust in the eternal validity of psychoanalytic practice—its fitness to survive for all times and for all time—there is tremendous passion, inspiration, and inventiveness in the field today. Even if psychoanalysis has lost some cultural significance, as it has within the United States, many psychoanalytic practitioners, patients, and enthusiasts believe that it will always have a place within the culture, because it continues to be effective and because its methods reveal knowledge that is subjectively *and* objectively valid. Here is how psychoanalyst and journal editor William Coburn describes the current scene:

> The cry for evidence-based treatments seems not to be deterring psychoanalysts and their respective patients from enjoying the discovery of their own personal odysseys …. Doubtless psychoanalysis, given its intense diversification of theories and sensibilities, could have Dodo-like perished in its tracks by now. But its continuing success strangely may lie in psychoanalysis' recognition that, indeed, each analysand, each person, is utterly unique and individual, each requiring a different clinical sensibility to reap the rewards of a therapeutic relationship. (Coburn, 2010, pp. 369–370)

Coburn indicates the robust and intuitive synergy between relational, contextualist impulses that characterize contemporary psychoanalysis, and the rise of the science of complexity that embraces chaotic and emergent phenomena. Psychoanalysts everywhere speak (even if in hushed, diffident tones) of a set of ideas and practices that seek to rouse patients from a kind of wakeful slumber, and that help them fulfill dreams of liberation and deep transformation.

Democracy and its rivals

Once seen as pernicious and recently teetering on the edge of irrelevance, psychoanalysis might seem to share little with democracy, which has proved to produce (relatively) stable social systems, and which—despite its own wildly oscillating and perhaps waning popularity—is now deemed relevant to nearly all. Regardless of their comparative fortunes, at the core they share a goal of freedom from repression. Each was conceived as a means of liberating people from repressive forces, of releasing otherwise censored or repressed opinions and desires—political or religious or even (as in Freud's thought) sexual or murderous. While psychoanalysis aims to cultivate individual emancipation, democracy aims for majority rule, though of course this is compatible with and may require the advancement of individual liberties and their protection from the tyranny of the majority. In any case, liberation, either of the individual or of the collective will, always involves pushing back against some counterforce, natural or artificial, and such counterforces tend to be stubborn. The call to freedom yields to conflicting, even contradictory, impulses, and then to endless contest. It would seem unsurprising then that neither psychoanalysis nor democracy has ever earned itself unquestioned legitimacy.

Psychoanalysis has had to assert and reassert its legitimacy for a mere hundred and twenty-some years, if we date it to the publication of Freud and Breuer's *Studies on Hysteria* in 1895. Democracy, on the other hand, has been at it for two and a half millennia, ever since Kleisthenes reformed the Athenian constitution in 507 B.C.E. to place the power of political choice in the hands of the "demos." It did not enjoy an auspicious birth. Our memories of Athens' political experiment tend to be both rosy and dim; we forget the internal contention and the ultimate external defeat. All of Pericles' (or rather Thucydides') inspiring rhetoric could not save Athens from itself or from Sparta.

Modern democracies trace back to American and French, rather than Greek, models, and these models have enjoyed a far more sustained success. This success is partly due to modern democracy's claim to advance "natural law," which was a core principal of the Enlightenment philosophy that inspired revolt against arbitrary power. Philosophy on its own has never toppled a king, but by the time of the American revolution, even those who'd never heard of Spinoza or Locke could still consider democracy "the most natural of all regimes," as it comes "closest to preserving the freedom which nature allows to human beings" (Dunn, 2005, pp. 66–67).

Ideas of natural law and innate rights would not just inspire revolt; they would also find their way into that enduring document, the

United States Constitution. They were tempered, though, in order to palliate those who thought the ideas nice but the application unpredictable. Some of the Founding Fathers, notably James Madison, were antipathetic to the notion of pure democracy and its threat of mob rule. So the drafters of the Constitution proposed an alternate formula for representative government that differed significantly from direct rule, but which nonetheless paved the way for a modern conception of democracy that was not only self-sustaining but ultimately inspirational.

Since then, democracy has been on the rise, but it has also experienced setbacks along the way. It lost a good deal of forward momentum, for instance, in the wake of its near total collapse in most newly liberated Soviet republics and client states. As our world today grows increasingly polarized, democracy has come to seem less a neutral and universally appealing ideal and more as a wedge by which certain cultures threaten to undermine certain other cultures. Moreover, in some cases, despite appearances, democracy's "success" depends upon the exclusion of "a vast number of fellow citizens in the hinterland from a decent share in the political and economic life of the nation" (Meaney & Mounk, 2014). David Harvey documents how democracy's entanglement with unregulated capitalism renders it but "a mask for practices that are all about the maintenance, reconstitution, and restoration of elite class power" (Harvey, 2005, p. 188). The term has been further degraded as it has been appropriated by many false claimants, including demagogues and aspiring tyrants, who use it to cloak their abuses.

It is questionable whether the term "democracy" any longer has a consistent or coherent meaning. At the least, actual, direct democracy—true rule by the people (as opposed to rule by detached representatives)—has become improbable and undesirable in today's populous, expansive, and complicated world. One might even say that we have given up the "dream of ruling ourselves" (Meaney & Mounk, 2014)—a dream that Freud had for humanity but also came to recognize as an impossible aspiration, and one that many people do not even want for themselves (Freud, 1927c).

Even so, despite burgeoning government incursions and surveillance, and despite the increasingly unchecked power of corporations to buy influence and subvert basic equality, representative democracy has no near rival as a system of government. In the words of political theorist (and gimlet-eyed democracy champion) John Dunn, "It is hard to exaggerate the singularity and mystery of democracy's rise to a global ascendancy, which, however disputed it may still be, is unmatched by any previous category the purports to shape political experience" (Dunn, 2014, p. 47). Dunn attributes this "global comparative advantage" to its "power to recruit allies and quell rivals" (ibid., pp. 41, 40), a power stemming from democracy's recognition of its citizenry "not merely as notional bearers of ultimate authority, but also as site of power in themselves, with a capacity to act and exert force on their own behalf" (Dunn, 2005, p. 133). This opportunity to assume responsibility for our own authority also entails our responsibility "to share, on notionally equal terms, in selecting the person or persons who is going to deploy it" (Dunn, 2014, p. 18).

Dunn's compelling narrative is music to a psychoanalyst's ears. Whereas Freud had revealed that the ego is *not* master of its own house, Dunn alerts us to "the distinctive imaginative deceptions" of democracy, specifically our tendency to fall into the "hypnotic spell" of over-authorizing our sovereignty. Beyond that, democracy's story, as he tells it, is actually the story of personal and political, individual and collective, agency. Furthermore, Dunn—possibly channeling Freud—tells the story of the *word* "democracy" itself: of that word's "spectacular" diffusion (2005, p. 137); its translation, interpretation, presumptive authority, enigmatic and elusive meaning; and of our complicated relationship with it, including what psychoanalysts refer to as our "transference" to it. Or, to borrow a phrase from French psychoanalyst Jean LaPlanche (1989, p. 126), it is the story of democracy as a quintessential "enigmatic signifier." It is the story of a word that defies any facile translation or interpretation, a word that inspires renewed efforts to grapple with what it means and what it authorizes. In short, the historical fate of democracy runs parallel to the fate of the word "democracy" itself, "in all its complexity and opacity."

The bewilderingly complex social and political forces that inculcate the word so deeply in our lexicons, and across so many languages and cultures, also saturate and burden the word with confusion. But Dunn's analysis of the enduring status of the word "democracy" prompts attention to a larger project: the conjunction between psychoanalysis and democracy and their shared commitments to speech. By studying this conjunction, we might find a path for psychoanalysis—beyond insinuating itself deeply into the lexicons of its adherents—to claim its own enduring cultural relevance and validity.

Psychoanalysis and democracy: basic principles

While everyone speaks of democracy at least casually and anyone in public life must address themselves to it, few casually ponder psychoanalysis, and the term has fallen out of everyday conversation.

And yet psychoanalysis may be the very theory that can make the most sense of democracy's story. First of all, as I hope to demonstrate here, psychoanalysis's true calling is to democratize desire—to unchain desire from its conditioned servility, to liberate desire to speak freely, through free association. The dispersal of the word "democracy," the word's very sovereignty and sheer resistance to subjugation, may be read from a psychoanalytic perspective as the story of desire's democratic impulse. Democracy emerges as the symbol of a people (in the civic sense) speaking freely, of "the people in their full sovereign indefinition" (Dunn, 2014, p. 28, citing Lenin!), signifying freedom just as it signifies desire.

The stories of democracy and of psychoanalysis each pivot on ideas and practices of freedom of speech and expression: they share many conditions, aims, and obstacles. As the Russian émigré psychoanalyst Moshe Wulff noted, "Where there is no freedom of speech, there can be no psychoanalysis" (cited in Zaretsky, 2004, p. 223).[3] Even more obviously, without freedom of speech there can be no democracy. So why have the two so seldom been considered together?

Let us note as a start that the analogy between (psychoanalytic) free association and (democratic) free speech, while persuasive enough to inspire this book, is nonetheless flawed on several counts. For my purposes here, I will treat them as closely affiliated in order to signify both that free association is that method whereby the patient speaks her unedited mental contents in an address to another; and that it is the means by which the patient claims that freedom of conscience essential to any valid claim to free speech. But there is an important distinction, not always explicit in my narrative: elemental free associations, more than sincere free speech, lie very near to unconscious, interior mentation. As I will explore in some detail, free association requires the patient to consent to frank, honest, and uncensored speech while simultaneously impelling her on an elusive and ever-undermined quest for true freedom, true speech. This is a quest, at the border of unconscious and conscious intentionality, to which the patient must commit if she is ever to acquire a sense of personal agency and sovereignty.

In other words, in analysis the patient is presumed to both assert and not to assert her free speech privilege. In her conflicted quest to claim her freedom of thought, and her free speech rights, the patient is assured of a partner, one that she both resists and insists upon. The patient does not only speak to herself; she aims her associations (however inadvertently) at an authentic (if only implicitly recognized or, even, actively disregarded) Other—the analyst. This Other, like the patient, will bypass conventional forms of social address for the sake of cultivating a distinctly psychoanalytical conversation.

By contrast, free speech, as per the First Amendment, is a "right" that protects expression against incursions by the government. Though I will overwhelmingly focus on the free speech clause (as much of First Amendment jurisprudence also has), its affiliation with other foundational ideas—freedom of conscience, press, association, assembly, and petition—creates what Burt Neuborne describes as a coherent and poetic "contrapuntal interplay between the collective practice of democracy and individual liberty" (Neuborne, 2015, p. 2). However, a beautiful and powerful blueprint, in itself, does not ensure that its design is realized. In civil society, the potential speaker may or may not recognize herself as possessing a free speech right, or as owning that right with a responsibility to the collective. She may or may not choose to exercise this right. She may not have ready access to a speech platform or audience. She may not know how, where, or when to engage in political speech outside of the implicit speech of casting a vote, for or against proposals that may be only distantly related to her needs, or for or against candidates to whom she otherwise likely has little direct access. Whether the citizen's speech is heard by an Other will be (to some large degree) a matter of privilege, both in terms of opportunity to find an audience, and in terms of position inside a context where her speech is meaningful and socially recognized.

While the right to free speech is given, its exercise must be actively assumed. Expressive liberty and civic engagement require active agency, yet the obstacles to claiming that agency remain daunting. Though the Constitution, by means of the First Amendment, asserts "sweepingly phrased" individual free speech rights (Abrams, 2013, p. 358), it does not require citizens to vote, nor commit itself to empowering the speaker's agency or to protecting the hearer's rights. However, it does name an ally in the right and responsibility to expose and to check abuses of power in this process: a free press. Like the analyst's function vis-à-vis the patient, the press has a special responsibility to serve the public interest, both by disseminating speech and by protecting hearers' access to a diversity of voices. (The press, by informing citizens about matters of civic concern, helps them to be well-positioned to bestow authority upon, or remove authority from, their governmental representatives.)

U.S. federal appeals courts have spent considerable time, over the past century, deliberating exactly how much freedom the American Constitution guarantees, or even contemplates, in its Bill of Rights. Various amendments have been the occasion of controversy, the First being a prime example. These controversies extend well beyond the courts; they are a persistent and characteristic feature of our political discourse, and of the political discourse of any nation with democratic aspirations. We use our freedom of speech to argue about how free our speech should be. How far do our individual rights—including our First Amendment rights to speech and expression—extend, especially when these rights "are derivative of and conditional upon citizenship" (Harvey, 2005, p. 42), and thus to some degree exclusionary? To what degree do our individual rights implicate a responsibility to others? How do we cultivate a practice of freedom that bears responsibility to ethical and social constraints? How do we build a Freedom Tower that is not a house of cards, and that does not seek to wall off social reality?

In the psychoanalytic microculture of patient and analyst, we tend to ask these questions (if only implicitly) within the clinical moment, within an ever-evolving relationship. Much of psychoanalysis's history can be read as an evolving story of locating lines between freedom and constraint. But while it has been ever preoccupied with how to cultivate that process by which we facilitate our patient's freedom to think, to reclaim (or claim for the first time) their speech, their bodies, their desires—we have less explicitly examined constraints to free speech.

In its early iterations, psychoanalysis conceived the psyche as the product of internal, intrapsychic dynamics (for example, among the id, ego, and the superego). Over time, much of its thinking has shifted in favor of, though not entirely to, conceptions of a two-person, "relational" process. In turn, free association and its practice of free speech as a dialogic and social discourse are ripe for reconsideration.[4] Attention to speech opens our capacity to hear it, to recognize its fundamental status as a democratizing practice. In fact psychoanalysis assumes at the start that speech—*free* speech, whether in the clinic or in the public sphere—is the means by which people's unconscious lives gain expressive freedom, and that treatment, if not cure, resides in that translation from symptom to speech. Jonathan Lear (1998), recognizing a natural affinity between psychoanalysis and democracy, emphasizes that both are vitalized and animated by the inevitability of reason's encounter with the disruptive but guiding power of the unconscious and the irrational.

Speech and space

That free speech and free association are grammatical pairs, and that they are so foundational and cherished despite their necessarily imperfect realizations, are not the only reasons they speak to each other. The connection goes deeper. In fact, studying the two side-by-side stands to benefit both societies and individuals that strive to be freer. The histories of the First Amendment and of psychoanalysis can each be read as a dramatic narrative, involving ceaseless (but progressive) uphill battle between truth and repression, courage and fear. The tales of both, in broadest view, though largely progressive, reveal many setbacks. These remind us that we may at best achieve degrees of freedom; the obstacles are inherent, intransigent, and incessant.

To be sure, sustaining free speech is a challenge even in nominal democracies, let alone under authoritarian rule. A similar challenge—sustaining commitment to a *patient's* free associations and to her speech—confronts psychoanalysts in their daily practices. They carry out a mission, analogous to those of transitional democracies and their institutional practices, that evolves gradually over the course of years of work, occasionally interrupted by episodes of cataclysmic, seemingly chaotic, motion.

What makes both this incrementalism and radical transformation possible is the therapeutic action of speech. In psychoanalysis, as in democracy, we glimpse how liberty, speech, and human relationship are entwined at the roots and mutually conditioned. Psychoanalytic clinical trajectories bear witness to the need for essential constraints if analytic practice is to advance any true approximation of free speech. In contemporary capitalism—at least in its libertarian varieties—the idea of mediation has been devalued; "regulation" has become something of a tainted word and concept, while the "free market" is seen as a path to utopia. As we study both psychoanalysis and democracy, if we are able to reappropriate regulation as a concept and as a practice from misleading and illusory binaries, we may recognize that it is a necessary precondition to freedom. After all, where democracy does prevail, "to a significant degree, law does rule" (Dunn, 2014, p. 34). In the experience of psychoanalysis, too, we find that liberation must walk a long and troubling path, one marked by impasses, false hopes, and violence, and subject to lawful practices.

Both free association and free speech require genuine human collaboration and compromise, and necessary—lawful—constraints. There is no free speech that is strictly private or strictly public; it all inhabits a dialectical space, a space between freedom and constraint, speaker and hearer, and mind and body. This space of mediation—a space *to mediate* and *that mediates*—is as essential to the practice of free speech in psychoanalysis as it is to democracy.

Freedom (of association, or speech, or assembly) can never be freedom *from* participation. For us to achieve the status of real subjects, of active agents, our freedom requires us *to contribute in* (Winnicott, 1965)—to claim our agency through relationship and "reparative gesture" (Winnicott, 1958a, p. 24). Free association, seemingly lawless, hinges on its transformation to speech, its recognition of lawful constraints that enable a mediating space. There we may discover each other through what David Lichtenstein calls "improvisatory speech" (1993, p. 233), what Evan Malater (2014b) refers to as "the movement of libido." For me, it is desire's voice, the speech of Eros. Psychoanalysis and democracy—and all of culture—blossom in this space between.

To understand why and how, to tap into "the spatializing or spacing essence of freedom" (Nancy, 1988, p. 145), I'm going to take a semiotic approach to understanding the special status of speech, for both individuals and for groups. My discussion will reveal some antecedents for recognizing the particular importance of triangular space, a space beyond a binary—what I'll call a space between. I will also examine some early quests to bypass that space in the precursors to free speech—attempts to achieve unmediated psychical communication, and (complimentarily) attempts to achieve direct physical communication. I will explore the genius inherent in our First Amendment ("Congress shall make no Law") and Freud's "fundamental rule" as they establish "rules" that grant primacy to open space, a third space of desire. This space is incarnated and instantiated by symbolizing feminine space, by naming a "feminine law."[5]

CHAPTER ONE

The space between

In one of his earliest defenses of what would evolve into the talking cure, Sigmund Freud confronted doubts about the value, and especially the healing power, of mere talk. At this point, Freud had yet to propose that free association is the "fundamental rule" of psychotherapy, that it is a privileged path to freedom of thought and thus to psychic release and healing. Nor had he yet considered the value of free speech in the consulting room. But he was already captivated by the mysterious power of speech and its potent, incantatory prehistory.

According to Freud, words are more than just sounds, more even than signs; in the form of speech, they inhabit a psychologically charged realm between *science* and *magic*.

> A layman will no doubt find it hard to understand how pathological disorders of the body and mind can be eliminated by "mere" words. He will feel that he is being asked to believe in magic. And he will not be so very wrong, for the words which we use in our everyday speech are nothing other than watered-down magic. But we shall have to follow a roundabout path in order to explain how science sets about restoring to words a part at least of their former magical power. (Freud, 1890a, p. 283)

1

Freud, who began his career as a hypnotist in a spiritualistic age, believed in the power of language to not only alter perception but also to effectively reshape the world. That's the very definition of magic: the ability to bridge the gap between wish and fulfillment, idea and reality, mental and physical. If not magic exactly, an indisputable mystery and majesty abound in the ineffable space between language and the world. This mystery and majesty is, for one primal example, woven into the biblical tale of creation, wherein God shapes the world through his word: he speaks, and the void surrenders to the material. Nothing becomes something, as speech bridges the widest possible gap. Freud sees in the Bible's "'Let there be light!' and there was light" a transference of magical power from words to religion, part of a growing expectation that words could be more powerful than mere wish (1933a, p. 165).

How language works its magic is a question that has arisen time and again in philosophy and theology since at least the founding of the Symposium. In Plato's *Phaedrus* (N.B.: a written text), Socrates considers the demerits of writing (a kind of absence and forgetting) in relation to the presence of speech, which has the power, in the words of communication theorist John Durham Peters, to directly bridge the gap between "person and person, soul and soul, body and body" (Peters, 1999, p. 37). But these dualities didn't mean exactly the same thing to Plato as they do to us. Even while Plato appears, at least in some texts, to privilege the immaterial and the pure ideal, he also understood (as Freud later came to) that our only access to such things is through the material. However, Plato, like his fellow Greeks and by contrast with Freud, lacked any concept of an "unconscious" or of anything like "psychology." To them, *psyche* was simultaneously "mind," "spirit," and, most literally, "breath": there was no real distinction between consciousness and embodiment. There might have been a transcendent realm of ideals, the exclusive realm of truth; but there was no duality of mind and matter, of spiritual and spatial.

By Freud's time, as documented in Carl Schorske's seminal study of that period, the notion of an unconscious was already widespread. Freud's innovation, according to Eli Zaretsky, was the idea of an "internal, idiosyncratic source of motivations peculiar to the individual" (2004, p. 16)—the idea of a *personal* unconscious. But this idea took some time to develop. Early in his career, Freud (quite unexceptionably) adhered to the currently accepted doctrines and treatments, which (as we shall see in Chapter Two) attempted to heal directly, without mediation. There was no concept of a gap between mind and body, no concept of a third space between psyche and soma, and so these early efforts attempted to bypass what Freud would come to discover as the most essential (and ultimately the signal) feature of psychoanalysis.

Freud initially believed that the mind operated mechanistically and that neuroses could be understood somatically. The inefficacy of hypnotic suggestion and physical stimulation led him to admit that unmediated communication is the stuff of myth. From there, he would gradually develop a greater, and ultimately revolutionary, recognition of his patients as speaking subjects, and of the key value of that speaking to subjectivity. Psychoanalysis would then become a science—and an art—of translation, interpretation, and mediation. His patients' symptoms compelled translation, and as Freud enlisted them as active participants in that translation, they (and their speech) compelled his attention. Human beings' capacity for language, that which situates them in a symbolic realm—beyond both stimulus-response physical prompting and also beyond suggestion—became a means of cure. In that sense, psychoanalysis "restor[ed] to words a part at least of their former magical power."

Freud certainly didn't see himself as a magician or a dealer in magical cures; nor did he believe in supernatural beings whose utterance of "Light!" could produce light. But one needn't believe in magic to recognize words' magical quality—that is, their instrumentality in making the spiritual, the mental, and the interior manifest in physical reality. Disenchanted with "therapeutic potions … the use of magical formulas or purificatory baths, or the elicitation of oracular dreams," Freud discovers "the magic of words":

> Words are the most important media by which one man seeks to bring his influence to bear on another; words are a good method of producing mental changes in the person to whom they are addressed. So that there is no longer anything puzzling in the assertion that the magic of words can remove the symptoms of illness, and especially such as are themselves founded on mental states. (Freud, 1890a, p. 292)

It is here that Freud's evolving theory intersects with that of the science of signs—semiotics.

Semiotics has two distinct founders and two distinct strains, one cultivated by the American philosopher Charles Sanders Peirce (1839–1914), the other by the Swiss linguist Ferdinand de Saussure (1857–1913). Despite their differences (which we shall consider later), both are concerned not only with signs (prototypically words) in and of themselves, but also with how meanings are made and how reality is represented through such signs. Freud's similar concerns made him a virtual semiotician. His focus on decoding the patterns of his patients' speech, and his use of that speech in making meaning of other signs, such as the hysteric's symptoms, long anticipated semiotician Roman Jakobson's declaration that "language is the central and most important among all human semiotic systems" (1971, p. 658) and Émile Benveniste's observation that "language is the interpreting system of all other systems, linguistic and non-linguistic" (1969, p. 239). Both Freud and semioticians of either stripe place their emphasis on the mechanisms by which reality is mediated for the mind through symbols. All deny that reality can in any respect speak for itself, whether the reality is perceived or not, objective or subjective, and mediating signs in turn require interpretation and translation, be they words, symbols, hieroglyphics, or the dream content that so fascinated Freud in his *Interpretation of Dreams*.

The disjunction between sign and reality, word and thing, may become obscured as signifiers become familiar over time, "naturalized," creating a "spurious identity between reference and referents, between the text and the world" (Tagg, 1988, p. 99). Naturalized signifiers may even acquire what Daniel Chandler refers to as "almost magical power" as the "medium of language comes to acquire the illusion of transparency" (Chandler, 2002, pp. 76–77). In the face of these temptations, we must keep asking, as Judith Butler reminds us, "What does transparency keep obscure?" (Butler, 1999, p. xix). In the wash of signifiers that seem wedded to their signifieds, we might slip into an atavistic, naïve pursuit for unmediated experience—if we don't fall prey to what Freud lamented as our "herd instinct" (Freud, 1921c, pp. 117ff.).

The power of psychoanalysis lies, in large part, in its semiotic mission: to defamiliarize us with what we take for granted; to challenge us to interpret our symptoms, dreams, and the like as meaningful signs; to question the power dynamics embedded in the codes that we adopt without reflection; and so forth. In short, one might argue that the power of psychoanalysis lies in its status *between*—between the word and the thing; between the quest for unmediated spiritual knowing and its corollary: direct, unmediated physical knowing; between hypnosis and physical manipulation. These are merely a few of the dialectics that sustain psychoanalytic inquiry.

Freud's thought would grow to encompass the ancient intuition (implicit even in Plato's idealism) that spirit and expression, discourse and intercourse, emerge in a space that is neither pure place nor pure idea. As it happens, hysteria played a large role in driving Freud to this conclusion, and in Freud's day (as in ours), hysteria was a gendered disease. As Eli Zaretsky argues, "In its association with overexcitement and theatricality on the one hand, and with passivity on the other, hysteria converged with 'femininity,' which the Victorian age opposed to autonomy" (2004, p. 24). Hysterics, it was thought, tended to be suggestible, responsive to unconscious currents, and therefore also responsive to the practice of hypnosis. Jean-Martin Charcot—the director of the leading clinic dedicated to the treatment of hysteria (the Salpêtrière), and an early major influence on Freud—believed that through hypnosis, "the 'lower' or 'feminine' parts of the mind" could be released and brought into connection with consciousness (ibid., p. 25).

But Freud (along with his collaborator Breuer, with whom he published five case studies as *Studies on Hysteria*) eventually recognized that hysterics, in place of speech, relied on the *body* to communicate. He came to hypothesize that hysterical symptoms represented a "resistance" against awareness of traumatic memory of "a presexual *sexual* shock" (Freud, cited in Makari, 2008, p. 90).[1] At first he believed that such shocks must have originated in events, and that the number of women suffering from hysteria must mean that early sexual abuse was widespread. But he could not long sustain belief in this "seduction theory." He still recognized that real experiences have psychological effects, and he never denied that sometimes his patients had actually been abused, and thereby psychologically damaged. But his theoretical focus shifted from the external to the internal: to children's native impulses and fantasies.

Simultaneously, Freud abandoned his practice of hypnosis (a form of seduction) in favor of close listening to the hysteric's speech and challenging her to find words that could take the place of actions (i.e., her bodily symptoms). Now "[m]ind would be linked to body, and the psychic would be rooted in the physical" (Makari, 2008, p. 103). And very specifically, the most private regions of the body, the genitals, would be implicated and exposed in a private but now also public discourse about very private (sexual and erotic) practices.

It has been commonly noted that the early analytic literature is replete with many explicit references to the genitals, but that as psychoanalysis evolved, it lost its foothold in the physical, let alone in the most personal and private aspects of our physicality. Study of psyche became the study of words and mind alone; we forgot that consciousness (let alone the unconscious) is not synonymous with the mental. We lost track of the way fantasy was (for Freud) and truly remains (for all of us) rooted as much in the body as in the mind. The resulting focus on interiority made it difficult for psychoanalysis to comprehend or cope with verbal impasses. And every analyst faces such impasses, as when after we urge patients (as Freud taught us) to speak freely, to share in unedited form whatever comes to mind, many insist they cannot do so.

The history of free association, like the history of free speech, has unfolded against a backdrop of longing for frictionless communication. Hidden within the concepts is a fantasy of the direct transference of thoughts, of a kind of telepathy, of a magical discourse in which freedom of speech means that it's unnecessary to speak, for even speech (like writing) is plagued with the impasses and misunderstandings. This longing is nothing new, of course. In *The Symposium*, Plato depicts the ideal of love as selves merging into one being, whose unity obviously does away with any need for discourse.

A similar mingling of selves, if selves they properly be, is presumed in the branch of classical and medieval theology called *angelology*. Among other conundrums, angelologists pondered the possibility and consequences of speech between beings who are pure spirit. The conclusion advanced by divines from Augustine to Aquinas is that angels are free from the need to use words; they communicate by sheer spiritual interpenetration, using a kind of telepathy. Freud, himself, never ruled out the possibility of telepathy;[2] even as he celebrated and harnessed the magic of speech, he harbored some doubts of its necessity. I suspect Freud knew that this was a mistake. Even if telepathy, by means of metaphor, helps us to capture subjective experience that we may attribute to what physicists describe as the nonlocality or quantum entanglement of an implicate universe, it is misguided to presume we can do without speech.

John Durham Peters hints at this mistake in his enlightening examination of Aquinas. He takes up the interesting suggestion by Stuart Schneiderman that

> angelology can be read as semiotics by other means. The bodies of angels and their couplings are allegories of signs and their syntax. But in the dominant Thomistic tradition, angels stand for communication as if bodies did not matter. ...
>
> ... Since [Aquinas's] angels have no fleshly bodies, nothing to hide, and no reason to conceal anything, the external speech of the voice "does not befit an angel, but only interior speech belongs to him." Since the purpose of mortal speech is to manifest what is hidden, what use would speech be among such lucidly intelligible beings? ... The speech of angels "is interior, but perceived, nevertheless, by another." ... Angels commune through a noiseless rustle of intelligence without the ministry of language or matter. (Peters, 1999, pp. 76–77)

In sum, angels "are unhindered by distance, are exempt from the supposed limitations of embodiment, and effortlessly couple the psychical and the physical, the signified and the signifier, the divine and the human" (ibid., p. 75).

This fantasy of instant communication, of a kind of quantum entanglement of understanding, was at least tempting to Freud. Perhaps he thought telepathy—angelic mental synchronicity—was the least implausible way to account for some clinical or hypnagogic phenomena. But the main course of his intellectual and professional development led to a different conclusion: any kind of communication, speech above all, presupposes a material gap. There can't even theoretically *be* symbolization where there is complete transparency and "mental" interpenetration, if we allow for the notion of the mental without the physical.

The philosopher Walter Benjamin places an ironic spin on mediation, defining it in terms that allow for a kind of telepathy, a seeming immediacy of mental communication. And "if one chooses to call this immediacy magic, then the primary problem of language is its magic. At the same time, the notion of the magic of language points to something else: its infiniteness. ... [A]ll language contains its own incommensurate, uniquely constituted infinity." He goes on to argue that "Name steps outside itself in this knowledge ... from what we may

call its own immanent magic, in order to become expressly, as it were
externally, magic. The word must communicate something (other than
itself)" (Benjamin, 1916, pp. 65–71).

Just as a word must communicate something other than itself,
so too must the symbolic in general attach itself to material objects. This
necessity is implicit in French psychoanalyst Jacques Lacan's claim that
the *speaking* subject comes into being where the "thing" *was*. And it is
at least implied in pediatrician and psychoanalyst D. W. Winnicott's
(1953) description of "transitional objects." Winnicott was addressing
the developmental process whereby the child comes to recognize that
his mother (or his mother's breast) is neither a part of him nor under
his total control. That is, he has come to realize that he is not the same
as mother, and perforce not the world, and (most woundingly) not
omnipotent. The child seeks special objects (security blankets, teddy
bears, etc.) that will comfort him and provide a sense of potency or
magic—objects that will simultaneously refute this fall and soften his
adjustment to the harsh reality of life in a world that is largely indif-
ferent to his desires and even to his needs. This wounding realization
is foreshadowed (at least faintly) in our first encounters with maternal fallibility, encounters that also puncture our omnipotence. The
"transitional object," like Benjamin's word, communicates something
other than itself. It occupies a *space between unnamed and named, between
the world of things-in-themselves and the named world*. By definition, it
occupies a space between material constraint and subjective omnipotence. Ultimately far more than a developmental phase, transitional or
"potential space"—the "place where we live," where all of cultural and
creative life takes place—was sacred for Winnicott, and its metaphoric
status has compelled psychoanalysts ever since.

Angelic communication is a fantasy akin to the infant's fantasy of
omnipotent control over his environment. If angels are all instantly
accessible and transparent to one another, then there's no need to communicate, no gap to fill, no unknown to know. The infant, in his original
state, not only has no capacity for language; like an angel, he has no
use for it, either. He may cry out in hunger, but crying is not language;
it is language's developmental (semiotic) analogue. Even animals cry
out in hunger. As we shall see, such cries are not symbols, though one
might call them "signs." Indeed the mother will interpret such signs as
the infant's expression of hunger, and therefore she breast-feeds. But
in Winnicott's evocative theorizing, the infant "hallucinates" the breast
into being (his fantasy is understood to be virtually coincident with

reality), and in this way the breast is both a confirmation (to the infant) of an emergent omnipotence, but also a precursor to the transitional object, to what lies beyond his subjective control. But sooner or later every infant approaches the gap: he is not his environment, he is not the master of his mother, he is not the totality of physical experience. With his evolving "invention" of transitional objects (which are not yet recognized as found objects), the child enters the realm of symbolization—the transitional space where language becomes necessary to bridge the gap between self and other, inner desire and outer reality (Winnicott, 1953).

The blanket as transitional object is comforting because the child both *makes* it that way and believes it has the *inherent* power to comfort. It is both discovered and invented. And this duality is cloaked under a spell of silence. As Winnicott puts it,

> the essential feature in the concept of transitional objects as phenomena (according to my presentation of the subject) is *the paradox, and the acceptance of the paradox*: the baby creates the object, but the object was there waiting to be created and to become a cathected [libidinally charged] object … in the rules of the game we all know that we will never challenge the baby to elicit an answer to the question: did you create that or did you find it? (Winnicott, 1969a, pp. 712–713)

Speech too is both discovered and invented; we produce it, making our own unique meanings, but to do so we have to take what we're given: the rules and vocabulary and common meanings embodied in a language. The blanket was already there, and so is language. Both transitional spaces and speech exist between the force of will and the resistance of matter, between fantasy and reality, the invented and the given. The notion of angelic communication is a fantasy of transcending (or never needing) this in-between, third space. But the beauty, and the tragedy, of our speech is that it both is and isn't magic. The magic blanket might "really" be a ratty piece of cloth, but the meaning with which we imbue our object is not unreal or impotent. The blanket is still magic.

This is a book about that magic. And it's a book about freedom. But it is also a book about law: how magic and freedom meet the material world that limits and constrains them but that also enables the soaring agility of desire. This "space between" a tethered and untethered desire enriches our lives with mystery and meaningfulness. This space is sometimes open, sometimes collapsed; it is sometimes shut down by fear and habit, but can be reopened through daring and dreaming, play and power. When it opens up, it provides the stage for exploring that third space of desire between freedom and repression, mind and matter, checks and balances. Here, in this mediated space, the unbounded exercise of free speech—and the freely speaking subject—paradoxically thrives.

But too often, the space between collapses, as we lapse into predefined roles, suppressing unfamiliar or unpredicted desires, slotting others into flattened roles, falling prey to our fears and the fear-mongering opportunism inspired (and rewarded) by those fears. In place of Winnicott's creative symbol, we tilt toward a defiant, boundless freedom (deprived of the condition of constraint) or toward a rigid subjugation to rules and limits (deprived of our imaginative flights). In the realm of civil society, we tilt toward a hubristic libertarianism or toward an adherence and subjugation to prescriptive authority. We retreat to what Emmanuel Lévinas calls the "angelism" of the law, the seductions of a purely spiritual dimension (Lévinas, 1982, p. 219); we elide our responsibility to a "symbolic dimensions of law that is limited by what can be articulated in speech" (McNulty, 2014, p. 141). We bypass the space between that spiritual dimension and the checking function of lawful constraint. Our imagination falters; the space for psychoanalytic speech closes—space which, as I aim to show, is also the space for democratic free speech.

In opening a space between the magical and the material nature of language, I will listen as (and shed light on how) desire and agency and yes, free speech, emerge in psychoanalytic practice—a free speech that is nonetheless conditioned by necessary constraints. This lawful space also emerges in the public realm, enabling us to become engaged citizens, to realize power and agency, individual and collective sovereignty, in our lives. Our struggles with and discoveries through free association light the way to a potentially dislocating discourse of desire, but also to *freer* free speech, the erotics of free speech.

Even in our knowledge that freedom is always limited, that the only possibility is of the impossibility of free speech, we still, perhaps more than ever, find ourselves striving toward it. For only by acting on the premise of ultimate freedom, by finding ways to exercise what freedoms we have now, do we even come within its grasp. We must build this tower with bricks that are molded in its image.

CHAPTER TWO

The fundamental rule: freedom in psychoanalysis

Antecedents to the talking cure

What is psychoanalysis? Most know it through endless cartoons of the bearded doctor, aloof, pen and pad in hand, eyebrow raised as the patient recites some misguided bit of self-analysis or lands on some comic epiphany. The analyst is often caricatured as an autocratic lawgiver and the patient as a bereft and oblivious subject. Psychoanalysis is in each case viewed as a paternalistic, one-way arrangement, in which doctor knows best and the patient's so-called free associations betray subservience and accommodation to authority.

While these pictures are wrong, they do depict two of the features that define psychoanalysis as both a distinct psychological theory and a technique. Even those who dismiss analysis accept one of its foundational concepts, namely that of the unconscious—or rather, of Freud's unconscious. Though Freud conceded that "the poets and philosophers before me discovered the unconscious," he claimed as his distinctive discovery "the scientific method by which the unconscious can be studied" (Isbister, 1985, p. 44).

A second defining feature of psychoanalysis, the "talking cure," was also not new to Freud, though he was the first to place so many chips on it. The practice of attempting to access hidden thoughts or beliefs through what we now call "free association" traces all the way back to late antiquity. As Lila J. Kalinich shows, something like it was "described in the spiritual literature of the early Christian church," in one notable example as a means of exposing the "unseen warfare" of the soul (1993, p. 210), and around 1890 Pierre Janet, a French philosopher and psychologist, proposed "'automatic talking' as part of his 'psychological analysis'" (p. 210).

At that time, Freud was still practicing the conventional methods for treating disturbed patients. The young Freud inhabited a culture whose faith in the tenets of the Enlightenment, with its emphasis on reason and order, had been jarred by industrialization, the emancipatory forces of mass culture and capitalism, and an increasingly gendered, modern world view. The psychiatric establishment witnessed the rise, in reaction, of a movement known as *associationism* (Zaretsky, 2004, especially pp. 18–22). Derived from John Locke's thought, associationism sought to restore reason in the disturbed person's mind, which presumably had become disordered or disrupted. That is, they sought to reorder the patient's associations, to manipulate their ideas.

But two other impulses had also emerged to challenge Enlightenment associationism: romanticism and the "somatic model." The romantic idea of the imagination, in part a reaction against the idea of imposing rational order, led to a blend of spiritualist and irrationalist currents known as *magnetism*, by which the therapist sought to heal through transmitting (or harmoniously distributing) a "magnetic" force. One variety of magnetism practiced by the Austrian Franz Mesmer (who called his force "animal magnetism") gave rise to hypnotism, which shunned interpersonal physiology and minimized the importance of the therapeutic relationship. While hypnosis requires suggestion, and suggestion is a vehicle for the therapist's influence, there was still *some* kind of relationship between doctor and patient. The futility of this attempt to erase the therapist foreshadowed Freud's project.

The somatic model (including phrenology), contra mesmerism, pursued an extreme physicalism. In this model, heredity shapes the mind and the causes of mental disturbance may be traced to biology of the brain. But, like mesmerism, it sought to transcend the mediating influence of relationship.

If magnetic therapy sought a purely mental (or at least spiritual) cure, hydrotherapy and electrical stimulation sought direct physical manipulation. It seems likely that Freud initially saw no need to choose between the romantic approach and the stimulative approach. He certainly practiced hypnosis; and while there is no direct evidence that Freud stimulated anyone's genitals, his writings indicate that he conducted "full body massage as he listened closely to his early patients, owned the best electrical equipment available, and claimed to practice all of the standard treatments of his day" (Starr & Aron, 2011, p. 375).

As time went on, Freud questioned the scientific benefits of these approaches, whose premises he had already begun to question, although he had not yet recognized the inevitability of mediation. (Nor was he overly fond of working with somnambulistic patients.) Meanwhile, he grew ever more intrigued by the work of his colleague and eventual collaborator Josef Breuer, who was finding some success with a new technique focused on simply talking. The aim was to direct the patient to speak her (and it was almost always her) story and to eventually experience in that story a kind of liberating and healing catharsis. Freud was especially influenced by Breuer's work with a patient, Bertha Pappenheim (better known to us as "Anna O"), who dubbed this self-narrating process "chimney sweeping" and who coined the now definitional term "talking cure."

The fundamental rule

Following Breuer's lead, Freud began to consider the value of mental associations, and the ways that "mere" speaking might uncover them. Speech in and of itself was not his real interest; rather, he focused on the ways a patient's speech reveals shapes and patterns of an unconscious symbolic landscape, where her hysterical symptoms take form. In his clinical work with "Elizabeth von R.," Freud observed that her feelings "were cut off from any free associative connection of thought with the rest of the ideational content of her mind" (Freud & Breuer, 1895d, p. 165). He came to believe that when a patient's speech is dissociated from usual conscious controls, it might reveal "pathogenic psychical material which has ostensibly been forgotten, which is not at the ego's disposal and … nevertheless in some fashion lies ready to hand and in correct and proper order" (ibid., p. 287).

Within the seeming messiness and randomness of free speech, Freud found an underlying order, a "proper" arrangement that spelled out the nature of the patient's "pathology." He ascribed this ordering to "an intelligence which is not necessarily inferior to that of the normal ego" (ibid., p. 287). Thus, by conceiving of the unconscious as a kind of parallel mind with its own language and symbolic capabilities, he revolutionized the science of the mind. This discovery launched him on a path that would diverge from Breuer's.

Freud became increasingly interested in finding ways to route around the conscious ego, with its many defenses and necessary blind spots, in order to make contact with this other intelligence. The search led him into the realm of dreams, which he first explored by analyzing his own. He began with dream imagery, to see what conscious associations it evoked, then moved back to other dream images. In this shuttling back and forth, he came to believe that when one is dreaming, one's energy is freed from the restraints endemic to consciousness and becomes more readily attached to "involuntary ideas" that signify powerful but somehow disturbing elements of memory and desire (Freud, 1900a, p. 102).

Meanwhile, in his clinical work with "Frau Emmy" in 1889, he began his experiments with verbal association as a means of supplementing hypnosis. At first, he tried to actively direct his patient through the process of association, using what amounted to leading questions. But Emmy bridled at this method and insisted that he listen to her without interruption. Her insistence proved to be the key to the method behind Freud's new science. As early as 1893, Freud had intuited that so long as a patient experienced physical pain, "she had not told me everything" (Freud & Breuer, 1895d, p. 148). Her pain was speech by another means.

As he worked with "hysterical" patients whose symptoms seemed to betray some mysterious, unspeakable underlying motive, Freud arrived at a crucial insight. When, by virtue of suppression or repression, it seems impossible to speak, speech still will out. However, this "speech," struggling towards its expression against powerful psychical forces, is usually unconscious and often physical. Hysterical symptoms were just such unconscious, physical "speech acts." By 1915, Freud concluded that the most direct path to the untold, unconscious mind—the most intangible realm of our being—led through the body (1915e). As the psychoanalyst Ricardo Lombardi has noted, the "enigmatic Unconscious" (the realm of the repressed and the unthinkable), denied access to spoken expression, seeks to discharge its energy by taking the only path left—corporeal expression—thus making itself even *"more tangible"*

(Lombardi, 2010, p. 880; Lombardi's emphasis). And so unconscious conflicts can, and perhaps must, be inferred from their physical effects, the way dark matter (given our current knowledge) can be inferred only from its gravitational effects.

Earlier, in his work with the "Rat Man" in 1907 (Freud, 1909d), Freud had developed a non-directed free association technique, approximating aspects of the dreaming state. He was soon referring to this—and its implicit moral injunction—as "the fundamental rule" (1910a, p. 39). Free association seemed to offer a more direct, less mediated avenue to revealing psychic conflict. But Freud noticed that for his hysterical patients, free association rarely led directly to the liberation of unconscious thought, to "free speech" for the repressed. Only through a translational process in which physical expressions—tics, mannerisms, involuntary gestures—gained verbal expression, did free association result in revelation. Furthermore, for some especially inhibited patients, Freud noted, "*the whole train of thought is dominated by* the element that has as its content *bodily innervation* (or, rather, the sensation of it)" (Freud, 1915e, p. 198; my emphasis). For such patients, that is, what they most need to say is utterly barred from utterance; instead, it is "converted" into preoccupying physical excitations.

Resulting from hidden conflict, these excitations are symptoms; they mark out and take shape from that conflict, they are signifiers—a kind of language. The body creates signs, sometimes with and sometimes instead of spoken words. Spoken words are also physical gestures; there is no signifying without the body, since we are not angels. As he progressed from patient to patient, Freud gained confidence that the contents of the unconscious mind could be accessed through direct verbalization, requiring no trickery to divert the conscious mind. Freud invited his patients to verbalize their conscious associations in order to reveal what lay hidden and unconscious. He listened both with a clinical ear, hoping that as his patients unlocked the secrets that burdened them, they would heal, and with a scientific ear, hoping they would reveal what lay hidden in the universal as well as the particular psyche.

Freud had discovered the mediating factor of language—how it links corporeal and subjective desire by means of a practice of "ritualized improvisation" (Phillips, 1993, p. 3). However significant this advance, and despite his better judgment, he remained captured by some yet elusive quest for unmediated access to the patient's unconscious. But he then encountered another mediating factor: that of relationship itself.

Freud discovered that his unconscious, however independent its reality might be, could only be "discovered" *contextually*. Far from independent, it became revealed within the constraint of *relationship*.

Freud named this relationship "the transference." The transference assured that free association could never be simply an act of mental communication between psyches. The transference grounded the analytic couple in their bodies, in their sensory experience, in their need to grapple with how memory and desire "spoke" through repetitions in relational behavior—between unconscious communication and speech, between body and mind, and (as a relational psychoanalysis now emphasizes) between two minds and two bodies.

Free association as transference address

To set the stage for Freud's discovery of the transference, let's look at his advice to the analyst on how to cultivate the patient's free associations. As he listened, the analyst was to grant these associations an "evenly hovering attention," betraying no special excitement by or approval of particular results. This sort of actively passive or humble attention with its surrender of authority and judgment and even of guidance, may be mistaken for the detachment or aloofness of popular caricature. But Freud, while urging analysts to present what would become known as a "blank screen" for inscribing the patient's speech, at least glimpsed that genuine healing would require mutuality between speaker and listener. The listener (analyst) must greet the speaker (patient) and open a space for speech to become free and real. The listener must be more than a tape recorder or speech is not truly speech but more like interior thought or soliloquy, which tends eventually to collapse into withdrawal or even delirium.

To some who later insisted that psychoanalysis is a two-way street, this lack was precisely the problem. They feared that free association serves to *avoid* rather than forge genuine communication, because it seems to lead only to what Henry Stack Sullivan called "parallel autistic reveries" (Aron, 1990, p. 448). In either case, understood as a form of address, free association aims to replace "silent soliloquy with spoken words, and it establishes a human relationship … in the service of a therapeutic objective" (Kris, 1996, p. 14).

Freud's own practice never fully evolved to this point, nor did that of other early psychoanalysts, who attempted to maintain their position in the clinic as neutral and uninvolved auditors, in order to optimize conditions for the emergence of their patient's unconscious contents and expressive freedom. And as Freud's thinking evolved, free association as a method became tethered to a particular model of the psyche: the "drive theory." Accordingly, the primary goal of analysis was, as Jacob Arlow put it, to ensure that "what emerges into the patient's consciousness is as far as possible endogenously determined" (Arlow, 1979, p. 193). Free association was seen as a means of burrowing down through layers of interior obfuscation to unearth the repressed materials of childhood conflict exposed in the flow of associations, free from the analyst's influence.

In practice, however, Freud discovered that free association cannot stop at the endogenous (prior to and outside of the treatment). No associations are truly "free" of the analyst's influence, and there can be no "free" in the sense of unearned. The analysand must *choose*, must assert her agency, even if only to discover what is not free or consciously chosen. What's more, Freud discovered that, within the clinic, repudiated desires are revealed towards and for the analyst, who is never a neutral figure. Far from being a blank screen, the analyst is implicated in each of the patient's associations. The patient's feelings and wishes toward the analyst, who substitutes for important persons in the patient's life, inevitably inflect process. The patient's speech thus unfolds in a context brimming with "transference."

This inevitable entanglement has prompted what's known as "transference analysis," whose focus is to interpret the ways complex feelings experienced in the analyst's office form a screen of resistance between the present and the past. In transference analysis, the analyst and patient strive—by penetrating the surface and searching for the gaps in meaning found in dreams, slips, symptoms, indeed any communication—to discover a "latent" substrate of repressed experiences and feelings. Perhaps ironically, despite and because of the power of transference, classical psychoanalysis evolved to ensure that the analyst is almost never a lived, three dimensional, discoverable human subject. Observing that the "three fundamental pillars of the [traditional] analyst's conduct became abstinence, anonymity, and neutrality," Stephen Mitchell (1997, p. 177), advocated instead for a relational turn in psychoanalysis, a move away from classical conceptions. If these pillars aimed to regulate transference—to distill an objectified unconscious and to ensure an ethical, if not also scientific, practice—their ossification into tenets of clinical practice undermined psychoanalysis's humanity and vibrancy. There is no safekeeping for the analyst in a protected, cordoned-off realm. As Freud had already glimpsed, analysis inevitably leads to a relational entanglement with the patient that becomes the true grounds for treatment.

Freud, in his own practice, was very much a real presence who, while self-conscious enough to normally sit where patients couldn't see him, still couldn't help but expose to them his large personality. Freud also recognized that free association is a form of address: the patient aimed her associations at an authentic, if only implicitly recognized other (i.e., the analyst). By virtue of this structural given, free association differs essentially from both interior monologue or dream, which Freud felt was "a completely asocial product; it has nothing to communicate to anyone else" (1905c, p. 179). Further, free association finds its greatest ally *in a relationship* that changes the very path of so-called freedom itself into an obstacle course that is as much about "resistance" as it is about desire—as much about repressed fantasy as it is about a repressed reality, as much about internal tyranny as it is about relational oppression. Free association begins at the site of an intense drama, seeking both reunion with that drama and freedom from it, a claiming of personal creative destiny from predetermined fate (Bollas, 1989).

Mutual (free) association

We return here to what might seem a commonsensical point, but it's one that took some time to dawn on analysis. As Mark Kanzer says "the fundamental rule involves a two-person relationship" (1972, p. 265), and it always has. Christopher Bollas describes the stakes: "by asking the person to think out loud," Freud anticipated "the dialogic structure of a two-person relation, a partnership one might term the *Freudian Pair*" (2002, p. 7). As relational or intersubjective models of psychoanalysis have evolved, the analyst's status as a real human presence in the clinic has come to be accepted. No longer a psychoanalytic Wizard of Oz, knowable only through the scrim of the patients' fantasy projections (and their interpretation), the analyst provides a human resistance or friction representing an "Other" for the analysand (patient). Only in this way does the analysand have any real chance at self-discovery and authentic social engagement.

While free association, understood as a relational activity, avoids the trap of autistic reverie, it can never be objective or free from personal bias, since it is cultivated in the context of a real and specific human relationship. By contemplating the transference as a "joint creation," the analyst's subjectivity and influence, rather than being avoided or controlled, "become active and analyzable aspects of the analytic process" (Aron, 1990, p. 456). Though the analyst's presence (in the transference) always "points to the absence of the original object" (Perelberg, 2013, p. 569) and exists in a complicated psychophysical space between *the patient's* past and present, between *the patient's* historical reality and unconscious fantasy, the analyst also is situated between his own past and present, reality and fantasy.

In this re-envisioned process, each member of the analytic couple becomes potentially knowable in distinct and mutually (if asymmetrically) reciprocal ways in and through the process. But what of the patient's singularity? By highlighting the contextualized and socially conditioned nature of the analytic encounter, psychoanalysis diverts attention from (when it doesn't actively dismiss or negate) the subject's personal signature, *her* free expression. The muddled status of free association in contemporary relational theory is relieved, to some degree, if we recognize that a relational or intersubjective lens, by illuminating the analyst's personal subjectivity, can also (paradoxically) expose the patient's distinct expression. As the patient evolves through relationship to discover the analyst as a "real" (if also still metaphorical) subject, with desires that exist independent of the patient's fantasy or possession, she also discovers herself as a subject of singular desire and symbolic agency.

At any rate, appreciating the mutuality of subjectivity has led us to engage in a conversation about how analytic speech deconstructs the tyranny of unexposed, hidden dogmas and unspoken truths, about how it preserves a dialectic between freedom and constraint, "between ritual and spontaneity" (Hoffman, 1998). Further, once we acknowledge the analyst's inevitable and essential status as a "personal subject" (Slavin, 2010), we discover in free association a path by which two human beings find their way, by means of a faithful and intentional practice, to a relationship of mutual respect, sharing, and healing. Occasioned as it is not only by a commitment to interpretation, dialogue, and unconscious encounter, but by both the analyst's real, human limits (including prejudices of technique) and subjective freedom, relational conceptions of free association have implications for how psychoanalysis might "free" free association beyond individual emancipatory goals towards shared and democratic ones—implications that remain relatively unexplored.

More immediately, once free association is no longer viewed as an antique vestige of the so-called "one-person model" of mind, it may be appreciated in light of what Freud at least implicitly intended: that it unfolds as a relational activity—*a conversation*—in a lived encounter with a personal but also metaphoric "Other" in the consulting room. This encounter is complicated both to experience and to describe. The lived complexity, with multiple facets, varies with the patient's (and analyst's) capacity for symbolizing inner states; with the patient's relation to the particular status of this both personal and impersonal figure located in the room and positioned on a mental stage; with how the analyst is used (and uses herself) as a lever for excavating the patient's desire in "a temporal collage" (Bollas, 2002, p. 56).

In Freud's evolving view, transference and resistance are but two sides of a coin. The cure resists itself, so much so that Freud came to conclude that when the patient insists she has nothing to say, she is captured, in effect, by the transference (Freud, 1921c, p. 126fn.). The analyst, for his part, contends with "countertransference," which works in the opposite direction. Countertransference, at first narrowly conceived as something disturbing or interfering with the analyst's function, would be later reconceived by many as co-determined and generated by the unconscious of both participants. Seen from this vantage point, it is as valuable as transference, implicating the analyst in a richly vulnerable and mutually collaborative process.

While a conception of the mutuality of free association is apt to raise questions of its (paradoxical) validity, psychoanalysis recognizes the analyst's asymmetrical responsibility to the patient's expressive freedom. Analytic neutrality—an often misunderstood or caricatured concept, even in actual practice by analysts—ensures that the analyst stays "on the patient's track," that he remains "focused on the patient's intentions" (Adler & Bachant, 1996, p. 1031; p. 1039). And so he plays the same game of tug of war as the patient—a contest between this surrender to an authority not of his choosing, and a more conventional tendency to discriminate, to impose judgment. At the same time, the analyst is still present, superintending the discourse, a figure of latent but real power supplementing an evenly-suspended attention with what French analyst Jacques Lacan called a "learned ignorance" (Donnet, 2001, p. 156).

Though we may employ different signifiers to make this point, what essentially unites psychoanalytic practices is this: the analyst can and should use her subjectivity to "to catch the drift of the patient's unconscious with his own unconscious" (Bollas, 2009, p. 20). The aim is to set in motion a discourse that expands the subject's expressive and symbolic freedom. This aspirationally unbounded discourse is liberated precisely, if paradoxically, *because it is bounded by constraints*. Constraints that the patient must grapple with as they ensure a space beyond unmediated wish fulfillment and angelological requitement. A space for speech, for Desire's speech.

Free association, transference, and the subject's democratizing agency

As we have seen, Freud's practice (if not his premises) already implicitly set the stage for a two-person view of free association—and for an essentially democratizing aspect to its practice. After all, the ironic definitional "rule" of free association was that there was *no* rule to follow and *no one's* rule. If free association was to prevail, the patient had to bypass conventional rules of conversational censorship, ceding herself to the impetuous yet also imperial authority of desire's voice, her unconscious desire. This is very different from law as what one might conceive as a superego injunction. It is a liberating injunction: a law or decree to speak freely—and a law bounded by an appeal to the patient's honesty. The familiar authority of prescriptive codes or "positive" law is upended by a less orthodox articulation of "'indestructible' ... laws of speech," which in turn depend upon lawful space (McNulty, 2014, p. 83, quoting Lacan on the Ten Commandments).

Though patient and analyst will many times over repeat and reassert familiar clinical power dynamics, in which the analyst holds interpretive authority and speaks in a privileged voice, the patient's free association offers a means for leveling the playing field, by assuming equal right and equal authority to speak. Her "imperial" voice discovers real limits, but also transgresses beyond familiar confinement. Freud conceded the analyst's authority is inevitably trumped by a prevailing truth—the voice of an emergent, formerly unconscious dimension— the voice of resistance and the unfree detours that are also routes that free desire. The analyst's mandate to "simply listen, and not bother about whether he is keeping anything in mind" (Freud, 1912e, p. 112), while impossible to uphold in practice, ensures a certain equality, a give and take in which *both* members of the relationship surrender to the realm of unconscious mental activity in order that the patient's disenfranchised, sometimes forbidden, often silenced voice—her intuitive knowing and transgressive desire—can claim for a time the freedom, opportunity, and *right* to hold forth.

Often, in exercising this right, especially at first, the patient is unable to bare some or even many of her frightening, embarrassing, unthought, and as-yet unnamed desires. Her effort to grapple with the hidden forces determining her feelings, by itself, positions her as a paradoxical agent of the method that aims to treat her symptoms and thereby free her. Consider Freud's famous instruction for learning how to free associate: "Act as though, for instance, you were a traveller sitting next to a window of a railway carriage and describing to someone inside the carriage the changing views which you see outside" (1913c, p. 135). Though her associations may be experienced as compliance with Freud's command, she may also discover elements of a choiceful surrender to what lies beyond her choice, a surrender that leads to an extraordinary experience of "ideational serendipity" (Mahony, 1979, p. 160).[1] She may discover a previously concealed sense of purpose to her associations, a sense of her own agency.

All the more does the patient's speaking, her revelation, require true courage, and this courage makes her power more real, and her speech more *free*. Baring her soul completely is impossible to realize in practice, but Freud's free association was an invitation to an open-ended conversation in which the voice of Desire speaks. Though this voice forever interrupts itself and is elusively insatiable, it also foretells the possibility of a cataclysmic, decisive shift in the distribution of voice. That said, free association remains constrained by its own impossibility—a fact that Lacan would make pivotal in his writings, equating desire with lack, with incompleteness and wanting. Mostly, analysts dance with this impossibility, falling prey (for the sake of their patients, despite Freud's and Lacan's insights) to the illusory quest that free association might be realized. For that reason, free association occupies, inherently, a *space between*—*between* its possibility and its impossibility.

Given this concession to impossibility, as Lawrence Kubie noted in 1950, "true free associations are not easily come by, and make up only a small portion of any analytic session" (1950, p. 48). Even approximations of free association are seldom described in the analytic literature. (Instead, one often finds references to literary examples of "free association," such as Molly Bloom's interior monologue in *Ulysses*.) Though we might wish more analysts took on this Sisyphean effort, this absence of examples is not really a failure of psychoanalysis. Any effort to describe free association is a form of capture, a betrayal of its essence.

But if we attend, as does Christopher Bollas (2009, p. 10), to Freud's frequent use of the metaphor of a weaver to capture a "zig-zagging line of thought," we arrive at different conclusion: we suffer not from a *paucity* of free associations, but from an *infinity* of them. A day "in our lives is a complex journey through a maze of associations.... We cannot even think all the associations sprung by a single evocative object" (ibid., p. viii). As we listen, free association reveals itself as ever present, a complex, intricate array of moving parts, both unseen and everywhere. Hidden patterns and new meanings are layered in an always freshly composed "symphonic score" (ibid., p. xii).

Commonplace, non-analytic approximations of the experience may be found in a familiar contemporary activity: our seemingly haphazard journeys by way of Googling. We start perhaps with a focused goal, but before we know it we've hopscotched our way from link to link, meandered to YouTube and back, creating an exploratory patchwork that reflects unanticipated or otherwise censored interests or desires that we have not consciously anticipated. Now imagine that same unbidden Google search has been conducted in the presence of an other whose own search queries and browser history are mostly unexposed, but who is watching us and begins to extract hidden meaning and order from our behavior. Immediately, we recognize our impulse to hide, to blush at the exposure of our surreptitious searches, to resent the eye of the intrusive Other who seems to remain impervious to her own taboo longings, and so disingenuously human. In this experience, we can begin to glimpse what is at stake in free association.

You might sense in this analogy a hitch in the free associative method. Not all online behavior is indicative of genuine interest or intention (conscious or otherwise); there is at least *some* "noise" in the data one might collect from our browser history—fumbled clicks, misleading links, dead leads. But it matters what story is told in the midst of all the countless untold stories, words that drop away unspoken, that don't make it into the spoken narrative that claims to be free association's odyssey. Which is the freer associative path? That which competes but fails to cross the threshold to language? That which remains at the borderland, just beneath that threshold? And yet without words, we have no story. We have only the story of what we do choose, of what we do speak, of what can be told and heard; this story marks the entry to free speech, if not always to all that is freely associated.

The analyst—who, as it turns out, is actually mining his own very human meandering contours of mind and its hidden, even locked, cubbyholes—must work at finding a true signal amidst the noise, a sense of directional agency within the metaphoric Google search, within the abundance of nonverbal and verbal communication that becomes available in any clinical session. This process partly requires that the analyst allow even the noise—between his and the patient's noise—perhaps especially the noise, to reveal the signal. D. W. Winnicott, for one, recognized the creative possibilities of the patient's finding his way into a "non-purposive state," a state of being at rest that may yield "non-sense," that is, noise (1971b, pp. 55–56).

How the analyst contends with noisy data both conceals and reveals the signal, a fact that frames Freud's suggestion that all analysts themselves be analyzed: To best tease out the signal from the noise, we develop our ears to amplify its traces, and then we follow where that detected signal takes us, investigating and deconstructing its meaning. British analyst Wilfred Bion writes, "I believe that the analyst may have to cultivate a capacity for dreaming while awake" (Bion, 1991, p. 215).

Through this process, as Julia Kristeva says,

> Freud invented a "speech," a certain version of language which is perhaps not its truth, but one of its potentialities, and it is the formidable privilege of psychoanalysis to reveal it .... [This speech] opens up another path in our relations to the signifying process which constitutes the human. And it is indeed this displacement of speech in relation to itself, this infinitesimal revolution, constitutive of our practice, which worries people. (Kristeva, 2007, p. 431)

After all, we might dare to conclude, free association offers a template for participation in the world outside the confines of a clinical session. It provides a template for *free speech*: shared participation and equal voice in a democratic order. Perhaps what is most terrifying about free association is that what appears to be a monologue is revealed as dialogue between a speaker and a listener, anchored in its unpredictability, in the irretrievability of words, in the incessant flow of language and history bookmarked in space and time. We as speakers both fear and desire that we have a listener, that we will be heard, that we will hear ourselves for a first time. We as listeners—much as we prefer the protection of predictability—might, if not must, hear that which we'd prefer remain shrouded in silence, unnamed and unknown.

CHAPTER THREE

The paradox of freedom and the first amendment

Speech and the ethic of surrender

How free is "free"? The allure of free association as an ideal, for both analysts and their patients, is quickly dampened in practice by obstacle, impasse, and interruption. Likewise, free speech functions as a democratic symbol more than as an achievable reality, as both lived experience and the fitful evolutions of First Amendment jurisprudence have revealed. Simply put, both in the clinic and in civil society, the pursuit of free speech reveals that speech is anything but free and that there are few (secular) concepts as vexed and contested as "freedom." It isn't just that freedom isn't free (but costs); it is that freedom has always (to some degree necessarily) entailed dependence, restraint, repression, obstacle, even impossibility. So freedom is (perhaps appropriately) conceptually indeterminate.

Freud acknowledged this contradiction at the heart of free association: even when "achieved" in practice, works only because it's anything but. In James Strachey's English (mis)translation, "free association" captures this tension in its two component words, as "association" also carries organizational, bureaucratic connotations. By contrast, Freud's original term was *freier Einfall*—"free irruption"—denoting "a spontaneous and coincidental falling out into the open" (Mahony, 1979, p. 21). As we listen to associations unfold, or fall out into the open, in the course of a treatment, we observe an always fascinating but also challenging interplay between a patient's free will and underlying determinants. "[F]ree is but a conscious reference, entailing the rejection of conscious or preconscious interference" (ibid., p. 157). Free association is the circling about a gravitational core of a collapsed psychic mass; it is free to roam only within a predetermined dimension. Its aim is to gradually expand that dimension, to bring it, if only faintly and flickeringly, to view and into the realm of language.

This is rarely a trip either we or our patients want to take. While Emmanuel Ghent (1990) glimpsed in his patients a "passionate longing to surrender," he also observed that this longing carries "that most unwelcome price-tag: dread" (Ghent, 1990, pp. 114–115). Further, our patients long for, and dread, release not only from stifling *relational* bonds but also from stifling *ways of thinking*. To "break free," our patients must *choose* free association, but they do so *only* when their options for controlling their discourse have reached a futile limit; they surrender from a position of desperation as much as from desire. At last they choose what has been a perpetually procrastinated conscious encounter with their elusive unconscious knowing and intentionality, with the "overdetermined" fuss that stifles their lives in repetitive patterns.

Given the various diversions and avoidances that he witnessed in his patients in pursuit (and in lieu) of free association, Freud added the following recommendations, when beginning the treatment, to the fundamental rule:

> What you tell me must differ in one respect from an ordinary conversation.... You will be tempted to say to yourself that this or that is irrelevant here ... that there is no need to say it ... [but you] must say it precisely because you feel an aversion to doing so.... [N]ever forget that you have promised to be absolutely honest, and never leave anything out because, for some reason or other, it is unpleasant to tell it. (Freud, 1913c, pp. 134–135)

Michael Guy Thompson notes that Freud's phrasing establishes free association as a pledge, introducing what Philip Rieff (1959, p. 315) originally called "an ethic of honesty" into the practice of psychoanalysis. As Thompson elaborates, by enlisting this pledge,

"Freud transformed the patient at the beginning of analysis from a person who simply tells stories into a moral agent who determines what is true by saying it" (Thompson, 2001, p. 400). Free association, linked with this emancipatory if also moral injunction (the *actual* fundamental rule), impels us to attend to what we typically conceal, to say whatever spontaneously comes to mind, so that we might expose unconscious secrets that we hide even from ourselves.

With this shift, the practice of psychoanalysis forfeited the "panoramic memory of the hypnotised subject" (Donnet, 2001, p. 159) for free association and its moral imperative, becoming as much a study of freedom as a study of resistances (Freud, 1924f, p. 196; 1925h, p. 235). But while discontinuities signaled limitations on associative freedom, before long they became the terrain of greatest interest, revealing that free association and *un*free resistance are but two sides of one coin. Discontinuity is an index to the quest's impossibility: by dint of the fact that words themselves are ambiguous, incomplete, and incapable of symbolizing the totality of experience, free speech is, in practice, impossible. Freud's response to the gaps in speech was twofold. On the one hand, he attempted to compensate for the gaps and resistances—the patient's unfree free associations—by adding his own interpretations. On the other hand, he began to study the ways in which the very situation of the psychoanalytic treatment insisted upon constraints—thereby enabling the patient's expressive, if *symbolic*, freedom.

Let's pause for a moment to consider the word "free"—an adjective whose imaginative power is proportional to its conceptual elusiveness. Patrick Mahony notes the "pregnant fact" that in Sumer, circa 2350 B.C., "'freedom' (*amargi*) as a word appears for the first time in recorded history" and that "literally *amargi* means 'return to the mother'" (1987, p. 130). If we fold this observation into our exploration of what "free" really means, we may begin to recognize the paradoxical encounter between what is determined and what is free that lies at the heart—and the "navel"—of the psychoanalytic conversation, which by dint of language will impose and create separation.[1] Tracing Mahony's etymological excursion, we discover that "the terms 'translation,' 'metaphor,' and 'transference' are synonymous; said otherwise, transference is an unconscious translation and metaphor, or as the early Freud would have it, 'a false connection'" (ibid., p. 7) but also one that will bring reunion, a new—if imperfect—joining or relationship. Patients will tend to transfer their childhood conflicts onto the person of the analyst, as metaphor, setting the stage for a reenactment of their developmental history and its blockages. Thus Freud became convinced that the interpretation of both transference and resistance was essential if the pathway between memory and symptom, between unconscious and conscious, between past and present, was to become decipherable.

Freud was beginning to recognize that it is *constraint* that ensures a space for honest, daring revelation. Constraints led Freud, just as they led his patients—and just as they lead us—to circle back to the very ground where he, they, and we have already planted our footsteps. Back, namely, to the figure of the analyst: the figure that Freud had discovered is never neutral in the clinic. Freud's fundamental rule bequeathed to psychoanalysis a paradoxical rule, and the odyssey of free association became a tale of the paradox of freedom.

Paradoxes of freedom

Bearing in mind the primal etymological link between freedom and a return to mother, let us return to the infancy of psychoanalytic thought. Free association emerged amid frustration with earlier, failed clinical methods. After a period of productive experimentation, it eventually became the general "rule" of psychoanalytic practice, the path to liberating a patient from the tyranny of her symptoms. This genetic model of frustration plus experimentation also characterizes the American Constitution and its Bill of Rights, in particular the First Amendment, which is to the American mind synonymous with guaranteed free speech. The Founding Fathers, bridling at the motherland's increasingly authoritarian and tyrannical restrictions on public expression as well as on commerce and governance, set forth the proposition that free speech and free assembly were essential to an informed and participatory public. Any healthy (implicitly democratic) social order would depend upon them, especially since open speech and assembly might lead to serious challenges against the very government that guaranteed these freedoms. In the end, free speech became for the incipient nation a different kind of fundamental "rule": a rule nominally aimed at animating democratic life, but more fundamentally intended to consolidate the new nation and stabilize relationships among both individual states and economic classes. It is debatable whether these operational considerations can be ascribed to any prior popular sentiment.

Freud would come to discover that the unconscious is governed by the laws of speech—laws that enable the unconscious to "reign" in a symbolically mediated but still unbounded exercise of freedom. But this freedom is still discovered and fought for anew in each analytic encounter and in each analytic coupling. The situation is actually more fraught in civil society, at least American civil society, where human rights such as equality and "freedom" are conceptually linked to and even identified with democracy, and thus where the individual/collective dialectic is a process of continual self-inflicted wounding. Again and again, the conversation hinges on how we understand "freedom," and its paradoxical constraints.

Karl Polanyi suggested that there are two kinds of (political) freedoms, "good" (e.g., freedom of conscience and freedom of speech and association) and "bad" (e.g., the freedom to exploit others). He credited the market economy with producing both, but he warned that it also degenerates freedom when "the freedom that regulation creates is denounced as unfreedom; the justice, liberty and welfare it offers are decried as a camouflage of slavery" (Polanyi, 1944, pp. 256–257). In American society today, our First Amendment rights set the stage for these controversies. Civil libertarians argue for strenuous protections of free expression, even when it may cause harm or be in conflict with other core values. Others support regulations that protect human dignity, social justice, and meaningful collective action, even if at the penalty of some sacrifice of free individual expression.

We find an echo of these tensions in Freud's discovery of the power of resistance, of *unfreedom*, as both a barrier to and enabler of the talking cure, of *free* association, which is oxymoronic because it cannot really be free in any usual sense. It is bounded by the very structures of language, by the constraints of transference, and by unconscious determinism that challenges any naïve conception of human liberty. Furthermore, he came to recognize that without a practice of *constraint*, the analyst cannot possibly offer the patient a means to win relative psychical *freedom*.

But it was the tension between individual liberty and collective interests that proved especially perplexing to Freud, and that led him to tilt his theory decidedly away from any pure, unmediated pursuit of free expression and toward a theory of compromise in which liberty is tempered by constraint. The Founding Fathers also actively wrestled with the paradoxes—and inevitable concessions—vital to any plausible Constitutional commitment to personal and national liberty. Explicitly influenced by Enlightenment thought, they sought inspiration from the common law of England and from John Locke's account of natural rights theory and the social contract. As we will see, the result was that similar tensions were not only embedded in the First Amendment but have continued to characterize its evolution.

In briefest overview, natural rights theory held that individuals had not only inherent but also inalienable rights to liberty. But Locke's social contract held that such natural rights were bounded by the competing rights of others (to equality and to freedom). Compromise was an essential part of the bargain: To some degree, individuals must alienate their rights to the community or government which stands entrusted and empowered to mediate between individual and collective rights. But the *sine qua non* of this republic (which would become known as a representative democracy) was that "we, the people" maintained a checking power—the right to oversee the proper conduct of the government entrusted with this function. For Locke, this right implied the right even to dismiss the government; and so it allowed for revolution.

Steven Heyman traces the influence of Locke's thinking on the early American political landscape and on the bills of rights in many early state constitutions. These created a strong precedent for privileging freedom of speech and of the press as important barriers against governmental incursions on the liberty of the individual. In a set of Radical Whig writings (*Cato's Letters*) that popularized Locke's views, freedom of speech—"the right 'to think what you would, and speak what you thought'"—"was not merely a barrier against government oppression; it was also an essential element of natural liberty" (Heyman, 2008, p. 9).

These sentiments influenced debates surrounding a federal Con-stitution. Although we tend to forget this, when the Constitution was first drafted in 1787, it had no bill of rights—a lack that sparked lively debate: Federalists, on the one hand, felt that such a bill was unnecessary because the people would retain all rights not specifically delegated to the government, Antifederalists, on the other hand, lobbied for federal protection of liberty of speech and press. James Madison subsequently introduced a bill of rights in the First Congress in 1789, and drafted a First Amendment saturated with a natural rights perspective in which free speech and press rights, "the great bulwarks of liberty, shall be inviolable" (Heyman, 2008, p. 13).

To draft a bill acceptable to Federalists and Antifederalists alike, the framers chose to bypass specific points of controversy, wording their amendment by invoking only general principles. This decision left a significant gap—not only between those favoring strong state governments and those favoring a strong federal government, but also between free speech libertarians and those seeking regulation and constraint.

If the Founders granted sovereignty to the Constitution, the Constitutions' inaugural amendment pointed to the means, continually fought and never fully won, by which the people might restore (or claim for a first time) their own share of self-rule. After all, the First Amendment may be short on detail, but it is explicit about its purview: the target was Congress. "Congress shall make no law. ..." And so the Bill of Rights emerged as a response to Anti-Federalists' concern that the Constitution granted too much centralized power to the Congress. Individual states were accorded far greater (albeit implicit) discretion to set their own limits on freedoms encompassed by the Bill of Rights. The problem it was meant to address was the threat of *central* power to majority rule—not *any* threat to individual or minority expression. For the first eighty years of its life, the First Amendment protected free speech only from federal censorship, not from state control or majority sentiment.

This balance would begin to shift in the aftermath of the Civil War. The antebellum experience had shone a bright light on the ways in which slavery bred oppression; the slave states violated nearly every right and freedom declared in the Bill of Rights. This oppression, once exposed, awakened the popular consciousness and conscience, prompting social action and outrage at the inequities, across states, in religious and civic freedoms. It also prompted the ratification of the Thirteenth Amendment, which abolished slavery in 1865. At last, a federal Constitutional amendment trumped state law. But Black Codes resurrected de facto slavery and it was only with the passage of the Civil Rights Act of 1866 and the Fourteenth Amendment that the Constitution came to truly embody the Bill of Rights—and to apply it to every citizen and indeed every inhabitant of any state—in our modern sense.

The Fourteenth Amendment's retroactive assertion of the Bill of Rights' (and thus the First Amendement's) supremacy made a resurgent appeal to natural rights theory and its common-law tradition, the same animating traditions that had inspired Freud's commitment to individual liberty and self-knowledge. It was thus not, as most believe, at the republic's founding, but during its reconstruction, that the Bill of

Rights came alive. The Fourteenth Amendment's principal draftsman, John Bingham, claiming "fidelity to the sacred cause of the Constitution," proclaimed the "sacred" and "immortal" nature of our Bill of Rights (Amar, 1998, pp. 190–191). His hierophantic rhetoric invigorated the Bill of Rights, helping to establish as law the Founders' ideals (if not intent) of freedom. It would no longer be so easy for states to intrude upon and regulate private matters of free expression and religious practice.

Gradually, after the reconstruction, as modern First Amendment jurisprudence evolved, courts afforded greater protections to individuals and minorities. But this advance in civil rights, perhaps not surprisingly, entailed its own evolving tensions, ones that reverberate with the original debates surrounding the amendment—ones that would come to perpetually plague Sigmund Freud as well: namely, how to negotiate a balance between individual and collective interests, and between collective and governmental or so-called "state" interests. These questions expose other core issues: how can we understand a collectivity divorced from individual citizens' participation and self-determination? And how can we understand state interests divorced from the collective?

Before examining how psychoanalysis addresses these matters, let's take a closer look at the partial resolutions, reconciliations, and setbacks characterizing the history of First Amendment jurisprudence.

Fuck the draft

While the framers put speech at the top of their list of protected rights and recognized its definitive significance for political liberty, that does not mean they ever believed that *all* speech ought to be permitted, or that *all* people should be allowed to speak. Nor did anyone at any level of government fight for the rights the First Amendment seemed to privilege. The vague and general language of that amendment certainly did not, to any early American's mind, cover seditious libel, blasphemy, or defamation, all of which were immediately and then for centuries successfully prosecuted (Strauss, 2002, pp. 40–44). Courts in general, not excepting the highest, cast a jaundiced eye on plaintiffs' claims that they ought to be allowed to express odious opinions, even if their harmfulness might seem arguable to us. As Anthony Lewis notes, "Claims for free speech regularly lost in the Court through the 1920s" (2008, p. 34).

Just as Freud's fundamental rule had ever so gradually achieved widespread acceptance, the tides in the US Supreme Court had ever so gradually begun to turn during the preceding decade, largely as a function of four opinions, two of them dissents: *Schenck* vs. *United States* (1919); *Abrams* vs. *United States* (1919); *Whitney* vs. *California* (1927); and *United States* vs. *Schwimmer* (1929). These created what has come to be seen as a "legal revolution" in First Amendment jurisprudence, largely because "their rhetoric was so powerful, so convincing, that it changed the attitude of the country and the Court" (Lewis, 2008, pp. 34–35).

The revolution began, somewhat inauspiciously, with the speech-restrictive decision in *Schenck*, a case involving pamphlets advocating draft resistance and distributed by the Socialist Party of America during World War I. The Court decided unanimously against a plaintiff asserting free speech rights, but in so doing they also began to define exactly what could be suppressed and what could not. Writing for the majority, Justice Oliver Wendell Holmes asserted that speech could be suppressed only when that speech is "of such a nature as to create a clear and present danger that they will bring about the substantive evils that Congress has a right to prevent" (249 U.S. 48 (1919)).[2] (Holmes's example, "a man falsely shouting fire in a theater and causing a panic," would become quintessential.) But in a Harvard Law Review article, Zachariah Chafee chided Holmes, asserting that "perplexing cases" involving the First Amendment "cannot be solved by the multiplication of obvious examples." He regretted that Holmes had done "nothing to emphasize the social interest behind free speech, and show the need of balancing even in war time" (Chafee, 1919, p. 968; Rohde, 2014).

Later that same year, in another antiwar case (*Abrams*), Holmes (joined by Louis Brandeis, in their first famous joint dissent) maintained that the prevailing opinion failed to honor this "clear and present danger" test. Obviously, Holmes's novel assertions in *Schenck* had failed to persuade the other justices; but even if they had, there would still have been room to disagree over what was clearly and presently dangerous.[3] Yet something *had* changed. Holmes—who had once been, in Alan Dershowitz's (2013) words, "a strident and often thoughtless defender of the power of government to punish controversial speech"— had changed his mind. He had come to realize "that the ultimate good desired is better reached by free trade in ideas."

In any case, Holmes's "clear and present danger" test, while initially more a rhetorical marker than a consensus view, represented at least half a step forward. As John Paul Stevens (2012) notes, now "federal judges began to see the power of the state as much more of a threat to the individual than vice versa." This step was reaffirmed eloquently, if to no immediate practical effect, in two significant opinions by Holmes and Brandeis in the following decade, opinions which set the stage for First Amendment rights as we now know them—or as we think we know them.

First came Brandeis's opinion in *Whitney*, the case of a woman convicted for helping to found the Communist Labor Party in California. Brandeis, joined by Holmes, concurred with the Court's decision but disagreed with its reasoning that speech may be censored and even punished if it has a "bad tendency" and might therefore lead to social harm. "Those who won our independence," argued Brandeis,

> believed liberty to be the secret of happiness and courage to be the secret of liberty. They believed that freedom to think as you will and to speak as you think are means indispensable to the discovery and spread of political truth; ... that the greatest menace to freedom is an inert people; that public discussion is a political duty; and that this should be a fundamental principle of the American government ... that fear breeds repression; that repression breeds hate; that hate menaces stable government. (*Whitney* vs. *California*, 274 U.S. 357 (1927), at 375–76)

After this rousing argument that authentic discourse relies on truly free speech, Brandeis and Holmes joined together for another opinion, this time actually dissenting, in *United States* vs. *Schwimmer*. Holmes asserted that "if there is any principle of the Constitution that more imperatively calls for attachment than any other it is the principle of free thought—not free thought for those who agree with us but freedom for the thought that we hate" (279 U.S. 644 (1929)). With these words, Holmes helped to spark our inspirational and aspirational love affair with the First Amendment.

All these opinions were in fact or in spirit dissents. But finally, in 1931, the Court upheld a free speech claim, narrowing the gap between First Amendment ideals and a real commitment to free speech. With the Court's decision in *Near* vs. *Minnesota*, it became difficult to issue a prior restraint on the press, even if what was published had a "bad tendency." The case involved a challenge to Minnesota's Public Nuisance Law, which prohibited the publication of "malicious, scandalous and defamatory" content. The Supreme Court stated outright that this law was a direct "infringement of the liberty of the press" and thus unconstitutional. The decision however was by no means a blanket absolution. There remained some types of speech that the Court considered obviously beyond the bounds of protection, including certain restrictions on obscenity, incitements to violence, and obstructions to the conduct of war. This grab bag of old and new limitations on speech would become collectively known as the "Near exception."

Tides were turning. Legal doctrine began to reflect the now central mission of free speech to protect currently unpopular ideas from a current majority; and the Supreme Court began to "incorporate" the free speech clause against the states by means of the Fourteenth Amendment. The Near exception would remain a basis for enacting prior restraints until the Court reversed course in its 1971 ruling in the "Pentagon Papers" case, *New York Times* vs. *United States*. But even before that decision, in its 1964 ruling in another case involving the same plaintiff (*New York Times* vs. *Sullivan*), the Court had already put an end to the idea of seditious libel and virtually immunized the press from subsequent penalties for what it publishes. That case set new standards for libel, freed the press from the threat of endless libel actions, and thus paved the way for a much bolder and more open press. But it did so at the price of setting a very high standard not only for government officials but for "public figures" of any kind to win damages for libel, as they now had to bear the burden to provide evidence of "deliberate or reckless falsification" to do so.

Even given this seemingly decisive tilt toward press liberty at the expense of public figures and institutions, the free speech rights of individuals were less than assured. In a noteworthy case of 1935, the Court rejected a claim put forth by a family whose children had been expelled from school for their refusal (based on their convictions as Jehovah Witnesses) to participate in a mandatory Pledge of Allegiance. Only in 1943 was this ruling overturned, paving the way for the First Amendment to stand guard for minority speech, in the face of majority oppression. By the 1960s, free speech advocates scored many a victory:

> Schoolchildren protesting the Vietnam War won the right to wear black armbands. A man's right to wear in public a jacket adorned with "FUCK THE DRAFT" was affirmed. Some types of sexually explicit speech got protection. (Wu, 2013, pp. 36–37)

Not surprisingly, as Tim Wu observes,

> it was also during these years that conservatives staked their
> original, parsimonious position on the First Amendment.
> Politicians like then-Governor Ronald Reagan and Richard Nixon
> denounced what they viewed as a misuse of the Constitution
> to protect "subversives." ... Conservative legal thinkers such as
> Robert Bork and Justice William Rehnquist led an intellectual
> assault on an interpretation of the First Amendment that they con-
> sidered sharply at odds with majority rule. ... The battle lines were
> drawn. To the left, the First Amendment was becoming sacred
> writ; to the right, it was a living symbol of judicial excess. (Wu,
> 2013, pp. 36–37)

Since then, free-speech skirmishes have continued to break out in
appeals courts across the land. The Supreme Court has ruled on the
issue scores of times since 1971.[4] Its views on who (or what) counts as
a legal person with the right to speak freely (and how freely, and in
which contexts), and whether spending money is a kind of "speech,"
are among only the most recent live controversies.

One notorious case, known as *Citizens United*, has led to a rapid
dismantling of First Amendment protection for the voices of people
with "fundamentally different views."[5] By granting First Amendment
status to corporations, just like any other "person," *Citizens United*
(and its antecedents) essentially rendered the *identity* of the speaker
irrelevant, prioritizing instead the question of whether the law "abridges
expression that the First Amendment was designed to protect"
(Wu, 2013, p. 37). Those who defend the decision tend to argue that
while money itself isn't speech, restricting the flow of money restricts
speech. As unsatisfactory as that logic may be, as Joe Nocera (2014)
points out, that's not quite the point anyway. The problem is the subtle influence that big money buys and corrosive collusions that follow.
What's the purpose of so much money in politics? "Big contributors,"
he observes "want something for their money ... they want to know
that their bidding will be done."

Citizens United was not an isolated decision. A series of rulings
followed fast on the heels of this watershed case. As documented
by Wu, these rulings expose a story of the "'co-opting' of the First
Amendment [by] economic libertarians and corporate lawyers who
have recognized its power to immunize private enterprise from legal

restraint" (Wu, 2013, p. 36). This story spans issues that confound most common sense notions we have about free speech, including how corporations "deal with customer data or are required to make disclosures regarding their financial standings or the potential downsides of their products" (ibid., p. 38).

Assessing this "hijacking" or exploitation of the First Amendment, Wu conclusively laments, "Few industries these days can resist First Amendment defenses of even the most outrageous conduct" (ibid., p. 39). Which brings us to the point of my exposition of high court free speech decisions: There have always been boundaries to speech; they have always been contested at levels low and high; and they are the product of cultural moments and judicial prejudice, not of any definitive founding intent.

As in the case of free speech, our understanding of free association has been continuously evolving, adapting to cultural moments, psychological dynamics, and practical experience. Both psychoanalysis and constitutional law remain (ostensibly) dedicated to the pursuit of freedom, or of certain kinds of freedom, even as both have needed to recognize that restraints are often not only advisable but also essential to the freedom under restraint. But Wu's assessment of how the "mighty, as well as the marginalized" (ibid., p. 37) have come to not only make use of but also to exploit the First Amendment highlights how the frankly insincere, cynical and even sinister imposition of restraints—and, perhaps more perversely, the anarchic and tyrannical freedom *from* restraint—breaks down any ethical framework for true democratic expression and its engagement with unsettling but also vitalizing unconscious energies.

There is, after all, an irony at the core of both the First Amendment and psychoanalysis's fundamental rule: Both imply that freedom is the rule, that constraint is the exception. But unbounded freedom is a myth. Constraints, far from the exception, are the keystone upon which freedom—the freedom of symbolic expression—becomes possible. How democracy and analytic treatment become vulnerable to degradation; how they are enhanced by thoughtful restraints that bear responsibility to specific relational contexts while endeavoring to preserve an ethic of freedom; and how psychoanalysis might help citizens and their leaders better understand the interplay of freedom and restraint—all these are the subjects of my remaining chapters. And they require that we elaborate a conception of symbolic freedom, freedom in a space between utter, unfettered liberty and necessary limits.

CHAPTER FOUR

What is special about speech?

Free association and free speech, as we're discovering, share much beyond that essential if aspirational adjective, "free." Both require genuine human collaboration and compromise. Both are conditioned by and subject to lawful foundations—constraints that (aspirationally) generate an open space for free, even unbounded, symbolic discourse. Both are riven by foundational tensions and paradoxes that arise in large part from such necessary, even intrinsic, constraints. But, as I noted earlier, raw free associations, more than sincere free speech, lie very near to unconscious mentation (and to its non-metaphoric inexpressible and inexhaustible origins), suggesting their bare dialectic with consciousness. I will return to this distinction later in this chapter.

Despite slow and sputtering gains in the free speech privileges nominally set forth in the First Amendment, and despite the more dramatic recent erosions to them, free speech has assumed a de facto primacy (its *firstness*) over other Constitutional rights. This valuation has been so seldom explicitly discussed (at least until recently) that Constitutional scholar Frederick Schauer (1995) described it as an implicit "orthodoxy," or more properly "an ideology" (p. 11). Worse, it seems there may be no "philosophically defensible" core to the First Amendment, except for what emerges from its common-law, opportunistic use (for often mutually exclusive ends) as "the first and last refuge of saints and scoundrels alike" (Schauer, 2002, p. 197; p. 193). In view of the practical results, the confusion and conflict among arguments and decisions, Robert Post laments "what is now generally acknowledged as the sorry state of First Amendment doctrine" (2002, pp. 172–173).

This state of affairs might have been predicted. The Constitution's framers never clarified the meaning or significance of free speech beyond the amendment's few words. They left no written legacy of their intentions, no record by which to understand this provision—though state constitutional antecedents are certainly relevant and provide rich insights into the federal document (Amar, 1998; Wood, 1969). It helps, as Burt Neuborne (2015) suggests, to read the First Amendment in its entirety. We discover that freedom of speech is embedded in other foundational ideas: it lies between two religion or conscience clauses (freedom from establishment and free exercise), and among three levels of individual interaction with the community: freedom of the press, freedom of assembly, and freedom to petition for a redress of grievances. Highlighting this sequencing, Neuborne credits Madison's "genius" with what he describes as his poetic, "carefully drawn, chrono-logically organized blueprint of democracy in action" (Neuborne, 2015, p. 17; p. 18). Nonetheless, the First Amendment ("Congress shall make no law ... abridging the freedom of speech, or of the press ..."), while explicit in its way, is ultimately opaque by virtue of its terseness and generality. What's more, we—and the Court—typically (and problem-atically) reduce it to the free speech clause alone. This reduction once more prompts the question: Why do we distinguish speech from other intentional and self-expressive activity?

This contradiction—so little speech about why speech matters—mirrors a similar ironic gap at the core of psychoanalysis. While Freud often revisited and restated his belief in the analytic preeminence of free association, "he never got far beyond some early core ideas; and it is just as surprising how often these same ideas have been reiterated in psychoanalytic literature with relatively little advance beyond them" (Mahony, 1987, p. 23). To be sure, there are several noteworthy medita-tions on the topic of free association, variously scholarly, clinical, and philosophical (to name a few: Bollas, 2002; Kris, 1996; Mahony, 1987; Thompson, 2004), and free association did for a period receive its due in the literature, at least until theory grew more keenly attentive to transference and resistance, and it became the "somewhat neglected handmaiden to those theoretical stepsisters" (Kris, 1996, pp. xiv–xv).

Still, today's psychoanalytic literature continues to suffer a surprising dearth of sustained studies on free association—what Mahony (1987) called its ironic "cryptomnesic fate" (p. 152). Our inconsistent attention to it not only in theory but also, for many of us, in clinical practice, echoes its inventor's. While we have never stopped discussing free association, it remains oddly situated. On the one hand, we apply free association idiosyncratically in practice, bending it to our purposes, adapting it to clinical situations—as per Harry Stack Sullivan's (1953) oft-cited recommendation to supplement Freud's bare guidelines with a guided "detailed inquiry." On the other hand, unreserved, unedited conversation is so primary a value that we tend to conflate it with the closely linked but not identical fundamental rule (Mahony, 1987; Thompson, 2004)—a "pledge" of honesty. This pledge enlists the patient's status as a moral agent (Thompson, 2004, p. 10) but also obscures it, as we tend (when we conflate the terms) to associate more freely to the "free" in free association than to the ethic to be "honest."

Declining attention to free association seems to have coincided with the rise of relational psychoanalysis, which rejects a one-person model of the mind and downplays (when it doesn't frankly dismiss) drive theory. These relational tenets run contrary to traditional conceptions (and methods) of free association as the product of endogenous processes of a singular mind (Aron, 1990). And just as First Amendment doctrine "veers between theory and the exigencies of specific cases" (Post, 2002, p. 153), today's psychoanalytic pluralism creates theoretical ambiguities which, it would seem, have ambiguous clinical implications. Citing Kris's contention (1990, p. 26) that "free association is the hallmark of psychoanalytic treatment conducted by analysts of all stripes," Fred Busch (1994, p. 365) wonders whether this homage obscures conceptual contradictions in methods and goals that warrant critical analysis. Perhaps this is why we seldom investigate what values underlie free association and its conjoined and implicitly esteemed partner, free speech.

But this blurriness stems in part from Freud's own. He did not begin with an a priori theory of the value of free association, let alone free speech. An explicit focus on language would have to wait for others— for example, Jacques Lacan (1957), who famously adopted ideas from the fields of semiotics and linguistics to elaborate a "linguistic turn" in psychoanalysis, arguing for a rigorous and renewed focus within psychoanalysis on speech and language in which free association as a form of unedited speech leads to truth of the subject's desire. American psychoanalysis has only haltingly integrated Lacanian innovations, and many of the thinkers influential to Lacan (notably, the Swiss linguist Saussure) were relatively unknown to Freud. But Freud, who set forth on his career in a spiritualistic age, infused both by naturalism and its neo-romanticist reaction, perceived the signal power of words long before he conceived of the fundamental rule. Freud's discoveries, more than clinical happenstance, emerged from intuitive but persistent experimentation with his patients, and reinforced his early conviction that speech has a curative potential. But the romanticist-scientist was more apt to speak of restoring the magical power of words (1890a) than to clarify underlying assumptions about what made speech special.

Oddly, this ill definition of the magic of speech persists. Despite Freud's early recognition of speech's promise, it is seemingly unprecedented in the talking cure's century-long history that a recent issue of the *Journal of the American Psychoanalytic Association* (December, 2014) was dedicated to the therapeutic role of language. Therein Jeanine Vivona writes that it's "both strange and true that contemporary psychoanalysis lacks a full explanation for the therapeutic action of talking" (2014, p. 1025). In writing on the First Amendment, Schauer similarly observed that there is "little free thought about free thought, little free inquiry about free inquiry, and little free speech about free speech" (Schauer, 1995, p. 13). Recent global challenges—think *Citizen's United*, the Danish cartoons, the aftermath of the Arab spring, the *Charlie Hebdo* massacres, the controversies surrounding the Confederate flag in America—have awakened us to the relevance of free speech to any intuitive notion of democracy, far beyond ivory tower rhetoric or of a muddled and too often tone deaf Supreme Court. These same challenges inspire and provoke psychoanalysis to reach beyond its historic professional insularity and to claim its relevance to the public sphere. Yet our capacity to articulate psychoanalysis's relevance to a robust free speech regime is limited because (at least by some accounts) we leave undertheorized, and lack a framework for, the therapeutic action of speech.

Given its central importance to at least one major democratic project and to an entire therapeutic model, it is puzzling that speech has received so little focused attention, at least until recent times, either from political scientists or from psychoanalysts. Its value is taken as axiomatic. More fundamentally, the conceptual ambiguities surrounding the primacy of speech—why it is privileged in both democratic discourse and psychoanalytic theory—reveal a self-contradiction that both highlights their mutual resonances and merits interrogation. It at least seems that, in psychoanalysis no less than in Constitutional literature, we have been mute about what we most value. Why did free association, relative to other forms of human expression, attain such special status that psychoanalysis became emblemized as the "talking cure," a phrase imprinted early on upon it by one of Freud's signature patients, known to us as "Anna O"? Further, why do we focus so much on the obstacles, and less on the means by which speech may aspire to "cure"? If the relationship between democratic discourse and psychoanalytic free association is surprisingly and rarely explored, is this because they both elude the challenging question posed by Schauer (1983), "Must speech be special?"

It is (to risk tautology) not only that we have too seldom explored the question of what makes speech special, but psychoanalysis has seldom explored its relationship to democratic free speech. Most arguments defending the special status of speech appeal to the tenets of Enlightenment philosophy, which was practically the blueprint for the American and French revolutions but also foundational to Freud's evolving thought. What I find especially compelling about this heritage is how an Enlightenment ethos of scientific experimentation insinuated its way into both the U.S. Constitution and Freud's thought; and how an experimentation with free speech figured prominently in both. What's more, it would be this key variable that would entwine Freud's scientific dream with what George Makari (2008, p. 245) calls the "liberal's dream" inscribed in Freud's new science—its promise to "further individual emancipation." In his experimentation with free speech, which amounted to a kind of Enlightenment ethos, Freud joined his scientific dream to his emancipatory one, and anticipated what I see as psychoanalysis's democratic calling.

Experimentation and enlightened speech

Timothy Ferris, tracing the historical links among the scientific revolution, the Enlightenment, and the spread of democracy, observes that the American Revolution was "carried out in disproportionate measure by scientists like Thomas Paine, Benjamin Franklin, and Thomas Jefferson"

(Ferris, 2010, p. 6). Liberal democracy, like scientific knowledge, is in his view based on experimentation, on provisionality and debate (ibid., pp. 114–115). James Madison came to recommend an "empirical course, … an 'actual trial,' for what would inevitably be a flawed and imperfect, but potentially also resilient, Constitutional launch" (ibid., p. 102).

In their discussions of the new nation and its developing constitution, several of the Founding Fathers borrowed from science the term "experiment." So too did Freud as he probed his patients' psyches and developed theories around what he discovered. He sought through hypnosis to reveal the unconscious as "something actual, tangible and subject to experiment" (Freud, 1924f, p. 192). Furthermore,

> Progress in scientific work is just as it is in an analysis. We bring expectations with us into the work, but they must be forcibly held back. By observation, now at one point and now at another, we come upon something new; but to begin with the pieces do not fit together. We put forward conjectures, we construct hypotheses, which we withdraw if they are not confirmed, we need much patience and readiness for any eventuality. (Freud, 1933a, p. 174)

Freud did not limit his use of scientific terminology to analytic practice and its revelations. He also (in this way like the framers) called "experimental" the development of social processes and political movements, such as Bolshevism, Marxism, and so forth.

Ultimately, both Freud and the framers entwined ideas of experimentation with ideas of liberty. And while rejecting traditional received authority, both drew a foundational inspiration from science, especially the natural sciences. The experimental tradition advanced knowledge, liberty, and truth born of observation and curiosity. If Freud was inspired by da Vinci, the "first modern scientist," it was because Leonardo aimed "to probe the secrets of nature," including human nature (Whitebook, 2008, p. 1771, citing Freud, 1910c, p. 122). Freud too might have drawn (unacknowledged) inspiration from Thomas Jefferson, who had championed not only press freedoms but the printing press as a means of promoting knowledge and liberty. Writing in 1813, Jefferson noted, "Science has liberated the ideas of those who read and reflect, and the American example had kindled feelings of right in the people. … There is not a truth existing which I fear or would wish unknown to the whole world" (Ferris, 2010, pp. 107–108).

Truth seeking was, of course, at the heart of Freud's scientific—and semiotic—mission. In developing his notion of the technique of free association and the fundamental rule that patients were to report on their mental activity without bias, he was striving to relieve his patients' suffering and to gather valid empirical knowledge of mental life and its unconscious foundations. Later, Freud would come to recognize the inevitability of our darker impulses, ones that (ironically per-haps) insinuated an anti-Enlightenment subtext of unruly, unseemly, passions into an otherwise too neat and domesticated Enlightenment tale of reason and personal sovereignty. His scientific claims, reflecting this tension, would be increasingly elaborated between speculation and myth.

If psychoanalysis, like speech itself, was situated between magic and science, Freud's magic was to situate himself as both "the romantic respecter of the unknown and the rationalistic scientist of the observ-able" (Roazen, 1992, p. 237). This duality would inspire his hopes to establish a scientific basis for the unconscious as a natural phenomenon, and thereby to establish psychoanalysis as a natural science; he would even eventually proclaim that psychoanalysis had no particular worldview beyond a scientific one (Makari, 2008, p. 450). However, this would be true only to the degree that natural science was no longer severed from human science, or from social philosophy. As we shall see, Freud's seemingly discordant dreams (liberatory and scientific) revealed themselves as entwined, like serpents on the caduceus. After all, speech—that experimental medium through which Freud would pursue his quest for scientific "truth"—was also the medium for revealing the emancipatory truths of our otherwise unspoken, symp-tomatic, captive desires.

Which still leaves the question: how did the Enlightenment inspira-tion for scientific and for democratic experimentation come to accord a privileged status to speech?

Moral and instrumental rationales for free speech

In modern contests between individual free speech and collective rights, proponents of the former will argue that free speech is special and worthy of special protection. They will ground their arguments in a Lockean natural rights tradition. From there, they may take one of two paths. Along one lie intrinsic or "moral" arguments based on a belief that free speech has value essential to human dignity and autonomy. This view is at least implicit both in the Declaration of Independence and in the Bill of Rights. Along the other lie arguments based on free speech's beneficial effects on (or consequences for) society. Such "instrumental" or "consequentialist" justifications for free speech include economic prosperity, personal happiness, or a more effectively functioning democracy.

Often enough, we discover that moral and instrumental rationales for free thought and speech are inseparable—that moral arguments *are* consequential. Any clear demarcation among theories favoring speaker's rights, listener rights, truth seeking or democracy, is hard to discover.

To the extent that psychoanalysis aspires to expand the symbolic capacity and emancipatory agency of the speaker, it too implicitly finds both moral and consequential bases for free association/speech. It finds resonance in Justice Louis Brandeis's evocation of the spirit that fostered the First Amendment: "Those who won our independence believed that the final end of the State was to make men free to develop their faculties" (*Whitney* vs. *California*, 1927). Further, Brandeis described the Founders' embrace of liberty both as an *end* (a good in and of itself) and also as a *means* "indispensable" to the principle of self-government. Perhaps unconsciously invoking Freud and the radical, even revolutionary nature of psychoanalysis, Brandeis links our individual liberty to our social collectivity.

Except that by this time Freud had concluded that civilization couldn't tolerate pure truths, preferring instead the illusions of wish fulfillment; and that ultimately civilized society requires renunciation (and thus discontent among citizens) rather than true liberty. But if Freud remained ever perplexed by the tension between individual and collective interests, he was at least vaguely confident that these were both relevant to the moral and instrumental aims of psychoanalysis. In his brief foray into the psychology of group processes, Freud concluded that

> In the individual's mental life, someone else is invariably involved, as a model, as an object, as a helper, as an opponent; and so from the very first individual psychology, in this extended but entirely justifiable sense of the words, is at the same time social psychology as well. (Freud, 1921c, p. 69)

If we could emancipate the psyche individual by individual, it would be possible to stimulate social reform and ultimately to create a healthy social space. He and many like-minded colleagues believed, "that curing the self could cure a society, and that conversely a sick society resulted in sick men and women" (Makari, 2008, p. 398).

Freud's remarks on these matters almost seem like side notes, addenda to his scientific pursuits. Along his "experimental" path, his main discovery was that, despite our or his wishes, there is no unmediated access to unconscious "data." His *scientific* quest for natural laws to account for unconscious processes led him to admit to what must be deduced, to a knowledge only partly accessible through a *mediated, hermeneutic, and truth-seeking* discourse. By recognizing the complexity of a natural science that includes our symbolic nature, Freud envisioned and contributed to an Enlightenment heritage that had as much to do with liberty as it did with constraints that enabled that liberty; and that had as much to do with rationality and order as it did with irrationality, the romanticist realm of the passions. He perceived the ineluctable tensions of a natural law *of desire's speech* that both governed human nature and to which human beings must be accountable. The laws of desire's speech bridged the gap between what otherwise seemed dissonant: the pursuit of an untendentious scientific truth was one and the same with a liberatory telos. By means of words, we might heal the splits between mind and body, individual self, and social collectivity.

On this view, the value of speech has much to do in both cases with an underlying concept of motility or directedness. It might even be said to be encapsulated in desire's law, a telos of speech as traced by Freud. Let us step back for a moment, past the Constitutional Convention, to the Declaration of Independence, which itself reaches back to the natural rights theory of John Locke. Locke's is the spirit behind declarations of the unalienable rights of "we the people"—including the rights to life, liberty, and the "pursuit of happiness." The *pursuit* of happiness. There's a crucial arrest latent in the phrase, a catch that is mirrored in the essential ethical push and pull of psychoanalytic practice. One may enter analysis in the pursuit of happiness; but, as its founding father insisted, psychoanalysis promises only the pursuit, and at that the pursuit not of desire's attainment, but of desire itself.

This pursuit involves the patient's own *declarations*, a word with enlightening roots in the French *declarer*, "to explain, to elucidate," and beyond that in the Latin *declarare*, "to make clear, reveal, disclose, announce." (The Latin verb *clarare* and adjective *clarus* are roots of the English *clear*.) Speaking, in analysis, would be the means by which we claim our self-sovereignty, partly achieved through dream material, slips of the tongue, and various parapraxes that betray our censored speech, our edited truths, our disavowed desires. Speaking is what lifts us out of infancy, literally the state of being unable to speak (*in-fans*), into the adult world, even if at first we are there only as guests. Freud's brilliance lay in his recognizing the daunting challenge this transformation entails, and of how we linger in the wordless world of childhood. But "men cannot remain children for ever" (Freud, 1927c, p. 49). That is, we must speak. The mute patient, or the patient whose speech (and wishful, conflicted fantasy) remains captive to illusory consolations of childhood, will remain imprisoned within a penitentiary of symptoms.

Why is speech special? The matter of truth

Let's now return to the question, what makes speech special? As I noted, free speech has enjoyed a special status among Constitutional rights, even if we never manage to articulate a coherent framework for it, and even if what is meant by the "firstness" of the First Amendment has in recent times become particularly confusing. We've also seen that free association claims a privileged status in the history of psychoanalytic thought, even if in today's pluralistic context it is muddled by conceptual ambiguities and contradictions. But however ambiguous the values underlying the privileges we grant them, freedom of thought and speech have attained a nearly sacred value.

What this means is that psychic emancipation, like political freedom, requires that we protect a space for speech, for desire's voice, or, we might say, for "lawful" desire. Psychic emancipation, like political freedom, must constantly and actively shield itself from tyrannical and coercive interference. Both are subject to Andrew Jackson's rule: "Eternal vigilance by the people is the price of liberty." While moral and consequentialist approaches, as considered above, help to shed light on the values that we attach to speech, be it therapeutic speech or public discourse, the special status of symbolic life and expressive freedoms lies in this eternal vigilance—in our eternal responsibility to recognize the necessity of constraint if freedom is to flourish. Constraints enable free association and its wellspring of new ideas, of novel, disruptive possibility.

Raw free associations that emerge at the margins of speech—sometimes hidden, sometimes sprawling, always overwhelming our capacity for coherent, consciously accessible thought and expression—might seem of questionable utility for the would-be democratically engaged citizen-agent. But once we grasp the laws of desire's speech and enable the structures that benefit symbol creation, we can also better withstand the rising tides of unconscious waters. From the free flow of symbols, a vibrant, awakening (if necessarily dislocating) discourse arises. The unconscious, through Freud's method for eliciting frank, uncensored speech and ideas, emerges unbidden and continually surprises us, being at once eternally uncontainable and also eternally grounding in its link to what is real and to what matters—truths and desires that transcend solipsism, petty politics, noisy chatter, identity politics, and group hegemony. Deprived of that elemental energy, we are left, individually and collectively, in a more vapid, static, and inert state.

From this point of view, a psychoanalytic vision of free association and free speech is compatible with a very broad model for democratic free speech, beyond partisan interests. It may guide jurisprudence exactly because it explicitly aims to cultivate dialogue between a speaker and listener, while also aiming to expose truths that otherwise will remain defended against, unformulated, and unheard. Seana Shiffrin (2014) wonders what might constitute a capacious and unifying theory of free speech. In a move that strikes me as rather psychoanalytic, Shiffrin suggests privileging the interests and needs of the underlying thinker, including an opportunity to develop the capacity for thinking (e.g., education, mutual associations). By adopting what she calls "a thinker-based theory," she asserts that we might "underwrite a freedom of speech protection that yields a fairly broad justificatory foundation for the freedom of speech protection" (Shiffrin, 2014, p. 85).

In fact, as psychoanalysis has evolved, its focus has shifted beyond exposing mental contents (for example, repressed conflict such as Oedipal fantasy). It has become highly attentive to *how* we think, *how* we organize experience, and how the psychoanalytic conversation might enable us to engage in what Thomas Ogden (2005) has called "dream thinking" and "transformative thinking." Related but not synonymous, these forms of thinking cultivated in analytic conversation both involve the patient's capacity for speech that plays with meaning and symbols, and that creates a sense of dreaming one's waking life into being, allowing the possibility to bear catastrophic and destabilizing new ideas.

Such "waking dreaming" (Ogden, 2004b, p. 1361), along with our night dreaming, inspires psychological and creative transformation.

Imagine the individual and collective benefits of building a society capable of bearing together unconscious, "undreamt dreams" (Ogden, 2005). A society that welcomes putting words and music to our fears and desires, that trusts itself to survive and to blossom because it has the capacity to elicit the emergence of the unknown, to be alive to a freer speech that provides ethical and creative direction, its erotic telos. By virtue of our human design, we concede to need each other, and to our need to grapple with unarticulated truths as we seek our symbolic freedom.

Perhaps, as Freud discovered and knew all too well, it is because our bodies are so implicated in our speech that his own more expansionist views on the possibility of freedom became more circumspect. Although he dedicated his clinical practice and scientific discoveries to the laws of desire's speech, he lost faith that society could sustain the ethical space essential for the exercise of unconscious emergent experience. Psychoanalytic ambitions, when divorced from any genuinely functioning democratic structural underpinning, could only wreak havoc.

However much Freud's hopes for psychoanalysis diminished in a world riven by brutal subjection, racism, and tyranny, he never lost sight of the fact that a greater ability to speak entails a greater status in society. But for Freud, if not for the Founding Fathers, to gain that ability we must begin by learning to speak the knowledge of the body. Psychoanalysis, then, can be understood as something more than putting thought into words: putting the body into language, and enabling desire to find words, its own words. A process of symbolization, it is also a project of gaining membership in shared culture, cultivating a space of democracy.

Despite Freud's foundering faith in society, and despite his fears that his psychoanalysis would not find acceptance as a natural (lawful) science, his fundamental rule was founded upon a "no law" that was not lawless, upon a liberating impulse that had socially valid goals. The truth Freud sought was the truth that lay concealed in his patients' symptoms; a truth that is psychical and not *merely* historical; a truth that, once exposed, sets patients (or their unconscious) "free," and this was ongoing. Unconscious agency continually—if also episodically, in dreams, gaps, and slips—was self-revealing, truthful. But something else was at stake too: the truth Freud sought requires courage in the face of fear, for it requires *speaking* truth, exposing secrets, in the face of inner forces that—*and others who*—favor repression and silencing. As such, the pursuit of truth, for Freud, was both indelibly moral, linked with human liberty and dignity, and indelibly instrumental in his dedication to healing human suffering and to expanding knowledge.

This kind of truth would fascinate him throughout his career. Although he "remained conspicuously silent in explicitly developing an ethics that would convert the instinctual drives towards building a social ethos" (Tauber, 2010, p. 173), he was nonetheless increasingly convinced that freedom from intrapsychic censorship—and from governmental hypocrisy and secrecy (Freud, 1915b)—was essential to the pursuit of truth. This despite the fact that Freud saw most political, and all religious, expression as mired in self-deception. (See, for example, Freud, 1927c.)

The patient's courageous exposure of truths that others prefer remain hidden is parallel to the dissenting speech ideally protected from governmental suppression in any society that purports to be democratic. Obviously, without a real measure of transparency, and without ready access to information about political decision-making, representative democracy, already precarious, is gravely imperiled. Governmental secrecy and withholding of information pertinent to the lives of citizens "is the most direct and also the deepest subversion of the democratic claim" (Dunn, 2005, p. 185), creating a deepening chasm between the government and the people who have entrusted officials with their representation.

Equally obviously, political elites in many societies at least favor (where they can't implement) censorship—and censorship not just of incendiary opinion, but of truthful speech. Censoring truth is a violation of what psychoanalysts refer to as an individual's reality testing, with far-reaching consequences for that person's sense of agency and capacity to trust. For example, in the wake of Tiananmen Square, Chinese authorities, "with the aid of some Western Internet Service Providers," sought not to censor "a view which they sincerely believed to be false," but to prevent "large numbers of people from learning the truth of the matter" (Warburton, 2009, p. 37). Closer to home, Edward Snowden has become a lightning rod: an enemy of democracy to some; a heroic truth-teller to others. While it is true that Snowden is not officially a member of the press, his case still has implications for press freedom. In an era of diminishing privacy rights and growing government surveillance in the name of national security, it raises questions about where state interests end and individual liberty begins, and to what degree an individual's need to speak his truth must be balanced against larger systemic interests that are at least purportedly those of the many.

For now, the freedom of the press to sustain its vigilant pursuit of truthful investigation remains fraught and in peril, and it is under increasing pressure to parrot rather than to question the statements it's fed by government officials. Psychoanalysts (at least aspirationally), recognizing the far-reaching consequences of censoring speech for the individual patient's sense of agency and capacity to trust, explicitly invites her uncensored, free speech rather than a voice of social acquiescence and accommodation. Lacking a metaphoric psychoanalytic function dedicated to the lawful discourse of desire's truths, governments (like individuals) are all too susceptible to appropriating (and infantilizing), rather than operating in the service of, the collective sphere. Without adequate privacy and personal dignity protections, there is simply no such thing as free speech, and individual liberties and collective well-being both suffer the consequences. But how special is speech, anyway?

One claim for speech's special status would have had special resonance for Freud, as a clinician and scientist. In his essay "On Liberty" (1859), John Stuart Mill argues that suppressed knowledge or ideas may contain truths that society needs to hear. Mill wrote that a free market of ideas, even one that includes false and offensive ideas, ultimately serves the interest of revealing truth. Without dissent and free expression, ideas, however erroneous, may be accepted as infallible. Living truths degrade into received, dogmatic, orthodoxies. The "peculiar evil of silencing the expression of an opinion," he wrote, "is, that it is robbing the human race" (Mill, 1859, p. 33). In 1919 (*Abrams* vs. *United States*), Justice Oliver Wendell Holmes (who had met Mill) was promoting a "free trade in ideas" as the best means to establishing "Truth," which in turn is essential to democratic progress. By that time, Freud had already reached the same conclusion, even if he put it in somewhat different terms.

Even Mill's expansive vision of free expression was far from absolute; he did allow for suppressing speech that incites harm. Indeed, truth seeking is a troubling issue for both psychoanalysis and democracy, as the history of each attests. In the clinic and in society, the denial of historical reality is a central concern, annihilating, as it does, not only itself but also psychical reality. Some laws, such as Holocaust denial laws, suppress speech in the putative interest of protecting truth (and limiting harm to society). False beliefs might lead to real harm; but the suppression of false beliefs—like the suppression of truthful ones—can create secondary problems. Suppressing falsehoods tends to lend them credibility among the suspicious; suppressing liars may turn them into martyrs. Suppressing lies may even block the discovery of deeper truths accessible only by way of crooked exploratory paths.

But none of this is to say that deliberately misrepresenting facts and lying to and manipulating the public should be beyond the reach of governmental regulation (Shiffrin, 2014). Such false and insincere speech, especially by those in positions of authority, expertise, or with privileged access to information, undermines social and political health because it erodes trust and diminishes the collective valuation of truthful speech. Fostering an ethos of sincere speech in the public sphere, as in the private one, is essential for both individual and collective agency, especially given that there is in many cases no bright line between truth and fiction; their nebulous intersection is the locus of pretty much all our cultural and symbolic life.

Many of these concerns are echoed in a 1950 opinion (cited in Schauer, 1995, p. 10) by Justice Learned Hand of the Second Circuit, in which he considers the more prosaic question of free speech's boundaries:

> The interest, which [the First Amendment] guards, and which gives it its importance, presupposes that there are no orthodoxies—religious, political, economic, or scientific—which are immune from debate and dispute. Back of that is the assumption—itself an orthodoxy, and the one permissible exception—that truth will be most likely to emerge, if no limitations are imposed upon utterances ... whose truth the utterer asserts, or denies. (Schauer, 1995, p. 10)

That is, the one orthodoxy that is a "permissible exception" to the corrosive powers of free discourse and dispute is that the truth is most readily discovered through the speaker's *sincere* free and unfettered speech. So in this form, at least, an instrumental justification for free speech must draw a line past which questions cannot be asked, just like the moral argument does.

Psychoanalysis and democracy: the ethic of symbolic life

I have suggested that Freud sustained a commitment to his scientific dream for psychoanalysis, but remained less certain of his "liberal" dream, his quest for individual emancipation born of truth-seeking discourse. The tension between them only grew more pronounced as he aged. Even while Freud "stressed his scientific ambitions more and more" (Roazen, 1992, p. 522), he turned increasingly to social philosophy and to cultural problems, describing his pursuit of the natural sciences, medicine, and psychotherapy as "a long detour" (ibid., p. 526). Psychoanalysis today tends, as to some degree did Freud himself, to split off its scientific claims from its emancipatory and healing mission, obscuring the basis of both in an Enlightenment spirit of experimentation, specifically experimentation with a quintessentially human ingredient: free speech. Psychoanalysis's founder thus shared a common if unlikely heritage with his predecessors, the American Founding Fathers, who also sustained an ethos of experimentation with free speech—the exercise of which was seen as essential to human (individual and collective) liberty.

Specifically, psychoanalysis and democracy, by enabling the primacy of speech, both join experimental and hermeneutic aspects, scientific and liberal dreams, and empiricist and emancipatory truths; and both remain, despite seldom being seen so, mutually relevant. Why then have free association and free speech, whose origins, aims, and methods dovetail in such interesting ways, so rarely been considered together? The answer is not simply that psychoanalysis has waxed but mostly waned in esteem since its introduction to American shores. For even in the days of psychoanalysis's greatest cultural relevance, even when it was seen as a pursuit as "political" as it was personal, there was no visible attempt to create an interdisciplinary discourse on freedom.

We may get nearer to what is at stake by reframing the question in a way that returns to the distinction between free association and free speech, which I've glossed over in highlighting their mutual resonances: Namely, free association's closer allegiance to the rich reservoir of unconscious mentation (and, by analogy, to the freedom of conscience clauses of the First Amendment). We might then ask the question, "What is the difference between the possibility of having a new thought and the freedom to say anything?" Part of the answer now follows more obviously: It lies in Freud's invention of a "novel kind of talking strategy"—to reveal "the boundless elusiveness of the unconscious" (Mahony, 1987, p. 154), a search that becomes as much about words themselves as about their affective music. It lies in how psychoanalysis "languages" the body, how it explains the human need to explore, to learn, to form communities, and to speak to one another.

At the core of Freud's theory was a belief that our restless energy, our drive to thwart death and to build civilizations, is rooted in sexual difference (in particular the fallout from our discovery of genital difference) and in the primal dynamics of family relationships. Of course, elemental physical and psychical forces, sexual or otherwise, played little to no (conscious) role in the Founding Fathers' conception of "free speech" or a democratic social order. For the Founding Fathers were male children of the Enlightenment, and theirs was a world in which reason was to be the basis for ordering human relations, and a world in which reason could be expected to prevail, at least among the educated white men who held a monopoly on civic rights. Not that Freud, also a man of the Enlightenment, did not privilege reason—but he also was dedicated to laws of unreason, to deciphering the realm of passion, to decoding the symbols and signs of disordered desire.

I will eventually pursue the implications of Freud's claims, and those of his followers, regarding the relationship of symbolization (above all speech) to physical experience and sexuality—especially female sexuality. For now, suffice it to say that Freud's project of languaging the body was rooted in the child's discovery of sexual difference. He recognized and named the scientific "research" interests of children, beginning with the child's assumption of the null hypothesis of no genital distinction between the sexes, one refuted by the discovery of anatomical difference. This discovery breeds further curiosity (if not utter denial), and curiosity piques the search for knowledge. This search becomes a quest, as it were, to fill in a perceived and real "gap," a quest at first to comprehend the mystery of sexual difference, but later to find one's own freedom in the space between the tyrannical realms of refused knowledge (repression) and imposed knowledge (dogma).

In short, the child Freud was able to recognize was a scientist with a liberal dream. That child begins to show "activity which may be ascribed to the instinct for knowledge or research ... [that is] attracted unexpectedly early and intensively to sexual problems and is in fact possibly first aroused by them" (Freud, 1905d, p. 194). She sought knowledge, just as she sought individual emancipation from a tyranny of muteness and ignorance. She sought enlightenment, by means of "experiments undertaken in the service of sexual research" (Freud, 1923e, p. 143). She sought a means for intuiting truth, for naming desire, and for speaking truth to power. Her transgressive quest was inspired by her recognition of a gap—an anatomical gap that Freud filled in with phallocentric theorizing. Yet it was his legacy of the method of free association—that gift of open space—that enabled the semiotic mystery story that would captivate psychoanalysts and their patients in an ongoing quest to bridge the gap between fact and fantasy.

Because this gap is in itself a kind of absence, a space that by definition lacks definition, and because the quest to bridge it is an incessant struggle for both individuals and collectives, it is not coincidental that both Freud's fundamental rule and the First Amendment were initially elaborated in very general and oblique terms, with little specific content that could be used to draw precise points of reference between them. In their bare articulation of their foundational precepts, the Founding Fathers and Freud both left "a space" upon which their aspirations—their waking dreams—for freedom of thought and speech might develop roots and flourish. Space—absence—emerges as a significant and pivotal *presence* in the evolution of both psychoanalytic and constitutional traditions and practices.

Let us note the resonance between Freud's "rule" that granted authority neither to the patient nor the analyst for censorship or abridgment of the patient's speaking of desire, and the Founders' "rule," granting no authority to Congress to censor or to repress speech. Patients, and analysts, and Congress were all beseeched to make no law; this legislated absence created a "potential space" (Winnicott, 1971a, p. 41) for freedom, as well as for complication and contention. As Jean-Luc Donnet has written of the fundamental rule, "in spite of the simplicity of its formulation, the rule contained all the ambiguities that would lead to the analytic situation and its complexity" (2001, p. 160). What goes for the analytic situation goes for the democratic situation. In neither is the "rule" of freedom a set of concrete guidelines, but rather a generalized embodiment of underlying core but unarticulated principles. The rules do not make us their subjects; rather, they call on us to be active agents. In the words of philosopher Jean-Luc Nancy, they "open the space that only freedom is able, not to 'fill,' but properly to space" (1988, p. 70).

What this means is that freedom is as freedom does, and that the ideas behind it must reach a limit where further definition is not only self-contradictory but impossible. The gap left by this silence about speech, this unfreedom in the signifying chain (of writing) on free association, is filled with reverberations, echoes of Freud's unresolved problematic: how to reconcile individual liberty with cultural demands. Toward the end of his life, he soberly predicted that "we shall still have to strug-gle for an incalculable time with the difficulties which the untamable character of human nature presents to every kind of social community" (Freud, 1933a, p. 181). Or, as Terry Eagleton reflected, striking a simi-larly unresolved but more optimistic note than Freud;

> Once these shackles on human flourishing have been removed, it is
> far harder to say what will happen. For men and women are then
> a lot more free to behave as they wish *within the confines of their*
> *responsibility for one another*. (Eagleton, 2011, p. 75; italics added)

Free by the very confines of symbolic life, our raw free associations might find and nourish each other in the incessant transformational telos, and Eros, of speech that becomes a form of desire's action.

CHAPTER FIVE

The polis, analysis, and excluded voices

Origins

The privileged status of speech in both psychoanalysis and democracy exposes inviolable linkages between a truth-telling telos and the (ever only partially realized) sovereignty of the subject and citizen to claim a freedom from subjugation. "The American commitment to freedom of speech and press," says Anthony Lewis, "is the more remarkable because it emerged from legal and political origins that were highly repressive" (2008, p. 1). In the context of the nation's infancy, the ideal of expressive freedom—freedom of religion, freedom of the press, both helping to preserve political discourse and to create a space for dissent— became synonymous with the pursuit of democracy.

This is not to say that the Constitution's framers intended to create a "democracy." They actively and insistently rejected notions of direct democracy, calling instead for a representative government—a republic. In a republic, government is controlled by the will of the majority; however, it is a majority of citizens only, and it is a will mediated through chosen representatives. When the framers turned to ancient sources for inspiration, they drew practical lessons from the Athenian model in which aristocratic power was attenuated by a series of democratic reforms that gradually fostered popular sovereignty, while sustaining a basic stability in the process. But the word "democracy" barely featured in the crisis that was the American revolution. Where it featured at all, says John Dunn, "it did so most consistently and prominently as the familiar name for a negative model, drawn from the experience of Athens, of an outcome which [the new government's leaders] must at all costs avoid" (2005, p. 72).

The ancient premise of Athenian democracy would have set a negative example for at least two reasons. First, in the minds of some Founding Fathers, such as Madison, Athens represented a form of direct democracy that in the new territories might easily devolve into mob rule. Such was the spin that the great seventeenth-century political thinkers, notably Hobbes and Spinoza, put on it. Hobbes famously derided democracy, viewing it as "disorderly and unstable" and vulnerable to domination by a "tyranny of orators" whose persuasive rhetoric wrecked havoc with any intuitive sense of egalitarianism (Dunn, 2005, pp. 61–63). Second was Athens' humiliating defeat by tyrannical Sparta and its allies in the Peloponnesian War, which occupied the later fifth century B.C.E. It was during that century that the Athenian "polis" had carried out the first known experiment in free speech. (*Polis* is the Greek term for *city, citizenship,* and/or *city-state* and is the root of our word "politics.") While they produced no immediately enduring results, the Athenian trials with democracy and free speech did at least set basic terms and generate interesting debates. Our understanding of those terms and debates is largely mediated by Thucydides and Aristotle; but more psychologically acute pictures are painted in various plays by the Athenian tragedian Euripides. Indeed, ordinarily translated into English as "free speech," the Greek word *parrhesia* is first recorded in his writings.

So we have an origin for free speech. What about free association? It began, as we saw in Chapter Two, as a collaboration between the "hysteric" Bertha Pappenheim ("Anna O") and her doctor, Josef Breuer, who invented the cathartic method that Pappenheim dubbed the "talking cure." Sigmund Freud experimented with and modified Breuer's method, then psychoanalysis evolved as a conversation that is unreservedly candid, exposing desire and fantasy, forbidden or at least inhibited by social mores and convention, and that means grappling with the silences and the speech that fill the vacuum. What has previously remained unspoken (including what remains unconscious) gains suscitation in time and space, between speaker and hearer.

In terms of where lines are drawn for what is exposed, psychoanalytic free association, like freedom of conscience, may tilt towards the private and intimate, while free speech tilts towards the public. But both straddle borders *between* private and public. There is simply no free speech, intimate or general, that is strictly private. Nor can any speech worthy of the name be considered strictly public (and here I'm excluding ritual speech such as pledges and prayers). The two freedoms are, as I have noted, more than just linguistic cousins. Even though there are obvious differences of scope, insofar as free association is traditionally conceived as discourse directed at one listener, while free speech is directed at a whole community, we will discover a similar underlying dynamic in that both free association and free speech constitute forms of address. And we will find in the history of free association a (partially successful) attempt to escape from repressive forces, an attempt that mirrors the origins of free speech.

The polis and parrhesia

The idea, or ideal, of becoming revealed between private and public was not Freud's invention; it is implicit in the Greek conception of the polis, which anticipated the bridging between free speech and freedom of assembly that undergirds the First Amendment. In turn, the polis and the First Amendment anticipate how psychoanalysis cultivates speech by way of the proximate encounter not only between two minds but also between two bodies in a physical "assembly." A psychoanalytic polis would ground itself in time and space between personal desire and the public sphere, between the pronouns of a speaking "I" and a listening "you."

To contextualize and clarify the idea of a psychoanalytic polis, let's look back to a time when free speech was a matter of considerable discussion and was considered highly relevant to the project of democracy: namely, the Classical period of the Athenian constitution and its experiment with *parrhesia*. An historical antecedent of free association and free speech, the notion of *parrhesia* foreshadowed later Enlightenment thought about the natural rights of man to self expression, and subtended the evolution of Freud's psychoanalysis as well as the Founding Fathers' vision of democracy. Though it seems that psychoanalytic theory has never treated this historical concept,[1] the Greek experiment with *parrhesia* is startlingly relevant to the field and its truth-telling practice. Further, it foreshadows the fundamental link between free speech and female embodiment, which is the ultimate moral of this tale of two freedoms.

Parrhesia, "to speak everything" and by extension "to speak freely," "to speak boldly," was "a fundamental component of the democracy of classical Athens" (Pasquino, 2013). As Michel Foucault concluded, *parrhesia*

> was a guideline for democracy as well as an ethical and personal attitude characteristic of the good citizen.... *Parrhesia*, which is a requisite for public speech, takes place between citizens as individuals, and also between citizens construed as an assembly. Moreover the *agora* is the place where *parrhesia* appears. (Foucault, 2001, p. 22)

J. D. Lewis notes that "One of the remarkable features of the Periclean democracy was the right of every citizen to address the assembly if he wished" (1971, p. 129). S. Sara Monoson usefully distinguishes between the formal right of free speech (*isegoria*) and the practice of free speech (*parrhesia*), translating the latter as "frank" speech. She notes that whereas an ethic of *parrhesia* stood for shared participation and democracy,

> an intolerance of *parrhesia* marked tyranny ... a symptom of the watched character of daily life. A citizen of a democracy, on the other hand, was expected to have and to voice his own critical political opinions. (Monoson, 2000, p. 54)

Furthermore, *parrhesia* was associated with daring and courage, for in ancient Greece there were certainly no free speech protections such as we enjoy in the United States today, let alone the confidentiality protections in psychoanalytic practice. Instead, a high value was attached not just to one's speech but also to one's *responsibility* for it, and sometimes that entailed a price (often humiliation and fines, and rarely, execution). Given the high value placed on truthfulness, efforts were made to protect against deceptive oratory and speech that might exploit the public confidence. After all, "both the speaker and the audience had personal and political stakes in the truth value of ideas" if democratic *parrhesia* was to flourish (Monoson, 2000, p. 64).

These personal and political stakes were understood as an essential element of freedom, which in turn symbolized Athens' successful (if temporary) defeat of tyranny and its status as a democracy. Foucault (2001), in a series of seminars examining the rise and decline of *parrhesia*, points to the fact that *parrhesia* was granted to all (including the so-called "worst citizens"). Consequently, he suggests, the odds were high that immoral and deceptive speech would prevail, thereby endangering democracy. Unsurprisingly—even necessarily—a tension emerged between *parrhesia* and democracy, "inaugurat[ing]," as Foucault put it, "a long impassioned debate concerning the precise nature of the dangerous relations which seemed to exist between democracy, *logos*, freedom, and truth" (Foucault, 2001, p. 77).

"Real" *parrhesia* in its positive, critical, truth-telling aspects was opposed by sophists, who made a living from rhetoric and had little use for truth. The sophists found a willing audience in a citizenry ("demos") that generally preferred false but flattering oratory to "honest" but insulting or upsetting speech. Foucault interprets the decline of democratic institutions in the fourth century B.C.E. in part as evidence that *parrhesia* in its positive, critical sense, "does not exist where democracy exists" (ibid., p. 83). Foucault's pessimistic conclusion underscores his suggestion that "truth is understood as an ethical value," and that the "figure of the *parrhesiastes* has an exemplary moral status because she eschews a safe life for a life of truth and accepts the risks that it may entail" (Ross, 2008, pp. 67–68). On this account, democracy became associated with a lack of restraint, liberty with lawlessness, and political *parrhesia* with sophism.

Foucault associates another form of *parrhesia* with Socrates (as we know him from Plato). Socratic *parrhesia* posited a concordance among *logos*, truth, courage, *and* the ethical (and ontological) question of how one lives one's life *(bios)*. Or, as Socrates himself proved, how one dies. Although there is no strict chronological order for these different types of *parrhesia* (Euripedes died in 407 B.C.E. and Socrates was put to death in 399 B.C.E.), "the target of this new *parrhesia*," says Foucault, "was to convince someone that he must take care of himself and of others; and this means that he must *change his life*" (Foucault, 2001, p. 106, italics in original). Gradually, parrhesiastic speech disappeared from the public realm with the collapse of the ancient *demokratia* and moved into a different sphere: that of private relations (Pasquino, 2013). In that realm, its focus shifted in the direction set by Socrates to become a spiritual practice—one of self-knowledge, of one's relationship to truth, anticipating the practice that Freud and his patients would set in motion some two millennia later.

The truth Freud sought, like the parrhesiac's truth-telling, requires courage in the face of fear, for it requires speaking truth, exposing secrets, in spite of forces that favor repression. Julia Kristeva asserts that the polis "invites everyone to demonstrate an original courage ... to leave the shelter of the personal in order to be exposed to others and, with them, to be prepared to risk revelation" (2000, p. 53). The unique power, opportunity, and indeed the challenge afforded by the polis lies in its provision of the "chances for everyone to distinguish himself, in word and deed, who he was in his unique distinctiveness" (ibid., p. 61; citing Arendt, 1958, p. 197). From a similar angle, Michel Foucault identified his concern not with the truth, but with "truth-telling as an activity" (2001, p. 169); he asks, "who is able to tell the truth, about what, with what consequences, and with what relations to power?" (ibid., p. 170). Foucault's questions might apply directly to the project of psychoanalysis, which functions as a kind of polis wherein each patient has rights to *parrhesia*. Indeed, his quixotically titled compilation of essays on the subject, *Fearless Speech*, proclaims the simultaneous courageousness and impossibility of this truth-telling project—for psychoanalysis, for the polis.

It's not that the polis, at least as conceived by Plato and Aristotle, has remained unexamined within psychoanalysis, though it is perhaps underappreciated. Its reality, and its metaphorical value, have been investigated by such psychoanalytically minded observers of democracy as Jonathan Lear and Hannah Arendt. Lear points out that Plato considered the polis "the only environment fit for human habitation"; human beings are "dependent on it for the very constitution of their psyches" (Lear, 1998, p. 58). ("Psyches" is Lear's word, not Plato's.)

Arendt (1958) extolled Aristotle's conception:

> The *polis*, properly speaking ... is the organization of the people as it arises out of acting and speaking together, and its true space lies between people living together for this purpose, no matter where they happen to be. "Wherever you go, you will be a *polis* ...."
> (Arendt, 1958, p. 198)

This idea—that human beings are dependent upon interaction with others (and specifically, as Lacan posited, upon a confrontation with the desire of the other) for their very constitution as subjects—is at the heart of contemporary psychoanalysis.

Arendt also captures the essence of free association, recognizing that an

> unpredictability of outcome is closely related to the revelatory character of action and speech, in which one discloses one's self without ever either knowing himself or being able to calculate beforehand whom he reveals. (Arendt, 1958, p. 192)

Freedom (of association, or speech, or assembly) is ours to claim *through* participation, through "contribut[ing] in" (Winnicott, 1965, p. 103). Arendt recognized in Aristotle's polis a "guarantee against the futility of individual life, the space protected against this futility and reserved for the relative permanence, if not immortality of mortals" (Arendt, p. 56, cited in Kristeva, 2000, p. 58). We as individuals and as citizens must make meaningful acts; only in that way do we transform events and private fantasies into affectively resonant, shared experiences and realized dreams. As we do so, we—patient and analyst, you and I—create a private-public "location," animated in the present moment, a textured, reverberant sphere of speech and action between our imaginations and sensate bodies, between our personal and our civic identities. This is an embodied polis, *our* psychoanalytic polis.

Boundaries, barriers, and women's place

Foucault emphasized that *parrhesia* (even for those who have this privilege, at least in its early and positive incarnations) presumes an asymmetry of power between the speaker and his audience. But the speaker is not himself powerless; in fact, by speaking he gains a position of agency, he rises above mute subjection. Over and over in the ancient texts, an inability to speak freely is likened to enslavement, and the ability to do so is equated with the care or education of the soul. Within the boundaries of those granted citizenship, free speech (and its accompanying democracy) thrived.

Once again, we encounter the paradox that freedom is inseparable from concepts of boundary and constraint. It's noteworthy in this context that the word *polis* derives from an ancient Greek word for "boundary." According to Cynthia Farrar, the precise derivation is from a root meaning "wall."

> This boundary was not merely a mark of security from external coercion.... [It] was directed inward, spurred by the need to institutionalize an intention not to practise or be subject to coercion. The ancient polis created a space between slavery and tyranny. This ... was a glorious achievement. (Farrar, 1992, p. 18)

However, the glorious achievement of the polis, in lived reality, fell far short of this ideal. The polis that created a space between slavery and tyranny was predicated itself upon enslavement and exclusion.

In classical Greece, women, like slaves, were denied the right to citizenship, let alone to *parrhesia*. In her fascinating exploration from a legal perspective of the history of women in ancient Greece and Rome, Eva Cantarella argues that the Greek city "represents the perfect realization of a political plan to exclude women" (1987, p. 38). The first written Greek laws dictated a code of behavior that "unequivocally shows the centrality of the biological function, which was governed by the *polis* in such a way as to guarantee the replacement of citizens." That is, the function of women was to reproduce (if they were "free") or to provide servile labor (if they were slaves). Laws established a woman's subordination to men and deprived her of social and political participation, confining her to a part of the house called a *gynaecacum*, thereby ensuring that she would be walled off socially, intellectually, and politically. Spartan women had greater influence over their children and husbands, and more liberal sexual habits, than did Athenian women, and both "Plato and Aristotle attributed the decline of [Athens] to this fact" (ibid., p. 42).

Cantarella documents the very emergence of the polis in classical Athens as a turning point, after which segregation of the sexes became total—while in the antecedent "so-called dark ages" (ibid., p. 39), women were accorded at least some flexibility of movement and some limited social (if not political) engagement. In classical Athens, revered as the first democratic state, there were "iron rules ... that the *polis* imposed on women, shutting them out and depriving them of practically every chance of freedom: rules that both considered them inferior and made them so" (ibid., p. 51).

Cantarella concludes that the Aristotelian classification of men as "spirit" and "form," and women as "mothers" and "matter," codified (and thus rationalized) the female essence and role in a way that ensured her inferior status for centuries (ibid., p. 51)—nay, millennia. Women, virtually enslaved (as were slaves) in "the realm of necessity," freed men to participate in the creation of the polis as the "sphere of freedom." The achievement of a private-public space or polis for men was based upon a rigid, patriarchal split between private and public spheres (Cornell, 1991). In short, democracy was founded in a social space that totally excluded women from any form of political participation, suppressed women's voices, and practically imprisoned their bodies.

Indeed, we find that even in so presumably advanced and enlightened a society as contemporary America, we are hardly more than a stone's throw from classical Greece. Gloria Feldt, the former president of Planned Parenthood, argues that legislation

> is badly needed not only to restore liberties systematically carved away out of *Roe v. Wade*, but also to shift the legal framework from one based on privacy to one based on equal protection. ... A woman's right to her own life and body has to be elevated to the moral position that supports a human rights framework. (Feldt, 2009, p. 84)

It would not have been news to Freud that the more things change, the more they stay the same. Freud proposed that the (unconscious) aim of such compulsive action was the suppression, if not repression, of sexual impulses. Freud himself was guilty of perpetuating this sort of repression, namely by repeatedly emphasizing women's anatomically-based inferiority complexes. To put it another way, he argued, in a fashion that feminists have neither forgotten nor forgiven, that *anatomy is destiny*. The body grounds us, forever and inescapably, in who we are. Anatomy determines the divide between the sexes, and to some real degree, the psychological development of sexual difference and identity.

But Freud, whose arguments are never easily reducible, also pointed toward the power of our subjectivity and its debt to our body. Even in his theory of "penis envy," Freud requires every female child to create her own personal meaning for her alleged lack; the child actively imbues anatomy with subjective meaning and interpretations.

The discovery of anatomical difference will lead to a grappling with meaning, with relationship, with personal identity and status (Birksted-Breen, 2004, p. 3ff.).

If it is true that Freud presents the imagination as an antidote to strict materialism, it is also true that his theoretical triumph in creating a dynamical tension between anatomy and interpretation is trumped by a myopic and (many have argued) misogynistic focus. Just as he empowers subjectivity and interpretation, he reduces imaginative freedom. He writes:

> We have learnt that girls feel deeply their lack of a sexual organ that is equal in value to the male one; they regard themselves on that account as inferior, and this "envy for the penis" is the origin of a whole number of characteristic female reactions (Freud, 1926e, p. 212).

Thus, female anatomy will (universally) signify a woman's lack, and this perception of lack will organize her identity and be linked to a high incidence among female patients of "frigidity" and inhibition associated with a failure to achieve "a true change-over towards men" (Freud, 1931b, p. 226).[2]

This Freud averred that the "great riddle of sex" had as its bedrock the "repudiation of femininity" (1937c, p. 252). For men, this means renouncing feminine passivity so as to overcome castration anxiety and attain masculinity. For women, this means renouncing "penis envy" so as to assume their proper sexual identity and their reproductive role.

So what does one make of the fact that *this* Freud also (for example, in several case studies on hysteria) dedicated himself to the female body's secret knowledge and power? He did so because he could not help but recognize that women's bodies, so often disembodied and so often plagued with bizarre conversion symptoms, also speak volumes. As Starr & Aron (2011), have shown, Freud's rejection of hypnosis for his female patients coincided with his rejection of another obscure clinical method: the "biologically, usually genitally, based somatic treatments of hysteria practiced by his medical colleagues" (ibid., p. 385). In rejecting these methods, Freud privileged the female psyche as author of her body's desires (and inhibitions). He taught us that her body not only remembers, it also communicates, and he came to be far more interested in that space between her mind and her body than in shortcuts to a climactic story.

Freud listened and learned. Spellbound, he discovered that he could not "evade listening to her stories in every detail to the very end" (Freud & Breuer, 1895d, p. 61). What he heard was the voice of women and sexual desire emerging from silence, a symptom of their disenfranchisement. Women freely associating. The din of democracy could be heard.

Of course, as Foucault concluded in his study of *parrhesia*, the din of democracy is a precarious achievement that requires a commitment to "fearless speech," and that also depends on critiquing authority. Furthermore, the moral fortitude of the *parrhesiastes* lies not only in speaking what is invisible to others, but also in speaking what others *choose* not to see. Freud's free association insisted upon restoring these links, between mind and body, between female desire and repressed knowledge, between authority and unauthorized voices.

Freud, a revolutionary of the mind and the body, a co-conspirator in discovering (and inventing) the talking cure, could nonetheless fall back on his own repressive solutions. To paraphrase Emmy von N's challenge to her doctor: "Let me speak these memories before you try to explain them or wipe them away with the tool of hypnotic suggestion." In response, Freud (Freud & Breuer, 1895d), not yet convinced of the value of "reproduction in states of uninhibited association" (p. 11), listened. But he would listen and learn only up to a point, and would then back away from the lessons.

For example, as Freud learned of the widespread incidence among his female patients of sexual abuse and incest, he initially articulated what became known as the "seduction hypothesis," which granted etiological significance in adult hysteria to paternal childhood sexual molestation and premature sexual stimulation. By 1897, he had already come to question the truth of his patients' reports of incest. Although he continued to believe that seduction and sexual abuse were real and appalling phenomena, he came to doubt that they were as rampant as the extremely high number of claims would suggest, and thus he reduced their contribution to a "humbler one, in the etiology of neuroses" (Freud, 1925d, pp. 34–35). Unable to accept that there were so many pedophilic fathers (including his own), and increasingly convinced that in the unconscious mind fantasy often passes for reality, Freud changed his mind (Makari, 2008, p. 100). He devised a new cause for hysteria: childhood sexual fantasy and the childhood masturbation that such fantasy inspired. While not disavowing the reality of abuse in some instances, he now reinterpreted many reports of abuse as symptoms or effects, fantasy rather than reality.

So while Freud was the champion of a certain kind of inclusive, democratic ideal, he was also prone to disparage and devalue independent feminine experience. By abandoning the seduction hypothesis, Freud may have steered psychoanalysis into mistreating already injured patients. But he also thereby intensified his inquiries into the worlds of fantasy and imagination, bringing psychological agency into bold relief. To make room for the truth to be spoken—to expose a true voice—requires, but is never so simple as, exposing historical events. Personal desire must also be exposed. Recognizing this made Freud's conception of the battle between repression and voice, truth, and desire ever more challenging and ever more fraught. Unconscious desires and historical truth were enmeshed in an inextricably tangled web.

For example, Freud came to recognize the metaphorical significance of hysterical "conversion" symptoms: that desire is inscribed—together with the refusal of desire—on the body. What's more, Freud discovered that hysteria reveals an "inarticulable desire that [keeps] on being displaced" (Verhaeghe, 1997, p. 15). Symptoms, in this semiotic mystery story, are compromises or substitutive satisfactions, written on the body, becoming "mnemic symbols" of what is repressed. And fear ("fright hysteria")—accompanied by a gap in the psyche (Freud, 1950a, p. 228)—is the result of a "faulty" process of translation (that had also successfully served another purpose). Recovering history and memory became inseparable from recovering desire. But this process pivoted on its own translational process, the process by which unconscious material becomes conscious and dissociated material becomes associated. If hysterical fantasies had been translated into the motor sphere and portrayed in pantomime, so too could they be translated into another sphere or script. Overcoming repression became a process of "reintegrating translation" (Mahony, 1987, p. 5), a process that that played out through transference as an unconscious translation or metaphor.

This process challenges us to heed "the ethical drive that inspired *parrhesia* and the ethical hearing that allowed for truth to be determined in the relation to listening" (Al-Kassim, 2010, p. 17). It invites us to consider the need for a genuine and inclusive polis—a relational space that honors the courage involved in exposing desire—if democracy in psychoanalysis, and in cultural life, is to thrive. Perhaps Freud only dimly perceived this fundamental insight, and so he stopped short of recognizing the significance of female experience—and of *embodied* female space—between speakers and listeners not only for psychoanalysis and its polis, but for its truth-telling political system counterpart, democracy.

CHAPTER SIX

Repression

As we saw in the previous chapter, Freud has long been taken to task for silencing women and for denying their real message, even as his curative power depended on their truly *free* free association. Especially with his female patients, he would at times interpret away, or outright ignore, the kinds of speech that conflicted with his agenda, oscillating between listening and silencing (or ventriloquizing), hemming in meaning and agency. On the other hand, Freud did seek methods for granting allowance to—for *freeing*—repressed, elusive, and obscured voices.

As Freud came to see it, the analyst's task is interpretive, encompassing not only translation of what is unconscious into consciousness, but also lifting repression and filling in gaps of memory (Mahony, 1987, p. 10). Despite early allusions to a receptive unconscious and belief in unconscious communication, it was a *repressed* unconscious that came to dominate Freud's thought. Overcoming repression would mean more than unearthing and indicting historical events (including real abuses); the patient would also need to take personal ownership of unacknowledged desires by translating and resignifying them. All of which is difficult enough. But a further, perhaps even more difficult, step is required: deciding to what degree forbidden wishes may be preserved and used, raw or sublimated, for the betterment of one's life and world, and to what degree they may need to be "forgotten" all for the sake of civilized and communal living.

As early as 1908, Freud had come to regard repression—the psychically damaging suppression of the sexual life (through the prevalent "'civilized' sexual morality")—as too high a price to pay for civilization (1908d). He believed that free thought, the freedom to know, was the only antidote to repression, the key to self-sovereignty. Yet Freud could rationalize the very repressive solutions he otherwise rejected. While being so committed to freeing the unconscious that he built a whole science upon it, he could neither embrace demotic desires and their illusory objects, nor accept the inevitable unrest of unleashing repressive forces, and their inherently elemental and eroticized potency. By tugging at the thread of desire, we might pull too-tightly woven psyches apart at their seams. The result would be libidinal anarchy.

To be sure, Freud welcomed the "spirits from the underworld" (1915a, p. 164)—the dark psychic powers whose concealment costs us so dearly—but only for a brief visit. He wanted the patient to make their acquaintance and then to be free *to some extent* from the tyrannical shackles of repression. By putting language to what had been repressed, she would release "strangulated affect," freeing a chain of associations linking to pathogenic memories, relieving her from her symptoms. Facing what had been repressed would tame the power of the instincts to a degree; but it would then be necessary to reimpose a measure of repression.

Though Freud would come to recommend "working through" and ideas of compromise (discussed below), this last point raises new questions: How valuable is repression to psychological health? And how far may one responsibly go in reversing it? Such questions, *mutatis mutandis*, animate contemporary discussions about free speech in civil society, although they are typically framed in reverse: How valuable is free speech for society? And how far may we go, again for society's sake, in constraining it? Maximizing free speech protection may have the unintended consequence of wrongfully invading the rights of others, and/or of sacrificing other individual rights, for example, the right to personal security. But protecting social and state interests sacrifices individual freedom of speech. Some advocate a solution that evades this binary conflict. Steven Heyman (2008), for example, proposes a modern return to the tradition of natural rights theory, which recognizes that individual and social liberties are interdependent, not exclusive, and that both contribute coherently to a larger framework of rights based on individual liberty and democratic self-governance. The balance between them, so fundamental to both psychoanalysis and civil society, bears further attention. We must ask to what degree we are able, or even want, to bear responsibility for self-governance; and to what degree, short of imposed repressive tyranny, we would rather choose, and even prefer, to alienate that responsibility. What are the implications for ideas and practices that prioritize freedom of thought and of speech?

Between subjection and self rule

Freud's experience over time with patients who fiercely resisted knowing themselves would have eroded whatever dim expectations he had, dispelling any remnant of hope for an enlightened society. As Adam Phillips says, "Knowledge seemed a poor container for our sexuality and our violence. And the insistent and often debilitating repetitions in modern peoples' lives seems to belie their expressed belief in progress" (Phillips, 2014, p. 52).

Following (if unwittingly) in the footsteps of the framers, Freud came to recognize that individuals must sacrifice a measure of liberty for the sake of a "civilized" society. In fact, he concluded that repression was actually somehow biologically inherited, perpetrated in a kind of collective unconscious, as a mechanism to protect us from the ultimate taboo: incest. In the course of evolution, this inheritance came to protect us from other wishes and impulses universally acknowledged to be socially destructive. Freud's doubts about popular enlightenment would eventually erupt in *Civilization and its Discontents*. That text embodies a "disturbing, anti-progressive vision" that the "civilizing process was always oppressive," and that it left people with "a surplus of themselves they could do nothing with" (Phillips, 2014, p. 40). This surplus energy seeks release, and sometimes that release is violent. In earlier reflections on the devastations of warfare, which expose "the primal [and barbaric] man in each of us," Freud had concluded that the state and the individual are macrocosm and microcosm. He came to believe that a "belligerent state" enables the individual citizen to convince himself of what only occasionally would "cross his mind in peace-time" (Freud, 1915b, pp. 299, 279, 284). Ethical state governance restrains the individual for the sake of the collective.

But Freud at times seems to have abandoned any quest for mutual restraint or accommodation. Towards the conclusion of *Civilization and Its Discontents*, he goes so far as to say that the "two processes of individual and cultural development ... [stand] in hostile opposition to each other" (ibid., p. 141). While he had once cautioned against the stifling degeneration of an overly repressed society, he now feared more the potential catastrophes attendant on explosive individual (instinctual) liberties. Never exactly a fan of mass opinion, he now distrusted it, believing it will rarely lead to enlightenment, which is more likely to be advanced by the minority opinion it crushes. Civilization's survival would require leaders who "possess superior insight into the necessities of life and who have risen to the height of mastering their own instinctual wishes" (Freud, 1927c, p. 8).

Some of the same contradictions that mark Freud's thinking reverberate in the views of the Founding Fathers. We like to imagine that the founders of psychoanalysis and of American democracy were devoted to freedom as a pure ideal. But the reality is more complex. Yes, they recognized the dangers of an "inert" people, of a society unable or unwilling to engage with troubling truths, and had appreciated the potential gains from individual enlightenment. Both Freud and the American Revolution's leaders, in their youth, waved the banner of natural rights, embracing Locke's account of freedom of thought. But over time they considered with increasing gravity what was really at stake, and what were the costs, in our quests for freer thought and freer speech. Time and experience took a toll on both psychoanalytic theory and democratic ideals. As practiced, both have always been based on exclusions—exclusions that betray a distrust of "the people." Those who framed the Constitution often placed more emphasis on the "atrocious effects" of mob rule than on the "favorable effects of democracy" (Abat i Ninet, 2013, p. 48).

For both Freud and the framers, reality proved more complex than freedom's ideal. In response, they continually sought to elucidate a dialectic that could hold the tensions of humanity's darker impulses, without devolving into darkness. If people are incapable of ruling themselves, then they owe a great debt to civilization, and for the sake of civilization, they need to sacrifice a measure of liberty, of free expression, of "instinct." "The final outcome," Freud wrote,

> should be a rule of all to which all—except those who are not capable of entering a community—have contributed by a sacrifice of

their instincts, and which leaves no one—again with the same
exception—at the mercy of brute force. (Freud, 1930a, p. 95)

But Freud never really believed in a promised land. He came to see for himself that free thought and free speech could expose an unspeakable human potential for inhumanity. Repression, that defense against speech and cause of psychical symptoms, also seemed to be a principal tool for quelling inner (and societal) conflict. Freud called not for a return to neurosis but to a new, tempered repression—enlightenment yes, but also sublimation in the service of eros, in the service of a sustainable society.

Repression and reconstruction

Freud came to believe that free association could be a vehicle for *redistributing* libido, revising repression, advancing civilization (1916–1917, pp. 455–456). As he saw it, liberating the psyche's disenfranchised "voices," while dismantling hierarchical, repressive mental structures, would allow life-animating desires to be channeled into a conscious interplay between psyche and body, individual and collectivity. Thus, society too would benefit, not only from richer and more widespread artistic and cultural expression, but also by having its complacent and hidebound mores challenged.

Freud's project for release and sublimation presupposed that a delicate, precarious balance is at stake. Culture and civilization concomitantly need the potent force of libido, and need protection from its explosive potential. Recognizing the compulsion to repeat as an obstacle to treatment and cure, Freud noted that people "feel an obscure fear—a dread of rousing something that, so they feel, is better left sleeping. ... [T]hey are afraid of this compulsion with its hint of 'demonic power'" (1920g, p. 36). Liberating this power entirely was no solution, for the patient or for the society; and so he came to develop the notion of "compromise formation" as the gold standard of cure—a compromise that inevitably resulted in new symptoms. The domestication of desire was essential in order ultimately to benefit and to sustain a mutually constituted individual and society. Capturing and perhaps capitulating to this recognition, Freud concluded: "The aim of all life is death" (ibid., p. 38).

The evolution of an idea of "compromise formation" in psychoanalysis is echoed by the historical evolution of free speech in America, which has also become about defining appropriate compromises.

Free association, that most liberating and potentially transgressive speech, was both generated and tamed by constraint, and we have seen that the advent of free speech laws advanced the possibilities of a transgressive, liberatory discourse, while also introducing the need for potential inhibitions or necessary constraints.

A World War caused Freud to reassess the claims of individual freedom against those of collective rights, of expression against repression, of liberty against order. It would simultaneously prompt Woodrow Wilson to set forth his vision of a "New World Order," an order not only consistent with but promoting democratic values. Wilson made little headway, but the next World War would effectively unite much of Europe with America in an effort to reassert stability and security, "beneath the banner of democracy" (Dunn, 2005, p. 156), that offered an ineluctable "new formula for civilized rule (rule of the civilized by the civilized) ... to a world in dire need of civilization" (ibid., p. 155).

The decisive post-war tilt toward order (which would manifest itself in America as a two-decade culture of conformity) set democracy on a new path. Its aspirations were tamed and domesticated, but increasingly global in reach. Meanwhile, psychoanalysis followed its own bifurcated path through the mid-twentieth century. On the one hand, it grew theoretically darker and more timid; on the other, it seemed to gain in credibility and influence. In America, increasingly influential cultural and interpersonalist critiques advanced psychoanalysis as a liberationist social theory. In Europe, it gained new energy through the growth of a creative and fertile British "independent" tradition. But in a story that is far more complex than any short narrative can do justice, psychoanalysis became both more fractious and more homogenized by libido-draining orthodoxies. The talking cure became more mute: it increasingly favored compromise and repression, and was tamed (especially in its American variants) by the rise of an abstract ego psychology that emphasized adaptation and autonomy, and by the increasing dominance of pragmatic, pluralistic, and to some degree "driveless" approaches that dispensed with libido theory.

Subversion and danger

If the many varieties of postwar psychoanalysis combined to domesticate the very desire that was the wellspring of freedom, did this domestication conflate *the need for* constraint (to secure liberty of expression) with constraint itself? What was to be constrained, and what to be liberated? Why has expression been more feared than repression? How do we reconcile the conservative, cautionary tilt in Freud's postwar thinking with the subversive and radical propositions of his earlier thought that catalyzed his own shifting concerns?

I referred at the beginning of Chapter Two to caricatures of psychoanalysis as a paternalistic but also comically feckless enterprise, presided over by a dictatorial analyst who dispenses arcane and thus useless diktats to a passive and confused patient. These cartoons are countered by another kind of broad critique, one that sees psychoanalysis not as comical and pointless but as a subversive, if not positively harmful, practice with the power to unhinge morality and even to derange society.

Perhaps this is not an entirely false claim. Freud himself believed in the radical potential of analysis; as the old story goes, while on a ship with Jung arriving in America, he half-jokingly called psychoanalysis a "plague" they were bringing to new shores (Mannoni, 1968, p. 168). William James, who actually considered psychoanalysis a promising endeavor, still famously proclaimed its foundation in symbolic interplay and interpretation "a most dangerous method" (James, 1920, p. 328). In Peter Gay's oft-stated view, Freud's work was "deeply subversive for his time," and that it was even more "directly abrasive" and "unrespectable" than Darwin's views in *his* time (Gay, 1987, p. 144; 1988, p. 149).

It is true that psychoanalysis might be called "dangerous" insofar as it champions individual desire and thereby runs athwart traditional social mores and inhibitions. Especially in regressive stages of a treatment, it focuses on identifying and liberating what would seem to an outsider to be licentious, perverse, destructive, even immoral forces. But its goal isn't even social reform, let alone social derangement. Its true goal, and its real power, is the healing of individual patients whose symptoms, as Freud saw them, had been "created so as to avoid a *danger-situation* whose presence had been signalled" by anxiety (Freud, 1926d, p. 129). Of course, individuals make up a society. By empowering his patients to claim whom they "might have become at best under the most favorable conditions" (Freud, 1916–1917, p. 435), Freud's psychoanalysis had clear social effects, consistent with the Enlightenment project of human freedom.

In any event, Freud did not take up the call implicit in his theoretical turn, instead remaining "conspicuously silent in explicitly developing an ethics that would convert the instinctual drives towards building a social ethics" (Tauber, 2010, p. 173). If Freud's vision darkened as he fixed his gaze on the naked face of human aggression, others called for a new, wider-angle lens. In broadening psychoanalysis's impact beyond the consulting room, a group of scholars and philosophers later known as the Frankfurt School had a significant influence. Inspired by Freud's cultural writings, the Frankfurt School critiqued post-World War II culture and insisted that fascism remained a critical threat to a "deeply ailing world" (Adorno, 1951, p. 200). Arguing that, contra Enlightenment notions of progress, postwar Europe was "sinking into a new kind of barbarism" (Horkheimer & Adorno, 1947, p. xi; Whitebook, 2008, p. 1165), Horkheimer and Adorno embraced what scholar Yirmiyahu Yovel (1989) has dubbed the "dark enlightenment." As Joel Whitebook explains, they thereby aimed to paint an "unflinching picture of human beings as they actually are—animality and all—and not as we wish them to be" (2008, p. 1170). The goal was to expose the subject's "subterranean history," a project that mirrors free association's mission to liberate unruly unreason and its transformational energies.

Whitebook challenges contemporary secularists to recognize Freud's own illusion, that "'infantile' wishes will magically 'wisther away'" (ibid., p. 1173), and to pursue ways of animating society by recognizing and accommodating our "darker" impulses. Striking a similar chord, feminist psychoanalyst Jacqueline Rose's recent book—aptly named *Women in Dark Times*—offers portraits of women as "truth-tellers" who confronted the darkness of historical progress with the unruliness of their own inner lives. In her review of Rose's book, Frances Wilson describes its call "to 'alert' everyone, men and women alike, to the 'unreason' at the heart of what it is to be human" (Wilson, 2014).

Despite Freud's political conservatism, his dangerous method is indeed, if not a fundamentally radical enterprise, at least a liberating one, because its effects (if not always its intent) are democratic. Yes, the explicit goal of any treatment is a cure, or at the very least the alleviation of a patient's symptoms. But in unleashing the plague of intuitive, irrational, disruptive knowledge, we may resort to brute force and tyrannical solutions because our wishes are so big and even murderous, and our speech arsenals so small and limited. "My discoveries are not primarily a heal-all. My discoveries are a basis for a very grave philosophy. There are very few who understand this, *there are very few who are capable of understanding this*" (Doolittle, 1956, p. 25, citing a 1933 conversation with Freud).

Freud's free association is uncontainable, its freedoms unpredictable. It is like the ideal of political free expression as Vincent Blasi describes it: "simply to leave people free to follow their political thoughts wherever that might lead—free that is, to think the unthinkable, regarding political loyalty, consent, obedience and violence" (2004, p. 39). As with political free speech, the implicit trajectory of free association, by virtue of its demands, is the preparation of a democratically capable and engaged subject. The patient, during treatment and in life, no longer bound by an authoritarian doctor's prescription, claims her own voice and participates in a shared conversation, as well as an open-ended one—a conversation that continues to offer life (desire) to the subject and her community even as it constantly and essentially meets with its impasse. And so this conversation must resuscitate itself again and again from the stifling of freedom, the frustration of equality, the strangulation of desire, the near death experience.

Psychoanalysis's positive, utilitarian impact, had potentially toxic side effects that one might frame in free speech terms: As Freud came to see it, too much expressive license for individuals can be damaging to society. But one may quibble—and this is a serious quibble—about whether he misjudged the risk of too much expressive license as a side effect of free association itself. Would it have been possible for Freud to overcome his prejudices, his own acculturation, and fully advocate an enlightened, impassioned, embodied, and publicly engaged—and feminine—space upon which a robust, implacable voice of the citizenry might blossom? What would it have meant to trust the power of the talking cure beyond the consulting room? What if he hadn't handicapped the potential of that cure by insisting on a return to repression? He would have had to gain and sustain a faith in the power for stirring conversation to triumph over the recklessness and destruction that are potential in unfettered speech. And, as others have pointed out, it would have meant trusting, as he did in the beginning, his patients' reports of incest and sexual abuse—and trusting, perhaps, his own childhood memories of paternal abuse (Lear, 2005, p. 69). For by turning away from their spoken truths (and his own history), by muffling inquiry into real trauma, Freud developed a theory that privileged the role of fantasy in the genesis of psychological symptoms, obscuring rather than highlighting the fascinating tensions between fantasy and reality.

At the same time, as Alfred Tauber posits, Freud's thesis was that humans have moral responsibility and must contend with their status "as legislators to themselves," situating themselves between choice and determinism and situating psychoanalysis as a moral or ethical project (2010, p. 221). Tauber interprets Freud as accentuating reason's agency. But Freud was also dedicated to unlocking the laws that determine us. Not for the sake of reason's primacy, but for the sake of exposing the laws of unreason, of deciphering the realm of passion, of decoding the symbols and signs of disordered and taboo desire. In Freud's exploration of the dialectic between release and repression, reason and irrationality, we discover—more than a search for reason and autonomy—his inclination toward lawfulness. Turning to Derrida to read Freud, one might say that Freud's quest was "precisely not to take 'emancipatory battles' beyond the law, but to take the law, or at least 'the element of calculation'" between truthful desire and compromise into the heart of psychoanalytic "appeals to justice" (Derrida, 1992; Glendinning, 2011, p. 97).

Still, disillusionment found its way to the core of his theory: despite years of allegiance to his conviction that libido lay at the root of all psychical life, he conceded to the possibility that "beyond the pleasure principle" lay another darker, more destructive, human drive or impulse: aggression. As Freud's mission and discoveries became darker, his conclusions grew more pessimistic. He unwound (as in *Civilization and Its Discontents*) a narrative of fear and mistrust, aggression and guilt. Repression, he felt, was universal (if excessive in the case of hysteria); repression had value for society in part because he couldn't sustain a faith in practices of translation, in free speech as a meaningful source of truth that society could bear. Nor could he sustain a conversation with the mind that created linkages with—and was predicated upon—the body, that source of so much initial and exuberant discovery. Beyond that, Freud came to recognize an inescapable link between trauma and the feminine: that "what is essentially repressed is always what is feminine" (1950a, p. 251). Femininity not only lacked a signifier in his psychical framework, but there was no adequate location for women in the symbolic system of his—perhaps of any—time.[1] (Freud arrived at the substitute signifier, passivity.) For now, he kept as an open and even unasked question the relationship between the lack of a feminine signifier, that bedrock of repression, and the dark impulses that led us to warfare.

Had Freud had a different psychology himself, had he lived in less troubling times towards the end of his life, perhaps he might have maintained the "evenly suspended attention" that he beseeched the analyst to sustain to the discourse of free association. He might have kept his attention trained on the conversation between silenced, imprisoned voices and the body, likewise imprisoned but eloquent in its symptoms. He might thus have developed an appreciation for faith, rather than merely holding it in contempt or rationalizing its function. He might have grasped the possibilities of sustained conversation between private and public, a conversation that acts as a living, breathing, vitalizing force as it creates a space where liberation and restraint may meet without requiring repression. He might have been able to envision a democratic space that became self-fulfilling and self-regulating, organized as much by the inner wisdom of transgressive but not lawless unconscious processes as by shared voices in an ongoing dialogue dedicated to the pursuit of meaning and the revelation of unexpressed truths. He may have sustained a faith in a talking cure that, under the lawful constraints of transference and symbolic speech, did not recoil into repression and pessimism. He may have instead anticipated and realized an even greater calling for psychoanalysis: its ambitions and implications for a theory and practice for democracy.

CHAPTER SEVEN

Free speech? For whom?

Enfranchisement and opportunity

The United States Constitution, in its original form, made it very clear that free speech, and political participation more generally, were not intended for everyone. The Founding Fathers were inclined to reserve for the educated few the power to govern. According to Howard Zinn, the Founding Fathers, on the whole,

> did not want a balance, except one which kept things as they were, a balance among the dominant forces at the time. They certainly did not want an equal balance between slaves and masters, propertyless and propertyholders, Indian and white. (Zinn, 1980, p. 101)

James Madison, warning that state governments might tyrannize minority voices, proposed an amendment barring states from adopting repressive laws; it failed to be ratified. Only during reconstruction would such an amendment be adopted. Only in the twentieth century would it be honored.

Although both the First Amendment and the psychoanalytic fundamental rule laid the groundwork for including previously marginalized voices, they both continued to exclude those voices. Barriers to free speech, and equal participation, have only gradually fallen. We've seen that slaves could not be citizens, and thus were excluded from the American polis, until the passage of the Fourteenth Amendment in 1868. (This same amendment nullified other discriminatory impediments to voting, such as poll taxes and literacy tests.) We've witnessed the repression of women's voices, bodies, and agency in fin de siècle Vienna, and their disenfranchisement in the U.S. until the passage of the Nineteenth Amendment in 1920. However, serious obstacles persist. Voter suppression, gerrymandering, and felon disenfranchisement remain means of (often racially motivated and discriminatory) exclusion. At the same time, concentrated wealth in a tiny percentage of the population translates into disproportionate "inclusionary" political power. To understand these exclusions and biases, these persistent failures of free speech and inclusive democracy, we must understand the role of, and reaction to, an embodied feminine space.

Freud, influenced as he was by Enlightenment thinkers such as Locke and Darwin, came to recognize that desire is inscribed—together with desire's entanglement with the enigmatic, often subsuming, desires of others—on the body. Though he had perceived links between trauma and the feminine, he later came to view repression as necessary, in part because he'd lost his faith in free speech. His notion of "compromise formation" followed from his perception that repressed impulses insist on release *and* that social forces, including internalized ones, insist on their burial. But this compromise inevitably results in new symptoms. A similar feedback dynamic—new freedom, new pushback—characterizes the history of free speech in America, and I will argue that, from a psychoanalytic vantage point, this history has manifested the same deficiency that weakened Freud: an inability to comprehend the mystery of female sexuality, which is linked to an inability to protect a vital, embodied space for the democratizing impulse of desire in civic society.

Exactly what the First Amendment says, what rights it guarantees, and whether it serves particular ends that might help us interpret its means—all these questions remain unsettled. And so they will certainly remain, even if we were able to ignore, to control, to bottle up the truth of unconscious, elemental desires. The ambiguity of the text (admittedly a key source of its endurance), the inherent partiality of interpretations, the ceaseless competition of political and cultural interests—all these factors apply constant pressure to any judicial position on when laws may stifle speech and when they may not.

The evolution of First Amendment jurisprudence is fascinating to observe and raises vital questions. But if the implicit goal of democracy, as embodied in the First Amendment, is to guarantee all citizens equal freedom to speak and an equal chance to be heard, then focusing on particular controversial speech acts, or particular controversial laws, is to presume what has yet to materialize, because these controversies are all about the limits placed on those who can *already* speak—those already poised, full of voice, on the social stage.

Yet there are many people, indeed entire groups, that don't just lack the economic means to engage in the sorts of speech that get heard in our debates and campaigns. The problem for many if not most of us is not that our voices are being stifled by laws, but that there is no space in which we could even begin to speak, let alone be heard. Feeling marginalized, we usually give up and silence ourselves. Or we resort to actions that speak more loudly than words, but that violate the very foundations—the laws—upon which a genuine free speech community prospers. Laws prohibiting speech censorship, be they the Founding Fathers' or Freud's, cannot even the playing field for the vocal and the silenced without an active practice dedicated to listening, to enfranchising the voices (and bodies) of the muted.

After all, power dynamics and communicative failures operate on many different levels—from the intimate (one-to-one) to the political (many-to-many). Recall (from Chapter Three) that the Bill of Rights (unlike the Declaration of Independence but like the Constitution in general) had remained "conspicuously silent on the question of equality" (Oppenheimer, 2009, p. 11) until the Fourteenth Amendment's mandate challenged this silence. Albeit at a dilatory pace, the Supreme Court gradually yielded to this mandate. Animated by significant legal dissents in the decade between 1919 and 1929 (testaments themselves to the compelling, even revolutionary, power of rhetoric), the Court finally upheld a free speech claim in the 1930s. Legal doctrine began to close the gap between the ideals and realities of free speech. What followed was a spate of victories expanding the free speech rights of individuals and minorities—the root of much of the robustness and popularity of free speech rights today.

This expansion of protections has almost always been aligned with liberal and progressive causes. Not surprisingly, politically conservative groups came to view free speech protections as onerous—until recently. The pendulum has swung. Today, free speech protections are being used to advance—and to exploit—conservative political causes: to knock down abortion rights and hate crime statutes, and to secure unprecedented freedoms from regulation of commercial speech. Its vulnerability to exploitation reveals both the power and the precariousness of free speech, its ability to service both sincerity and masquerade. Truly "free" free speech requires lawful regulation that both encourages and protects speech. But what are the guideposts for that regulation? And to what degree is a commitment to equality (one nominal promise of the Constitution) pertinent to this conversation?

In psychoanalysis we work with patients mostly on an intimate level, but our aim is to help them find their voices in broader contexts too, if they are to constitute themselves both as subjects *and* as citizens in the polis. But as a profession, psychoanalysis has had to contend with institutional impediments to the sort of inclusiveness and empowerment to which it is nominally dedicated. Of course, free speech in psychoanalysis emerged as a largely one way conversation, with the analyst's "equality" enshrined in his acts of listening and evenly suspended attention. But that conversation has widened as relational practices have evolved to emphasize the mutuality between analyst and analysand in a shared, if asymmetrical, dialogue.

This shift has foregrounded a number of questions that can be translated from psychoanalysis into free speech or "natural rights" questions. Freud had discovered the psychosomatic benefits of promoting speech and decreasing self-censorship to gain access to his patients' unconscious desires and to develop their increased capacity for self-governance. Liberty was clearly good (at least up to a point) for the patient.

Although Freud remained preoccupied with the tensions between individual and collective interests, he never quite framed the technical clinical issues in terms of human rights, including the analyst's. He never recognized that the analyst's own "bill of rights" is an implicit boundary to the patient's expressive license, or that the analyst's rights could serve to advance the free speech rights of his patient. In Freud's era, and in the classical traditions that followed, the analyst's rights and dignity were cordoned off and treated as irrelevant to the treatment paradigm. Clinical tensions between the patient's expressive freedoms and the analyst's human needs and rights remained shrouded by technical guidelines—a kind of analytic positivism—that protected analysts by dimming the light cast on their vulnerability.

The need to negotiate between one's own and others' rights and desires is now a focal point of a reconceived psychoanalysis (e.g., Pizer, 1992; Slavin & Kriegman, 1992). Contemporary literature documents the challenges involved in conceiving the therapeutic endeavor as fundamentally intersubjective, involving two (relatively) equal if asymmetrically arranged subjects (Aron, 1991)—but we rarely do so while simultaneously considering the therapeutic action of speech. We must ask to what degree is any treatment actually therapeutic if it does not substantially honor the *mutuality* of human desire and need within relationship, while also fostering and cherishing the patient's *singular* voice and expressive freedom. I believe that to advance the goals of a treatment, an analyst must both welcome a patient's particular discourse and work to enable a discourse that is genuinely liberatory.

In this chapter, I will focus on how our institution has (only partly, I admit) worked through its own struggles with the dialectic between singularity and mutuality, between free speech and repression, between desire and transgression. This is as an unfinished story of basic inclusion and exclusion. Whose speech has been cultivated? Whose speech has been silenced? This survey might help us find a way to honor the aims of free speech by providing more equal opportunities—the occasions and the power—to speak. This will allow us to investigate further how free speech, in both psychoanalysis and the Constitution, ultimately rests on foundational human laws that regulate at a most basic level all communication: the lawful processes that protect and facilitate the life of the symbol.

Between absorption and marginality

If we follow Freud's lead and recognize the many dimensions of human communication, without insisting on verbal speech as the only or truest mode of valid expression, then we begin to glimpse a more inclusive model of free speech, and a more inclusive democratic vision than is set forth in the Constitution. At its founding, psychoanalysis expanded the realm of signification: even the most disenfranchised, the practically voiceless, might be heard and amplified, even despite their wishes and desires to hide, to camouflage, to remain mute. Of course, much of the art (if not also the science) of psychoanalysis depended upon a new form of hearing. From its inception, it was a practice dedicated to drawing disenfranchised voices into a shared discourse. It explicitly sought to free the speech of those whose silence had resulted in behavior, or physical "speech," that made them seem abnormal or ill.

Yet even in his early studies of hysteria, as Paul Wachtel (2002) has demonstrated, Freud (who still held to the "seduction hypothesis") could not help but view its etiology through the screen of social class. That is, he came to believe that hysteria was more frequent among upper-class children—despite a probable greater incidence of sexual abuse in "the proletariat"—because such children were morally and intellectually more sophisticated. Given their more developed sensibilities, they were prone to a disease resulting from necessarily more forceful defenses.

This odd sort of reverse discrimination, whereby only the well bred were qualified for treatment, makes for a somewhat sad but also illuminating and even potentially inspiring story. Psychoanalysis, in its very foundation, embodied and fostered an inherently democratizing ideal—the right to free speech—while at the same time reinforcing social inequities and class prejudice. On the one hand, Freud and his followers, by drawing out and then interpreting the voice of the unconscious and the suppressed, by getting patients to speak through words as well as through the music of the body, contributed, one patient at a time, to sowing the seeds of democracy. On the other hand, even as their practice was dedicated to enfranchising marginal voices, they actively marginalized certain other voices—and not, as we shall see, just those of the "proletariat." Eli Zaretsky has described these contradictory impulses within psychoanalysis as a mark of its historical situation "between absorption and marginality" (2004, p. 66).

What Zaretsky means is that, in parallel with its own inclusionary and exclusionary views of the patient pool, the psychoanalytic profession was itself subjected to cultural biases. Even if at times "absorbed" into the social life of a culture, analysis was still treated as marginal, other, strange. He attributes this odd duality to the fact that "*all* of Freud's early associates were Jewish" (ibid., p. 70). Drawing on the work of Sandor Gilman (1993) and others, Zaretsky notes that Jewish men were often depicted as feminine and were associated generally with women and homosexuals. To the degree that this prejudice held, psychoanalysis was to that degree and from its beginnings marginalized and viewed as "other," and, in what one might view as Freudian irony, Freud himself channeled the same kinds of prejudices. For example, according to Gilman, Freud took the traits that anti-Semitic literature ascribed to Jews (circumcised and thus symbolically castrated) and projected them onto women, even as that same literature had ascribed feminine traits to Jews (Zaretsky, 2004, p. 58). This tendency in Freud's thinking (and in psychoanalysis generally) has recently been explored with candor, complexity, and depth by Aron and Starr (2013).

Nevertheless, psychoanalysis would gradually emerge from the margins and begin to shed its stigmatized cast and stigmatizing presumptions. Like many intellectual developments first seen as strange and "other," it would become something of a fashion among the elite, and from there it would be part and beneficiary of general cultural-attitudinal shifts. In Zaretsky's analysis, the most significant intellectual trend of the early twentieth century was a shift away from property and family position as defining markers of the self. In their place arose ideas of autonomy rooted in personal choice and motivation, accompanied by a new recognition that the mind, like the body, is a complex organism susceptible to injury and amenable to cure. At the same time, around the turn of the century, America was embracing the notion of "mind cure"—that is, the idea that positive subconscious thoughts could cure both mental and physical ailments (James, 1902, p. 93). Where nineteenth-century psychiatry had "exclud[ed] and isolat[ed] those deemed 'mad,'" the new notion of mind cure "stressed the *universality* of the 'subconscious' … [and so] helped create a consumer market, an audience, and intense interest in Freud" (Zaretsky, 2004, p. 78).

Even as the popular culture grew more receptive to Freud's revolutionary concepts, psychoanalysis was embraced by the fledgling American psychiatric community, which claimed it as a scientifically based form of healing and granted it institutional acceptance. In exchange, however, American psychoanalysis paid the price of conformity and professionalism, becoming "alien in spirit and content to its original insights" (Zaretsky, 2004, p. 68).

Psychoanalysis would prosper in the United States, thanks partly to this edge-dulling professionalization, which removed the sting of Freud's more outlandish ideas. Not that the ideas themselves mattered so much—most Americans had no idea how much more analysis was about sex than it was about positive thinking, nor were they intimate with the methods of the talking cure. But Freud as an icon of the power of the unconscious, if not as an unmasker of the Oedipus complex, helped spur Americans' widespread optimism in the power of the *individual* to overcome obstacles and to engage in mental healing. This psychoanalytically-bolstered impulse, bottom-up and counter to traditional authority, was "ideally suited for democracy" (Zaretsky, 2004, p. 78). It culminated in Freud's 1909 lectures at Clark University, which not only granted his ideas scientific legitimacy but, given their generalization and accessibility, further ignited the sparks of consumer appeal for psychoanalysis—its Americanization, as it were.

Meanwhile, in Europe, psychiatry remained conservative and established, and so it tended to exclude from the university Freud's psychologically interpretative and speculative investigations. And so European psychoanalysis arose in opposition to the traditional, patriarchal order; it was claimed by the marginalized, by intellectuals, and by elites. But this de-centering granted it another kind of appeal, different from the kind it enjoyed in America: the appeal of the avant-garde and the socially progressive. Many of the original members of Freud's circle were Social Democrats, whose identification with the working class resulted in a socioeconomic as well as cultural marginalization.

But after a few decades in the wilderness, psychoanalysis found more fertile ground in the socialist-Marxist political views that were increasingly popular in the aftermath of World War I. Suddenly, analysts found themselves newly relevant, intellectually and socially. All of Freud's inner circle worked with shell-shocked populations, displaying the authentic benefits of their humane impulse to offer non-coercive treatments. Franz Alexander and Sandor Ferenczi, among others, experimented with time-limited treatment and "active" techniques to reach frayed, unmoored populations. Although such innovations came, in part, to be seen as degrading and diluting psychoanalysis, they also empowered it, enhancing its reach and effectiveness across diverse and marginalized populations. Freud certainly contributed to this expansionist impulse, but his signals could be a bit mixed; he sometimes implied that the common people couldn't handle his truth. For example, he famously concluded that "in applying psychoanalysis to the psychological problems of the lower classes, one must alloy the 'pure gold' of psychoanalysis with suggestion to create a psychotherapy for the masses." (Wachtel, 2002, p. 201; Freud, 1919a, pp. 167–168).

Alloyed or unalloyed, European psychoanalysis did make strides toward greater inclusiveness. In the process, it signaled that the treatment itself should and would be sensitive to social class and to the dialectics of enfranchisement and disenfranchisement. These expansionist impulses were tinged with elitism; and analysts' calls for social justice remained undergirded by class prejudice. Nonetheless, the Great War and its aftermath catalyzed a democratic impulse within the profession, altering views of who was fit for treatment and how analysis might advance social justice. Contemplating the massive destruction and displacement of people, Freud anticipated a day when "the conscience of society will awake" (Freud, 1919a, p. 167), compelling a psychological *and* material responsiveness to people in need (Gaztambide, 2012). Furthermore, he made tantalizing allusions to the broader social implications of psychoanalysis. For example, he told his Vienna Psychoanalytic Society that from case studies we learn "what is really going on in the world.... [A]nalyses are cultural historical documents of tremendous importance" (Nunberg & Federn, 1962, p. 251).

However, the promise of a psychotherapy for the masses was still contingent on another determination: who was analyzable, and who was (still) not. At each turn in the history of psychoanalysis, we see two contrary forces in action: the empowerment of disenfranchised voices, and renewed efforts and new methods to re-disenfranchise those voices. This latter, antidemocratic and authoritarian impulse within psychoanalysis would be especially dominant in post–World War II America.

World War II barely spared psychoanalysis in Europe, where it was pushed further to the margins, even while the same conflict contributed to its expansion (albeit with a decidedly, and paradoxically, conformist streak) in America. As George Makari writes, the Nazis

> had perpetrated a genocide of European Jews and massacred leftists, sexual "deviants," and those deemed degenerate or mentally unfit.... [O]nly the Dutch managed to keep a clandestine psychoanalytic group together. The French, Italian, Hungarian, and German psychoanalytic communities were either destroyed, dispersed, disbanded, or Nazified. (Makari, 2008, p. 467)

Otto Fenichel inherited the leadership of the analytic Left and sought to codify psychoanalytic technique in order to ensure its survival, but he did so from Los Angeles, not from Vienna. With psychoanalysis practically crushed in mainland Europe, English-speaking analysts acquired a dominant voice. The aforementioned conformity of American psychiatry was reinforced by the influx of "orthodox" Viennese émigrés, who had faced the silencing, annihilating perils of fascism.

In the aftermath of World War I, the flourishing of psychoanalysis had been of one piece with a growing consumer culture, with ideas of sexuality that were independent of reproduction, ideas of a "primitive" unconscious and its realm of desire. These changes in the culture were reflected in the growing presence of women and homosexuals within psychoanalysis itself. But again, as European nations set out on the path to yet another cataclysmic war, democratizing impulses were countered by anti-democratizing ones. The spread of fascism, the opposition of the Catholic Church, the increased professionalization of medicine, and the medicalization of psychoanalysis—all these contributed to stifling creativity within the field. In the late 1930s, ideas of social control emerged in tandem with the rise within psychoanalysis (and particularly within American psychoanalysis) of "ego psychology." Ego psychology attached primacy to the ego as the agent of reason and control, downplaying the importance of the drives that Freud's early followers had privileged. Analyzing the confluence of these factors, Eli Zaretsky concludes that "postwar psychoanalysis became a veritable fount of homophobia, misogyny, and conservatism, central to the cold war project of normalization" (2004, p. 276).

Not surprisingly then, the "talking cure" that Freud and his associates developed also came, over time, to disenfranchise some voices—and some bodies. We have already begun to explore the contradictory signals sent and the status granted to women in classical psychoanalysis (a far more complicated history than I shall be able to do justice to here). The voices of others too were excluded—for instance, those of gay individuals, including gay psychoanalysts—by marking them as "pathological," and thus illegitimate. Other patients too were excluded from the talking cure because they were judged unfit to participate. While homosexuality was once seen as a diagnosable condition *requiring* psychoanalytic treatment, other patients carried diagnoses that rendered them *ineligible* for treatment. For example, persons who were diagnosed with what became known as borderline and/or narcissistic disturbances were viewed as incapable of utilizing the stock tool of the trade, free association; thus they were also systematically denied access to the means by which they might win free speech.

As psychoanalysis evolved, it fell short of its implicit democratizing ambitions, becoming instead a venue for the psychological "haves" of society. Those with psychopathologies judged unsuited to analytic treatment were cordoned off from access to care. The treatment that had invited symptoms—signifiers of disembodied voices—to "join in the conversation" (Freud & Breuer, 1895d, p. 148) barred those with the symptoms most in need of attention and inclusion. In this respect, the psychoanalytic profession could claim little difference from society at large, whose very judgments and power dynamics it aspired to transcend. And so it betrayed its own radically liberating potential, and let down the democratic project.

Facilitating environments and voice

But this largely disappointing history is not a simple tale. Within the psychoanalytic community, some dissonant and dissident voices did emerge; and they were prominent voices, capable of righting the profession's course. Post-Great War devastations entailed an emergent socially conscious ethos, including Freud's call for a "psychology for the masses." Where World War I had fueled psychiatric attention to shell shock, the devastation accompanying World War II spurred psychiatric attention to the plight of homeless and orphaned children, and to the needs for mothering and for a comprehensive response to environmental devastation and deprivation. The impact of the sociocultural on the individual; the impact of the environment on psychopathology; the impact of separation and loss, especially of traumatic rupture, on the psychological primacy of attachment and the family: all these now came to the forefront of analytic attention. The former accent on Freudian drive theory—with its intrapsychic orientation and its central focus on the Oedipus complex—gave way, at least to a large degree, to a focus on early maternal care, dependence, and environmental factors.

This progressive turn in psychoanalysis, fueled as it was by wartime devastation, spurred a reconsideration of some core tenets of clinical practice. Whereas Freud had recommended that the analyst maintain a technical stance of neutrality and "abstinence" from gratifying his patient's longings (1919a, p. 162), the Hungarian analyst Sandor Ferenczi, a close collaborator of Freud's with socialist political leanings, argued against the attitude and practice of abstinence. He advocated instead for a technique in which the analyst provided *active* emotional responsivity and involvement in order to counter their patients' childhood deprivations, environmental and emotional.

Later, D. W. Winnicott insisted that analysts needed to foster a "facilitating environment" that might actively counter such deprivation. Daring to point out that economic class factored into deep societal fissures that were, to some degree, revealed in the clinic, Winnicott wrote

> there is this terrible contrast between those who are free to enjoy life and who live creatively and those who are ... all the time dealing with the threat of anxiety or a breakdown.... [W]ell persons are the "haves" and the ill people are the "have nots." (Winnicott, 1969b, pp. 234–235)

Psychoanalytic conventional wisdom held that neurotic problems are rooted in individual intrapsychic conflict and not material conditions. But Winnicott dared to implicate reality. "It always seems strange," he admitted, "when the analyst puts stress on the environmental factor." Nevertheless, "in matters of ultimate ætiology the important thing is the environment" (ibid., p. 236).

Winnicott's statement remains provocative, even if it today it seems obvious that material deprivation and its associated degradations must take an emotional toll. More tender sensitivities have not in fact produced more equal societies. In fact (as I imagine would not surprise Freud), the gap between haves and have-nots has only widened in most contemporary societies, developed or developing. As David Harvey has chronicled, while capitalism spreads, barely checked and rarely ameliorated,

> some populations are held to be more disposable than others, with the result that women and people of colour bear most of the current burden and will probably do so even more in the foreseeable future. (Harvey, 2014, p. 111)

As capital seeks "class domination," it inequitably extracts income and wealth from vulnerable populations, dehumanizing them as it further impoverishes them. This is as true in the United States as it is anywhere; in recent decades social mobility has in the U.S. almost ground to a standstill, "so everything rests on a social reproduction process that is highly unequal and tightly channeled, if not outright discriminatory" (ibid., p. 196). As alienation, human degradation, and fury mount, the emancipatory potential of human desire, including freedom of thought and speech, is stifled. But its implosive tensions are also stoked, threatening to exceed and to rupture the contours of a speaking and hearing community.

Free-market economists deride as "soft" and conducive to dependency rather than to "freedom" any meaningful social program aimed at supporting vulnerable populations. Similar opprobrium greeted early efforts by Winnicott and like-minded reformers to provide active clinical intervention, beyond the relative "neutrality" valued by classical analytic listeners. Such expansionist innovations were denounced as too gratifying of patients' emotional needs, wishes, and wants; they were belittled as "supportive psychotherapy" rather than true psychoanalysis.

Today, however, expansionist impulses have been absorbed into mainstream psychoanalytic practice. After all, we cannot hope to help produce a freer *and* healthier society for all unless we attend to the needs of the disenfranchised and grant dignity to their speech and to their status as hearers and as speech targets. Winnicott may himself have harbored this sort of grand vision, but he focused on building a clinical foundation for those whose care and developmental needs were most arrested, most neglected, and most at risk.

And so we might hope and be persuaded, along with Steve Botticelli, that clinical psychoanalysis, through actions in and beyond the consulting room, might "take its place as one small endeavor through which we struggle to bring into being the as yet unimagined possibilities of human life" (Botticelli, 2004, pp. 649–650). Along that path, we begin to recognize how any notions of free speech and free expression are fundamentally embedded in a larger context of human rights (security, privacy, equality, freedom from violence, and so forth). Moreover, we begin to appreciate psychoanalytic insights into the non-negotiable primacy of a space between having and not-having, a space of mediation, if free speech *and* mutuality are to emerge. But this recognition requires, minimally, that all voices be included in that emergent space and that the space (and its tensions) be sustained. Inclusion and sustenance in turn require "regulation," so that all voices may have a chance to be heard. The continued exclusion of patients, due to economic factors and to disenfranchisement from health care generally and psychotherapy resources particularly, still plagues psychoanalysis and its implicit democratizing ambitions. This exclusion yet again raises the critical question: What are the fundamental laws of free speech? And why are they ever so prone to violation?

CHAPTER EIGHT

Facilitating speech

Failed environments and psychoanalytic outreach

Freud played down environmental factors when he discarded the seduction hypothesis in favor of a theory that viewed childhood fantasies (typically of incest) as the key determinant of neuroses. He still held that it "would be a mistake to suppose that [reports of incest] are never characterized by material reality; on the contrary, this is often established incontestably" (Freud, 1916–1917, p. 369). Nonetheless, he would preoccupy himself far more with the neurotic's inner battlefield than with "external" environmental conditions, remarking (perhaps too casually) that psychoanalysts "are not reformers but merely observers" (ibid., p. 433).

Yet Freud remained concerned with the profession's broader social impact, believing that

> anyone who has succeeded in educating himself to truth about himself is permanently defended against the danger of immorality, even though his standard of morality may differ in some respect from that which is customary in society. (Freud, 1916–1917, p. 434)

As we've seen, other psychoanalysts, not content to bank the fate of material inequities on psychical and moral enlightenment, sought to fulfill the progressive social promise of leveling the playing field, not only between conscious and unconscious factors, but between environmental and individual ones.

One of the deepest and most influential thinkers to appreciate the role of environmental failure in psychic suffering was D. W. Winnicott, whose concept of a "facilitating environment" was introduced in the previous chapter. Winnicott believed that traditional interpretive techniques—when imposed by a too wise, too clever, and too certain analyst—were at least in some cases rather more poison than antidote. They might in fact replicate the brute imposition of others' signs and agendas that had characterized the very environments that had failed the patient. He did not discard standard techniques, but he urged psychoanalysts to supplement them with new *behaviors* and ways of being that could conjure, for at least the length of a therapeutic session, a nurturing and healing environment. The analyst might, by analogy, provide the "good enough mothering" of which the patient had been deprived.

Winnicott wasn't the first to try guiding analysis down this path. To some extent, his work recalled and revived interest in the earlier, but in its day harshly critiqued, work of Franz Alexander and Thomas French, who in the 1940s had advocated providing the patient "a corrective emotional experience" (1946, p. 66). Heinz Kohut, a Viennese-born, American-trained psychoanalyst, would pursue similar notions, and suffer similar criticisms. Arguing for the theoretical and clinical validity of a "structure building" approach based upon empathic listening and active analytic provision, Kohut established a new American school of analytic thought, "self psychology." Like Winnicott and others in the British object relations tradition, Kohut sought to extend psychoanalysis's mission to enfranchise initially disenfranchised patients.

Elisabeth Young-Bruehl has shown that the rise of postwar socialism in Western Europe dovetailed with and accelerated developments in psychoanalysis that shifted attention away from diagnosing sexual repression and neurotic conflict and towards treating traumatized populations and addressing environmental deprivations. In Young-Bruehl's analysis, postwar social democrats found a pragmatic partner in psychoanalysis and its modernized therapeutic ambitions.

This "psychoanalysis-socialism" synthesis, at its best, prompted leaders to look

> to the causal interactions among inequality and poverty, violence, and war.... Social democracy came to mean, in this sense, maximally inclusionary democracy, and the European social democrats designed programs for bringing excluded peoples into citizenship—and into the welfare states. (Young-Bruehl, 2011, pp. 188, 193)

The mutually recognizing generativity between social/political intentionality and psychotherapeutic advances has not survived into our current era, which has instead seen both social democracy and psychoanalysis retreat into defensive positions (ibid., pp. 198–199). Nevertheless, psychoanalysis has remained steadily, even increasingly, interested in understanding and providing treatment for pathologies that result from failed environments and failed relationships. The principal aim of such treatment is to reignite a stymied, but not extinguished, developmental process, one that advances a patient's symbolic and genuinely free free-associative capacities. In this sense, psychoanalysis, so often caricatured as a luxury treatment for the neurotic elite, has—notwithstanding the very real and ever burdensome economic factors that remain barriers to equality—made significant inroads in leveling the playing field for those otherwise denied access to free association and so to free speech.

From clinic to constitution: towards an active public sphere

It is not unusual for social, scientific, and cultural movements to veer from the course set by their founders, to lose touch with their original inspiration. Sometimes it happens because the forces these movements counter are pervasive and highly resistant. Sometimes even the founders can't handle all the forces they once tried to unleash. And so within ten years of publishing a three-volume defense of America's new constitution, John Adams led a willing Congress to pass the Alien and Sedition Acts, in clear violation of the plain text of the First Amendment.

As we have seen, psychoanalysts (including Freud) were not always willing to honor the ideals of liberation, empowerment, and inclusion inherent in its theory and aimed at in its practice. But the analytic community did listen to those courageous and conscientious dissidents who confronted its shortcomings in principle. Psychoanalysis has produced no utopias; nor would an outsider assessing its internal politics find models of inclusiveness and empowerment. But it has in fact provided a template for at least progressively and consciously opening the space within which a true democracy might slowly take shape. For democracy is in fact the goal, however indirect, of psychoanalysis.

Its area of expertise is helping people gain their voice. What Freud recognized, and what shaped the psychoanalytic project from the beginning, was that human beings on the whole lack a certain capacity for agency (ownership and self-assertion of intent and desire), and that their "autonomy" and "free will" are illusory. To achieve a real measure of personal agency requires a surrender to unconscious desires and dreads that we did not choose, and a humility and mastery born of that surrender. In that sense, all psychoanalytic patients achieve inclusion through an enlightenment obtained

> by an elite technique to which to a degree, the patient can, by reason of his own gifts, also aspire. Although he may have failed and so needs help, he enjoys a privileged status *vis-à-vis* the people out there on the street. (Percy, 1975, p. 213)

Once enlisted into a discourse aimed at enhancing free speech, patients have the opportunity to fully realize themselves as human beings, which is to say as symbolizing creatures. By contrast, as Chris Demaske has observed,

> First Amendment doctrine assume[s] a level of equality *already exists* among members of the citizenry and that so long as the government remains neutral, every autonomous individual will be capable of equally contributing to public debate. (Demaske, 2009, p. 51, emphasis added)

Many have challenged this assumption, pointing out that free speech ideology masks (and indeed perpetuates) a set of power imbalances. Critical legal theorists, among others, have noted that the mere existence of the First Amendment hardly guarantees that all are enabled to speak. The Supreme Court has recently been of little help. While First Amendment jurisprudence has created and sustained several limitations on unfettered speech (constraining defamation, blackmail, and so forth), it has thus far stopped short of protecting oppressed people from expression that harms them, both directly and indirectly. Instead, the Court has tended to favor "more speech" as the best antidote to malicious speech; free speech is viewed as its own correction. But at the same time the Court has done little to actually foster the solution it proposes, averting its eyes from the dread Medusa of judicial activism, perpetuating the comforting and self-sustaining libertarian notion that if left alone people can empower themselves.

So the Court, and American courts in general, stop short of mandating or even encouraging the positive use of public power to help citizens find their voices. But, as lessons drawn from psychoanalysis suggest, it would be only through such concerted public action that the scorned and silenced and abused could finally supply "more speech" and share their realities, their concerns, and their world view. In the words of Martin Shapiro,

> If free speech is instrumental to democracy, the government might ensure some basic equality of access of all ideas, groups, and individuals to the "market-place of ideas" by reducing the speech rights of the rich and powerful and increasing those of the weak-voiced. (West Publishing, 1983, p. 306)

In recent years—as the Court has been compelled to consider the excluded voices of sexual assault victims, the power of media monopolies to distort democracy, and the many ways that in American politics money talks the loudest—more observers have begun to conclude that "more speech" isn't enough of an answer, especially given the Court's decisions in such cases. What we need, they say, is government action that *actively provides* positive incentives for greater inclusion. Cass Sunstein, in calling for a "New Deal for Speech" (1995), argues that *laissez-faire* simply does not work in the market for discourse; it only allows existing power dynamics to harden. As Sunstein points out, it often happens (contra libertarian dogma) that in an unfettered market for speech, a great deal of speech is actually inhibited, and that in a regulated market, a greater diversity of speech is encouraged. Some sorts of government intervention in markets (e.g., limitations on media ownership) are important and even necessary to leveling the playing field and fostering freer speech.[1]

Jensen and Arriola urge legal scholars and jurists to seriously question the basis on which the law decides what is and isn't "speech." "What has long been thought of as outside the purview of the law (e.g., the silent cry of rape or incest)" (1995, p. 209), they note,

> can be defined as a central issue in First Amendment jurisprudence. Recognizing that some women may want to speak but cannot out of fear, or do not because of restraints imposed by existing doctrine (e.g., libel suits), would force society to redefine the meaning of freedom and the meaning of speech. (Jensen & Arriola, 1995, p. 209)

Citing Robin West's views, these authors advocate advancing beyond the liberal position which views speech as primarily expressive, with a focus on the individual, towards a more progressive view that frames speech "as primarily communicative, something that creates community and 'a social soul'" (ibid., p. 211).

Similarly, for Chris Demaske, First Amendment considerations of speech protections ought be based not in the illusory conception of autonomous individuals but rather in the "relational space" between speakers. Drawing from what legal scholar Kathryn Abrams refers to as "partial" agency, she asserts:

> Not everyone begins with the same level of cultural or social freedom, so the First Amendment, as a negative liberty, does not create a "free" citizen. In order to create active democratic citizens, the First Amendment would have to be read in a way that would both recognize incomplete agency and facilitate movement toward more complete agency. (Damaske, 2009, p. 65)

Sharing responsibility, sharing ownership: bridging private and public

Despite these appeals, the Court rejects speech regulation based on contextual factors such as unequal distributions of power in civil relationships. Psychoanalysis, by contrast, has taken on the task not only of enabling speech, but also of reducing the power barrier between analyst and patient, as well as of extending its reach to previously disenfranchised (and so voiceless) groups of patients. In this sense, psychoanalysis has implemented its own "New Deal for Speech." Through a kind of bootstrapping, the analyst's active provision of "emotional supplies" enables the patient to gain a foothold in the meaning-making process that we call psychoanalysis. This investment not only empowers the individual patient but also psychoanalysis itself. It creates the possibility for a win-win scenario that has mutually beneficial effects, enriching both members of the relationship as a capacity for genuine, mutual recognition develops. It creates the template for the patient's symbolic freedom, a shared and choiceful participation in one's life, beyond fated and determined scripts, and also beyond the therapeutic realm.

In this vision, psychoanalysis is an emancipatory and democratizing practice. The therapist's job is, in part, to shoulder that burden, too long managed alone by patients through their psychological suffering and physical symptoms. In parallel, society may need to shoulder a disproportionate burden for members who have been excessively disadvantaged. We often forget that the very members of society who become most marginalized are bearing the burdens of a kind of solitary confinement—psychical and material. This confinement, originally intersubjectively (including socially and culturally) constructed, is also sustained by a dynamic (often unconscious) enactment of accommodating the experience of feeling unwanted, unheard, silenced, and oppressed—an experience cultivated in a far earlier relational story, typically a family story.

At the same time, in the clinic we frequently confront acts of opposition and defiance, grounded in feelings of spite and resentment, the sense of being a "have not" among "haves." The stories behind such feelings usually remain unspoken and so unheard, even unknown to those who suffer through them. Such feelings, which the patient fears to examine too directly, are transformed into symptoms, and they sometimes become obscured in the stories that other people tell. When such resentments and injuries are manifest on a social level in conflicts between groups and classes, we often miss the transgenerational narratives, burdened by the accrued tolls of censorship, indoctrination, and racial or class based stigma, that tell the tale of their genesis. But in the quiet of the consulting room, we invariably come to hear the silent screams of oppressed voices—their fear and their longing, our guilt, our collusion—but also our own fear, our own longing.

Psychoanalysis has benefited from an active conversation about how to best help on an individual level. We create a space for dialogue that may stretch the boundaries of civilized discourse while stopping short of heinous actions. Words, which are irretrievable, can of course hurt. But we invite the conversation *and the relationship*, one in which both analyst and (ultimately) also patient bear responsibility for their speech impact. Some speech, it may be said, belongs in the consulting room exactly for this very reason, so that the speaker may assume status *as* a speaker, gaining the fortitude not only to voice what would otherwise remain shamefully silenced (or violently enacted) but also to bear the moral consequences of his speech impact. The analyst has no rights to bypass the laws of speech, and we must welcome bids for recognition, especially the bids that our patients make in desperation and when they bypass conventional morality. But civil society too needs to create outlets and conditions that favor the transformation of (otherwise disenfranchised) citizens into responsible speaking agents.

Ultimately, it is the capacity for signification—to create signs and symbols, and to own our communicative intent and impact—that empowers us as communicative agents, in analysis and as members of democratic society. Psychoanalysis, on this account, offers a template for what one might describe as "transitional democracy." That is, the analytic process enlists the patient into an inclusive and equal human relationship, based on its commitment to the patient's speech. And it has learned to take seriously the idea that some sorts of affirmative action are essential to the creation of the patient's initiation of agency and voice. Likewise, the Court may need to take seriously the importance of a public with agency and voice, and consider what sorts of measures are essential to the creation of an active public sphere so that, as James Madison hoped, "the people, not the government possess the absolute sovereignty." For popular sovereignty to prevail, marginalized voices need the chance not only to speak but to be heard. In this sense, it is the distribution—or redistribution—of voice that is at stake. As clinical experience demonstrates, when boundaries are redrawn, self and mutual respect may be restored. In turn, an emerging space between private and public, invisibility and visibility, silence and speech becomes possible, setting the stage for shared participation and a greater experience of genuine freedom. Such limits and commitments also prepare for a strengthened free speech regime, one dedicated to enabling individual and collective symbolic agency and to replenishing itself in an indefinite process of grappling with muffled voices, with yet ineffable truths.

If free speech is a shibboleth more than a reality—if the legal guarantee that most people may say mostly what they want excuses the lack of speech afforded to the less powerful—then perhaps part of the solution is to find a way of applying psychoanalytic insight to a revived discourse about how to equalize speech. How we think about regulating speech—at first blush a decidedly undemocratic prospect—begins to shift as we contemplate speech as a *relational* event. That challenge becomes all the more daunting in the context of "hate speech," to which our attention now turns and to which psychoanalysis, I will suggest, offers a nuanced approach.

CHAPTER NINE

Hate speech, survival, love

Offense, injury, and danger

Psychoanalyst D. W. Winnicott and Justice Oliver Wendell Holmes arrived from two very different angles at the same conclusion. If our fears and hatreds are left unspoken, we remain their hostages. Both men implicitly acknowledged that speech connects and brings to consciousness otherwise disconnected thoughts, feelings, and sentiments, making them available for transformation.

Free speech in psychoanalysis developed only fitfully as a practice, and some might say that it suffered setbacks. Even though Freud valued free association as an analytic tool, only gradually did he give due weight to the actual voices (and bodily utterances) of the women he treated. Even then, he remained ambivalent about the degree to which we can seek truth without compromise. Though he came to reckon with the need for limitations to free expression, Freud's fundamental rule still recognized, as James Madison had, an inviolable "apolitical interior of the human spirit" (Neuborne, 2015, p. 97).

How we might reconcile these tensions in practice, and not only in theory, in the clinic and in society (and not only in time of war), is a question ever subject to controversy. Take, for example, the Supreme

Court's ongoing attempts to deal with "hate speech." Such speech may *embody* what Justice Holmes called "thought that we hate," but it is not the same thing. Should it, too, be "free?" Or is hateful expression inimical to the sort of society the First Amendment was intended to promote? Hate speech is often directed at relatively disempowered groups. Might it therefore be considered unprotected and subject to prosecution in civil courts under group libel laws, as suggested by Jeremy Waldron (2012)?

As we saw in Chapter Three, today's expansive First Amendment rights for ordinary citizens emerged only gradually, through a series of challenges and equivocal decisions, all of them within the last century. These fitfully secured First Amendment protections have been watered down if not seriously undercut as, citing the First Amendment, courts have granted private enterprise unfettered rights to "speak" through advertising and political contributions. Far from limiting speech, courts have set an ever higher bar that challenges to free speaking must clear.

But nobody seems to want to put the bar out of reach. Even free speech advocates, as Nigel Warburton has noted, "almost without exception recognize the need for some limits to the freedom they advocate. In other words, liberty should not be confused with license" (2009, p. 8). This may be because, as the political philosopher Tim Scanlon puts it, "What people say can cause injury, can disclose private information, can disclose harmful public information. It's not a free zone where you can do anything because nothing matters. Speech matters" (Warburton, 2009, p. 4).

Scanlon's notion is nothing new. In *On Liberty* (1859), John Stuart Mill judged that there are necessary limits to expression. He argued for far-reaching protection for speech because of its immense value in preserving a free market of ideas, in exposing truth, and in eliminating error. But he excluded from protection speech inciting harm or physical violence (Warburton, 2009, p. 9). This became known as Mill's "Harm principle."

Mill's views were echoed by Justice Oliver Wendell Holmes in the previously noted case of *Schenck* vs. *United States* (1919). Holmes would soon, in a different case (*Abrams* vs. *United States*), remind us that we "should be eternally vigilant against attempts to check the expression of opinions that we loathe." But in *Schenck*, widely cited for its *expansive* views on free speech, Holmes asserted that we *should* not and *must* not protect expression that poses a "clear and present danger." Holmes's example was the humble but intuitively compelling case of "shouting fire" in a crowded movie theater. Legal arguments have ensued over the meaning and extent of almost every word in "clear and present danger." But the basic idea is still widely respected: Society could not survive free speech without limits.

A sort of "clear and present danger" test also holds in today's psychoanalytic practice and in therapeutic practices generally. In theory, patients are free to speak with impunity, as analysts are obliged to maintain patient confidentiality. However, ethical and legal duties regarding absolute patient privacy end if the analyst determines that the patient intends to inflict bodily harm on another or to exact a life, including his own. And so, in the clinic as in society, Holmes' general point holds: What people say can cause injury; there is no unconditional "free zone" for speech.

If as a society we've come to agree that we can draw limits in at least those cases, we have to wonder what guidelines should courts and psychotherapists use? This question harks back to Frederick Schauer's (see Chapter Four): "What makes speech special?" Psychoanalysis and free speech theories only ambiguously answer this question, making it hard to establish a unifying theory of free speech or to assert consistent guidelines.

In Chapter Four I remarked on the mutual relevance of Seana Shiffrin's (2014) "thinker based theory" and psychoanalytic aims to foster individual psychical and symbolic freedom. Both Shiffrin's and the psychoanalytic paradigm join free thought and free speech in promoting the autonomy and moral agency of the "thinker." Both also recognize that such agency is founded upon relationship, upon one's freedom of associations with others. A hierarchy of values follows. For example, Shiffrin posits that personal speech deserves protection equal to that of political speech. (Theories that place a higher value on democratic discourse would yield a different conclusion.) She also reasons that private, noncommercial, and political (especially dissenting and incendiary) speech merit more robust protection than does commercial speech.

How does Freud's novel talking strategy aid Shiffrin's quest for a unifying theory? Free association, as we've seen, carries an implicit ethical imperative, appealing to and requiring both the speaker's and the listener's moral agency. It also aims to create a space for raw and novel unconscious truths and intentions to be thought, spoken, and consciously known. Yet the free speech rights of the patient and the analyst are not the same. While both parties are obliged to sustain a truthful conversation accountable to unconscious desires and fears, the analyst's responsibility is to translate and interpret free association. That is, the analyst's position (especially following the inventions and modifications by later analysts, notably Bion, Winnicott, and Lacan) is to enfranchise free association into curative speech. Through this "free speech" practice, otherwise stifled and even previously unthinkable and unbearable thoughts can be revealed, shared, and symbolically transformed. Now, how can our experience with this asymmetrical yet generative process help us grapple with free speech issues that arise in the thorny, complex case of hate speech?

Hate speech, Winnicott, and survival

Over the course of its history, psychoanalysis has learned a good deal about hatred and hate speech, often first hand. Initially, Freud took pains to understand hatred as well as destructive impulses in general. According to his early thinking, we destroy and kill only for self-preservation; there is no independent drive to destroy. Over time, Freud changed his mind, partly as a result of observing that sadism and masochism are widespread and inherent, if often only weakly expressed, elements in the human sexual makeup. By 1905, he had concluded violent urges and sadism were rooted in sexual frustration; and, of course, his elevation of Sophoclean drama into common family romance, the "Oedipus complex," implicated sexual frustration in murderous competitive strivings within the family. What society viewed as "perversion" could generally be traced to society's taboos and parental censorship barriers to satisfying common sexual urges.

This relatively simple picture, in which most of what ails us can be traced back to erotic blockages, grew more textured in the following decades. The carnage of World War I drove Freud to consider a possibility he'd previously resisted: that life is governed not by a single instinct, but by opposing ones—Eros *and* the death instinct.[1] His emphasis here was on the conservative nature of the death drive, which typically found expression (as in transference and in cases of trauma) in the compulsion to repeat, to return to an inner state of constancy or homeostasis.

In a somewhat ironical turn, Freud conceded the powerful allure of a death drive that sought peace, even if also extinction, rather than active destruction and violence. His views took an even darker turn late in his career, as the atrocities of war took their toll. He now embraced what he had formerly excluded: that *destructive* aggression was an ubiquitous dimension of psychic life, situated "alongside of Eros and which shares world-dominion with it" (Freud, 1930a, p. 122).

But for the better part of his career, he contended with his patients' aggressive and "negative therapeutic reactions"—that is, as another kind of transference, beyond the standard "libidinal" or sexually-motivated transference. Moreover, he viewed these reactions as a great obstacle to recovery, because in them the patient maintained a "negative attitude towards the physician and [clung] to the gain from illness" (Freud, 1923b, p. 49). Freud's followers in the classical psychoanalytic tradition continued to focus on analyzing and dissolving the libidinal transferences; but, as one of them, Otto Fenichel, noted (1939), analysts could not ignore an excess negative transference which itself had to be analyzed. In this dimension, psychoanalysts professionally and personally endure hates and resentments that might otherwise remain underground and fester, resulting in individual psychic symptoms, and from there perhaps in social ills.

Our clinical work provides a living testament to the fact that hate speech violates human dignity in fundamental, deeply scarring ways. While psychoanalysts have always sought for the unconscious agency and fantasy that impels behavior and expression, it also now recognizes hatred's roots in real relationships, and in real cultural contexts, that is, economic inequality and racial prejudice. Whatever the roots of the patient's hateful feelings, the analyst remains part of the power dynamics that arrange themselves in the course of treatment. Furthermore, the analyst has to bear the impact of these dynamics in a real way. With or without all the possible layers of personal prejudice or resentment, which frankly may be reciprocal, all analysts pay a price simply by inhabiting the position that they do. They must, for the sake of a "cure," invite and hear each patient's expression of cumulative social resentment and hate. The degree to which the patient is vulnerable and "needs" the analyst in order to heal compounds those resentments. Vulnerability exacts its own price; and at least for a while someone else needs to make the payments. The same is true in civil society as in the clinic. As legal scholar Arthur R. Miller notes, regarding the preservation of free speech,

> Perhaps it is inevitable that [it] will involve occasional discomfort, disgust, even anguish, to the listeners. The notion that this is the price we pay for our freedom to express ourselves is not an empty one, for it truly is a price. (Miller, 1982, pp. 34–35)

Most of the time, for most psychoanalysts, it is a price worth paying, because they are able to remain connected to their love for their patients, to retain a vision, "however rudimentary" (Loewald, 1960, p. 18), of who they might become once freed from enslaving fears and resentments. In this way, psychoanalysts sustain a faith in the power of love to mitigate hate, and so to provide a means, albeit on an individual by individual basis, for combating hate speech. To do so, they rely on what free speech advocates refer to as "more speech."

In free speech contexts, "more speech" or "counter-speech" refers to public discussion and the airing of multiple points of view. In psychoanalytic practice, the "more speech" equivalent is allowing the patient to continue speaking without retaliation. This creates, albeit subtly, often painstakingly and slowly, a space for healing transformation. We bear the price of corrosive hate speech so that another, "better speech"—that of Eros—may prevail.

Winnicott, in a seminal essay (1969a), made this point so compellingly that his writing has spawned a revolution of thought about the possibilities for mutual recognition and entry to symbolic life through the analytic process. Challenging the analyst to endure a patient's expressions of hate and aggression without retaliation or withdrawal, Winnicott sets the bar very high. The analyst, he says, must "survive" the patient's destruction, so that the patient can discover a world of others who have an independent existence of their own. This is the *sine qua non* stepping stone to creative living, to play, to love and genuine relating.

Winnicott's insight was anticipated by Freud, who said in 1923 that "clinical observation shows not only that love is with unexpected regularity accompanied by hate (ambivalence)," but also that "hate is frequently a forerunner of love" (1923b, pp. 42–43). In treatment as in society, we may encounter a great deal of "thought that we hate"—and sometimes "hate speech"—en route to liberty and to love. Though we don't usually (even within the clinic) say it so directly, our hateful expression is what humanizes us; hateful expression conditions us to be capable of love. But none of us can achieve this alone. We all need the other to hear and to translate our hate—and to sustain their humanity while doing so. This requires faith. "Deeper than 'belief systems,' faith sustains the turbulent test of how 'two humans can learn to survive one another'" (Eigen, 2014, cover blurb by Meg Harris Williams).

Still, there will always be a remainder, an excess of hate. We'll always resist symbolization, even as we aspire to it. And part of what resists symbolization, said Freud and Winnicott and Lacan, is the female and her sexuality. As he developed his thinking on transference hate, Winnicott (1950) insisted on the psychologist's responsibility to draw attention to unconscious factors, linking our deep-rooted fears of the female to the widespread social accumulation of unconscious hate for her.

Asymmetrical regulation: speech content in context

We are left to question how we reconcile calls for the regulation of hateful expression with our psychoanalytic understanding that hateful expression is part of the path by which we condition our humanity and discover otherness? Let's return to Winnicott who, in another seminal essay, frankly asserted that,

> However much [the analyst] loves his patients he cannot avoid hating them and fearing them, and the better he knows this the less will hate and fear be the motives determining what he does to his patients.... The main thing, of course, is that through his own analysis he has become free from vast reservoirs of unconscious hate belonging to the past and to inner conflicts. (Winnicott, 1947, pp. 195–196)

Winnicott, who began his career in pediatrics, often understood the analyst's role as an analogue of the mother's, and applied lessons from the clinic back onto childrearing. So he called upon the mother to also know her hate, to recognize that "she hates her infant from the word go," and he listed a litany of reasons for the mother's hate, for example that her child is

> a danger to her body in pregnancy and at birth … an interference with her private life.... [H]e is ruthless, treats her as scum, an

> unpaid servant, a slave ... [and] having got what he wants he
> throws her away like orange peel. (Winnicott, 1947, p. 201)

"The most remarkable thing about a mother," he says,

> is her ability to be hurt so much by her baby and to hate so much
> without paying the child out, and her ability to wait for rewards
> that may or may not come at a later date. (Winnicott, 1947,
> p. 202)

The mother may not know that baby's love is around the corner from
this hate, and she may scarcely feel her own love during these times.
But she—and her baby—are greatly helped if she does.

For our purposes, let's note that within the necessary asymmetry of
the psychoanalytic arrangement, the free speech rights of the analyst
are, de facto, "regulated." It is exactly this asymmetry in power relations
to which proponents of hate speech reform call attention. Current First
Amendment doctrine protects dissident speech, even if hateful, from
the tyranny of the majority. But it fails to take into account the harmful
effects of hate speech. However, as Steven Heyman argues, "because
hate speech inflicts deeper injuries than other forms of wrongful speech,
it is reasonable to subject it to greater regulation" (2008, p. 183). If we
take by analogy the parent-child or therapist-patient relationship, we
can begin to recognize the humane appeal of calls for reform—and also
the complex challenge they pose.

It's not only that defenders of traditional First Amendment jurisprudence argue that content-based hate speech restrictions may lead down
a slippery slope to the censorship of any speech that the government
finds offensive. They also oppose taking account of the contextual,
power relationships between members of society, arguing that a permissive approach is the best way to ensure that the disempowered have
equal opportunity to speak and be heard. In turn, the familiar libertarian argument goes that "detestable speech" is constitutionally protected
"not because we doubt the speech inflicts harm, but because we fear
the censorship more" (McConnell, 2012). Another version—intuitively
and rhetorically appealing but also frightening—goes that "without the
best defense of free expression, everyone's right to speak and write and
paint and create music is endangered, because freedom is indivisible"
(Hentoff, 1992, p. 228).

The issues at stake become vexingly complex. Consider the case of Flemming Rose, who was the features editor of the Danish newspaper that commissioned and published satirical cartoons about Muslims, including Mohammed (with a bomb in his turban). That publication spawned vociferous global protests and violent demonstrations against what many indicted as blasphemy. Rose describes the erosion of free speech rights—which he designates a "tyranny of silence"—in the wake of these escalating tensions. Rose, like many others, had imagined that as societies become increasingly "multiethnic, multicultural, and multireligious," they would recognize the need to accommodate a greater freedom and heterogeneity of expression. "Yet," he writes, "the opposite conviction is widely held.... At present, the tendency in Europe is to deal with increasing diversity by constraining freedom of speech" (Rose, 2014, p. 9).

But treating underprivileged groups as blocs rather than individuals, and shielding such groups from possible offense, has its problems, not all of them political. For example, Rose asserts that intolerance has increased in Europe as a function of treating minorities as collectives, rather than as individuals. As he tells it, in this arrangement, "freedom of speech" devolves into "refraining from speaking anything potentially critical of, or offensive to, another group. That form of tolerance closes its eyes to intolerance of individuals within the minority group" (ibid., 2014, pp. 178–179). A similar dynamic has been playing out with increasing frequency on today's American college campuses, where student protest has succeeded in blocking commencement speeches by politically tainted individuals. Similarly troublesome is the recent proliferation of disclaimers known as "trigger warnings" that purport to protect a vulnerable audience from exposure to potentially traumatizing content—another vector of attack against diversity of speech. These trends beg the question that Salmon Rushdie (1990, p. 396) rhetorically posed, "What is freedom of expression? Without the freedom to offend, it ceases to exist."

The question isn't whether anyone has a right to not be offended; the question is when does offense become the kind of harm that erodes the grounds of the freedom that allows it. And the corollary question is how measures to protect disadvantaged groups might stifle rather than promote diversity. These issues continually challenge us and elude facile solution. Nevertheless, it's clear that all paths to freedom require limits. Of course, people raised in a society that continually trumpets its devotion to freedom are apt to mistrust restraints imposed from above, say by the Supreme Court—that "most purposefully antidemocratic element of the Constitution" (Dunn, 2005, p. 126). But of course the Court isn't creating boundaries out of thin air; they were already there. The question of free speech is always a question of how free, and the answer always depends on some collective sense of what sort of speech is dangerous, and how likely that danger is to occur. Judge Learned Hand, in an oft cited (1950) opinion, suggested that we must always judge "whether the gravity of the 'evil,' discounted by its improbability, justifies such invasion of free speech as is necessary to avoid the danger." All of this is well understood by most free speech advocates as well as by psychoanalysts, who recognize that not setting boundaries is as likely as setting them to leave us hostage to forces that have nothing to do with freedom.

We can illuminate what is at stake by taking an example close to home: Imagine raising a toddler without ever setting boundaries. Any parent can predict the likely outcome, and some parents have experienced it first hand—namely, that the beloved child will become a little monster. In the absence of boundaries, the child's omnipotence may swell to fill the available space. (Not that this experience is fun for the child either; while toddlers might protest when a parent says "no," it's pretty scary to be the boss of one's own parent, let alone of one's own self, at such a young age.) As children gain in physical size, this growing sense of omnipotence, left unchecked, becomes far more difficult to manage, and is obviously more potentially threatening than the already challenging temper tantrums of toddlers.

While raising a child is obviously very different from building a society, in both cases we are faced with the always difficult and sometimes angst-ridden need to draw lines around not only what one may do, but what one may say. This line drawing isn't a simple matter of checking the runaway power of the powerful. Sometimes, as in the analogy of the toddler, we must decide the degree to which we extend special protection to the less powerful. And we must also take care not to merely invert the power dynamics and let the oppressed become oppressors. Our aim is to hear the toddler's tantrum, but also to translate it, and to enlist the toddler as an empowered member of a speaking and hearing community. In establishing boundaries, we aim not to suppress speech, but to create space for dissent and for airing differences—and for recognizing each other's humanity. The release and expression—of fury, resentment, frank hate—requires, as Winnicott recognized, some human and humanizing encounter in which our destructive urges are met with firm but healing "survival."

The decisive questions for a psychoanalytically inflected free speech practice become: What rules of thumb cultivate the unbounded symbolic potential of speech? How do we sustain a robust space for speech that advances this goal—that enables "destructive" speech to meet with humanizing "survival"? How do we discriminate coercive rhetoric and aggressive acts of dominance (under the cover of speech) from a discourse in which we can sustain together often aggressive and competing desires?

Additional necessary questions follow, for example: How do we ensure a space for the most disadvantaged members and groups within society to speak and to be heard, and that is sensitive to the vulnerability of speech targets? And perhaps most fundamentally: How do we create social contexts that enable us to speak together? How do we, as a speech community, facilitate the speaking, hearing, translating, interpreting, holding, and surviving functions that the analyst and the treatment situation aim to provide?

As scattershot hate speech finds it way to listeners and translators, it meets its counterpart when we dare to refute it. But we must clear a proper space for the argument. Christopher Hitchens tells this story:

> I went on *Crossfire* at one point, to debate some spokesman for out-raged faith, and said that we on our side would happily debate the propriety of using holy writ for literary and artistic purposes. *But that we would not exchange a word until the person on the other side of the podium had put away his gun.* (Douthat, 2015)

Given Hitchens's talent and taste for the unabashedly provocative and mercilessly persuasive, he may seem an unlikely candidate for us to invoke in fashioning a shared space that respects the voices of the disempowered and marginalized. As Ross Douthat put it (in the same *New York Times* editorial (2015) that cites Hitchens, written in the aftermath of the *Charlie Hebdo* attacks),

> the kind of blasphemy that *Charlie Hebdo* engaged in had deadly consequences, as everyone knew it could … and *that* kind of blas-phemy is precisely the kind that needs to be defended … because

> otherwise the violent have veto power over liberal civilization, and when that scenario obtains it isn't really a liberal civilization any more. (Douthat, 2015)

And yet psychoanalysis cautions us. The vulnerable, but also the violent, are often those of us without outlets to symbolic discourse. Not everyone has equal access to the symbol and its incredible versatility and power, including its power as a weapon or means of wielding power. What we intend as symbolic expression is experienced as violence by an other, who has been marginalized and is unable to find a foothold in symbolic realms. When received by an Other whose access to shared symbolic discourse is blocked, the symbol will be construed in either/or terms, as brute fact.

This means that certain speech that begins (in the imaginative intent of its creator) as symbolic if also inflammatory will be registered by some in ways that are experienced as invasive, coercive, and even annihilating actions, and we are all vulnerable to collapsing the space for symbolic life. Under stress and in the aftermath of trauma, we all remain ever vulnerable. We experience many of the signs and symbols that interpenetrate us in a brutish way. We are "hit," "assaulted," "raped"; we lose our capacity for metaphor. What's more, when we are deprived of symbolic capacity, our own bids for communication are apt to fail. We stumble in our efforts to gain a foothold in symbolic life as agents *with intentionality* for the hate we communicate. We resort to our bodies, to silence, or to blindsiding speech in ways that violate the very laws of symbolic life. We are struck anew by the remarkably enduring and startling insight and challenge posed by Freud's epochal claim that "the man who first flung a word of abuse at his enemy instead of a spear was the founder of civilization." (Freud, 1893a, p. 36).

Psychoanalysis—and public life—all too vividly demonstrates that we have no choice but to contend with startling and unnerving raw free associations, flung words of abuse, between unconscious and a conscious intent. *In search of the analytic function* of being heard and translated and known, our hate speech is our unbecoming calling card. It too often summons fear and hate in exchange, though it longs for recognition of its desiring intention. It's not that anything goes. But when we respond with retaliation and rebuke, we miss a mutually strengthening opportunity: to enlist raw, unfettered, often hateful speech into something socially purposive.

To put the matter differently: To counter a patient's hate, and hateful expressions, we require more than just "more speech," or "better speech," or what Judith Butler has referred to as "counterappropriative speech" (Butler, 1997), though these are useful and necessary conduits. We also must enrich the hatred with its counterpart: love, or Eros, which as Freud (following Plato) understood had as its purpose "to combine single human individuals, and after that families, then races, peoples and nations into one great unity, the unity of mankind" (Freud, 1930a, p. 122). Lofty and unworldly as Freud's words may sound in the context of discussing the brute actions of hate speech, they call for us to recognize a space between, an embodied relational and discursive space in which persuasive but not coercive or brute force dynamics may prevail. In the courts and in the clinics, there are no universal solutions, except for a surrender to the lawful primacy of this space, a primacy I will call feminine law. Perhaps Freud said it best when he simply said, "all cures are cures of love." Level playing fields are also loving playing fields.

CHAPTER TEN

Enshrined ambiguity: drawing lines between speech and action

Local contexts and boundary setting

At their origins, Freud's fundamental rule and the Founders' First Amendment were abstractions intended as universal rules. In the case of Constitutional rights, they were to be adjudicated by the popular body of a jury or by an "independent" judiciary in a neutral way, with all (white) men treated equally. Freedom to speak was to be independent of context. In Freud's conception, free association was to be met with the analyst's non-authoritarian, "compassionate neutrality" (Kris, 1996, p. 38), abstracted from any relationship of personal influence with the patient. It is in this sense that he should be a "blank screen."

But contemporary legal scholars have called into question the very concept of First Amendment neutrality. Neither "freedom" nor "speech" is a metaphysical given; and no court is neutral or free from popular pressure. Indeed, at its very origin the Constitution was seen as subject to popular enforcement. Madison, for example, while championing the idea of internal checks and balances among the branches of government, conceded that "*[t]he people* who are the authors of this blessing [constitutional liberty], must also be its guardians" (Amar, 1998, p. 132; citing Rutland & Mason, 1983, p. 218).

On a pragmatic level, any universal or sovereign right to free speech is complicated by the tenuous line between speech and action. If speech can't be distinguished categorically from conduct, then there is no sacred impermeable realm in which speech exists and may receive special treatment. Regulating speech is, like regulating behavior, dependent on situations and contexts.

Likewise, in today's era of theoretical pluralism and clinical innovation, the tyranny of a central orthodoxy in psychoanalysis has been under assault. Contemporary theory questions the notions of a neutral analyst and neutral free associations uninfluenced by the analytic relationship.[1] As psychoanalysis has evolved to appreciate the mutual influence between patient and analyst, it has recognized that setting boundaries and making clinical decisions happen in a "local" context (*these* two people in *this* analytic relationship). Analysts increasingly view their own subjectivity, and thus partiality, as vital to the process by which patients claim their own status as human subjects.

Enshrined ambiguity: "regulated" freedom

The practices of psychoanalysis and first amendment jurisprudence have evolved not only (not even principally) in the academy, but through case studies and case law, by trial and error. In his mature career, Freud found himself perpetually balancing two contrary psychotherapeutic actions: eliciting desire (including destructive desire) from the recesses of the unconscious; and imposing restraints on that desire. Finding this balance has challenged psychoanalytic discourse and practice ever since. This interplay of liberation and repression, evolving dynamically over time and leaving inheritors to find their own balance, is a pattern also repeated in our understanding of the First Amendment.

The contours of this evolution are shaped in considerable part by the text of the Bill of Rights. The First Amendment, as David A. Strauss points out, began as a pretty weak statement, and it is only over time that we have invested it with the strength it claims today. "The process was distinctly evolutionary; the key principles were developed over fifty years, often through trial and error, with false starts and subsequent corrections" (Strauss, 2002, p. 44). Said principles emerged in what he regards as a textbook "common-law" fashion, gradually establishing themselves as commonly understood legal principles that were accepted as givens. We begin to appreciate the wisdom of the First

Amendment text when we take a long, retrospective, view. As Thomas Emerson puts it,

> Governments strongly prefer acquiescence to dissent. The long-term benefits of tolerating the views of others are often not immediately apparent. The system, in short, is a sophisticated one, requiring the education and re-education of each generation. (Emerson, 1984, p. 32)

As I have suggested, the very "weakness" of the First Amendment is the source of its strength, durability, and resilience. It had to be, in Winnicott's iconic words, "good enough"—and *only* good enough. Situated in a "space between," both strong enough and deficient enough, this text could flower in a way both suited to the times and faithful to its germ. In its ambiguity, the First Amendment leaves enough space to be interpreted broadly, even to be seen, by some, as anything but ambiguous.

The entire United States Constitution is, as Jill Lepore observed, a mere 4,400 words (not counting amendments); and she observes correctly that it "doesn't exactly explain itself" (2011, p. 72). The even more terse First Amendment spells out still less, leaving open an interpretive space that has yet to be completely filled. One might likewise observe that Freud didn't exactly explain himself when he set forth the fundamental rule of psychoanalysis (Mahony, 1987). And as Michael Guy Thompson puts it, "Like so many of the technical rules that govern psychoanalytic technique, … there isn't a definitive description of what free association entails anywhere in the psychoanalytic literature, not even in Freud" (2000, p. 35).

By creating minimalistic and abstract blueprints, both the Founding Fathers and Freud created a space "that enshrines an ambiguity" (Laplanche & Pontalis, 1973, p. 4). They set into motion a dialectic between absence and presence, between boundedness and unboundedness, between what is essential and non-negotiable and what may be elaborated and interpreted. They provided building blocks rather than completed structures—a "bounded formlessness" that characterizes its (and Winnicott's conception of) "potential space" (cited in Summers, 2013).

The Court, in each generation, visits and revisits these issues, as it seeks to balance the claims of freedom and restraint—a debate that engages scholars and occasionally the general public. Psychoanalysis, on the other hand, has been less explicit in addressing the balance, or tension, in Freud's founding rule, though most other core tenets have been openly debated. Discourse around free association, as we've seen, is oddly situated, scattered among essays and edited books. On the one hand, it is met with silence and dismissal as a "technique" neither suitable nor epistemically valid in the wake of today's intersubjective turn, in which analytic discourse is mutually constructed, rather than centered on the patient's free expression. On the other hand, the value of free association is often taken as an article of faith, an unquestioned axiom. Still, at least in theory, psychoanalysts aim for an unrestrained and candid, if asymmetrical, conversation with their patients. But we tend to be less explicit about the boundaries inherent in that conversation. After all, free association is fought for and gained in relationship to a real human being. The boundaries established during the treatment are keyed to a real relationship.

But if subjectivity and locality are so essential to the analytic process, how then can we generate general insights and develop useful guidelines and practices? And on what general basis can we understand and justify the ways we set boundaries to our patients' free speech? How do we understand the idea of natural rights in the context of localist, intersubjective frameworks? What does it mean to us as practicing psychoanalysts to acknowledge that our cherished commitment to "free association" is a shared fantasy? And what implications do these considerations have for civil society? Not only do our patients never fully realize free association, and not only is it necessarily constrained in theory, but we also do actively set (mostly unacknowledged) limits on our patients' speech. What kinds of boundaries do psychoanalysts set, and why?

To get a sense of how this process plays out in a real situation (local context), and to see how line drawing between speech and action in the clinic might apply to civil society, let's consider a series of sessions and some illustrative exempla from my own practice.

An illustration from clinical practice

My patient had been suffering uncontrolled, intrusive sexual fantasies that obliterated her experience of agency and voice, and so obviously of free association. During her long treatment, she initially used our relationship as what Winnicott called a "facilitating" or "holding" environment in which I provided her some of the soothing and self-regulatory functions (for example, mood and behavioral regulation) that she was as yet unable to provide herself, at least in large part, because of previously unmet developmental needs and unaddressed environmental deprivations. The goal at this stage of the treatment was to help her release and share with me her unwanted thoughts, in an enclosed and safe space within the boundaries of our sessions, in order to cultivate her sense of interiority. (This is what free speech advocates might regard as an active implementation of conditions for free speech.) This would begin a long and gradual process of eliciting her own sense of agency, and her capacity to bear her experience without retreating to either deep withdrawal or abject dependence.

Little by little, she began to experience increased self-delineation and capacity to self-regulate her own inner states. And she began to reveal an ownership of her independent gestures, including self-initiated motoric activity and self-generated fantasy (that was no longer *strictly* conditioned by her disowned, unconscious agency and its co-option by overdetermined historical and relational factors). While we were still mired in this challenging process, she began to experience physical "startle" responses in our sessions, perhaps responding to my spontaneous movements. She seemed to be invoking a deep sense that her very life, her spontaneous being (signified by her capacity to startle someone else), had been stymied, oppressed, obliterated. Was she startled? Startling me? She was startled and so was I. I understood this startle behavior to be my patient's attempt to claim her own aliveness, by way of affecting me; we would both find our way to connect through being startled and startling to each other. Here were the seeds of an emergent freely associative process and of mutual discovery of each other's independent being.

But as so often is the case with developmental evolution, my patient's progress suggested (*and* concealed) the remnants of an earlier traumatic story, in which aliveness is achieved at the peril of the other's deadness. This recalls the Founding Fathers' early recognition, inspired by John Locke and by a work from the 1720s called *Cato's Letters*, that free speech meets its natural (law) limit where it obstructs the freedom of others. My patient's quest to reclaim her inalienable rights involved a complex interplay between her natural rights and mine, and between her developmental needs and others' impulses to suppress them. This is a story that encompasses much of what

Freud called "repetition compulsion" in the transference, and of what relational psychoanalysts refer to as enactments of dissociated trauma and self-other configurations. In other words, her behavior suggested not only a kind of liberation but also a kind of enslavement to unprocessed, if not unconscious, early traumas.

Accordingly, my response to my patient's startles shifted as she repeated the behavior with increasing frequency within the session and across multiple sessions, and as I grew more irritated. She had gained a greater sense of volition and intentionality for her gesture; and this was a goal I'd held for her. But a subtle further change impinged upon our relationship: it began to feel as if she were *exploiting* the impact of startling me, seeking to silence me, to disarm me and punish my independent gestures. She also seemed impervious to my efforts to process this active dynamic with her. Our work now compelled me to respond differently: to use my speech to challenge hers, so as to help her engage in "real" speech rather than in coercive action. I felt the need to use my voice not only to welcome her nascent agency and aggression, but *also* to set boundaries.

I suggested to her that I no longer experienced these behaviors as reflexes, but rather as aggressions; they were choices, even if partly disowned choices. Although I wanted to welcome expressions of her assertion and aggression, I did not welcome the experience of feeling blindsided, as if she lacked intentionality. Seeking to help her engage in "free speech" rather than in disowned action, I decided to tell her that I intended set some limit in response to her further (behavioral) efforts to bypass the space of speech, by (physically) startling me. My goal was to open up the space for her agency, for her ownership of intent, by linking her choices with explicitly stated consequences. I told her that this limit would involve ending the session early. My patient protested, insisting on her right to use the session as she needed, to fill it with her speech and expression.

Although she did not explicitly invoke her "free speech" privilege, she did call me to task on the hypocrisy of my so-called invitation to free associate, to say whatever came to mind in the context of our sessions. She rebuked me for setting capricious and arbitrary limits—limits that I did indeed improvise because I had not anticipated they would be necessary. I recognized then the validity of her rebuke for unfairly censoring her and sending mixed messages. But a point of psychoanalysis— one that lacks a sufficient analog in the public sphere—is to emotionally process these imperfect decisions and the shared humanity that inevitably enters intersubjective processes.

Any real conversation about free speech, and its limits, must take up questions of impact, responsibility, and context. Although I began to set boundaries with my patient when her speech act (action that is a form of speech) aroused my genuine discomfort, her behavior did not lead me to feel "harmed." But I did anticipate that, without an explicit verbal interpretation of her behavior and exploration of her fantasied (and real) impact on me, the treatment might get derailed into progressively more destructive disowned actions (enactments, in psychoanalytic terms) between us. Instead, my hope was to help her to claim her status as an intentional subject, whose speech was not aimless. It was an address to me, and would perhaps necessarily seek to startle me, awaken me, unnerve me. Indeed, part of what makes psychoanalysis compelling—and reflective of dilemmas faced in civil society and by the Court—is that it takes place at the very line where a patient's speech dares to make the analyst uncomfortable.

Bearing discomfort on behalf of one's patient, while perhaps necessary, is not an aim in and of itself; it is only useful insofar as it serves a therapeutic function. In this case, my discomfort helped me empathize with my patient's history and find words to communicate my understanding. But my discomfort also helped me set a boundary, which in turn helped her take ownership of a previously disowned behavioral enactment and intention by locating an emergent line between action and speech. It also helped her feel increased empathy for herself, including empathy for her struggle to acknowledge her fear, hates, desires, and her conflicted tensions about being in a relationship with me. My goal was to facilitate her own experience of conscious choice and personal agency.

Conversation about boundary setting arises in most therapies, as it did here, when an ever-precarious and intangible line between speech and action threatens to collapse. After all, in psychoanalysis, we make meaning not only of speech but also of silence, of facial expression, and of physical gesture. We do so in a way that challenges us to become aware of what is (or formerly was) unconscious and is now available to become conscious—of what is (or has been) disowned and is now capable of being owned. For example, when my patient introduced her body into the treatment in the provocative yet mostly disowned way, seen above, she signaled to me (as I came to understand it) that she was ready to acknowledge how our verbal communications were expressions of her bodily experience, and of her own history of physical violation and vulnerability. These were necessary steps toward owning her status as an embodied, visible, speaking subject. Whatever its idiosyncratic pathways, as Freud discovered early on, psychoanalysis achieves freer speech by means of a dialogue with the body. All the more reason for our conversation to address boundaries.

Speech and action: line drawing

My patient's progress lay in claiming her own agency, constituting herself between body and speech; this achievement required both mutual recognition and the mutual drawing of lines between action and speech. Her achievement followed from more than just speaking; it was itself an action, and action that she gradually was able to *own, with a sense of intentionality*. What was true in this clinical encounter is true for us as we assume our place as contributors to our societies. Just as the American Constitution is "not just a text, but an act—a doing, a constitut*ing*" (Amar, 1998, p. 27), so too is one's claim to speak freely, to speak authentic speech. *Speech requires action*.

What do I mean by "authentic speech"? In psychoanalysis, we aim to cultivate symbolic speech: speech that emerges from an open space, a space of desire in which the erotics of free speech prevail and symbols can blossom. I distinguish symbolic speech from the speech that often appears at difficult moments in life and in treatment: speech that flattens, collapses, and deadens discourse; speech that degrades human dignity. Symbolic space and thus symbolic speech are difficult to sustain: Discursive space is ever subject to violation and collapse. Preventing this collapse depends not only on the courage to be open in one's desire, but also on a willingness to draw lines, the sort of lines that enabled my patient to claim her agency, as a subject with a distinct voice.

Speech requires action—such as drawing lines, or resisting the impulse to wound—to avoid degradation into unmediated action, and sometimes speech requires action because a moment calls for marking a line itself, for a symbolic gesture between speech and action. Of course, it can be difficult to distinguish speech from action or to specify what actions rise to the level of the symbolic, a difficulty we often face in psychoanalysis, and which has often beset First Amendment jurisprudence. Both fields have evolved as defenders of expression rather than deeds; and yet there is no clear and fast rule for telling the two apart. Where is the line at which speech crosses over from expression to action, from symbolization to aggression or coercion? And were this line clearly defined, how far does a commitment to free speech compel us to protect speech that is not symbolic, but closer to action? Conversely, how far does that commitment compel us to protect actions that might be considered modes of speech because they are primarily symbolic? (I shall consider one quintessential example, flag burning, below.)

The notorious difficulty of discriminating between speech and action, symbol and deed, is a topic frequently taken up by Stanley Fish. As he sees it, "speech always seems to be crossing the line into action, where it becomes, at least potentially, consequential" (1994, p. 105). Finding this line becomes ever more challenging when one recognizes that the very point at which the status quo is subverted—when the line between speech and action vanishes—marks the space between them, the space upon which symbolic speech is born and where false substitutes die off.

Some have attempted to fudge the distinction between speech and action (as perhaps I did here with my patient) by distinguishing not only between speech and action, but also between what became known, after *Chaplinsky* vs. *New Hampshire* (1942), as "low value and high value speech"—with "low value speech" being granted less than the extraordinary protection afforded political speech. As David Strauss explains, the Court, having evolved to consider political speech as centrally important in free speech expression, had to concede that not all speech could be afforded the same extraordinary protection (2002, p. 54). Although the Court has expanded free speech protection for a broad range of expression throughout the last century, it continues to regulate large realms of expression and communication,[2] and provides "categorical" exceptions for four categories: obscenity, defamation, commercial speech, and "fighting words." The Court, by granting certain categories of speech the greatest protection, also defines unworthy categories.

The Court draws lines, but it also redraws them. What might be considered fighting words unworthy of First Amendment protection was winnowed in cases following Chaplinsky. The Court instead seeks to maintain a high threshold of protection for such speech, which is punished "only when it is both intended and likely to bring about 'imminent lawless action'" (Heyman, 2008, p. 115). In a 1972 ruling, *Police Department* vs. *Mosley*, Justice Thurgood Marshall espoused the view that the government may not restrict speech because of its content, nor may it discriminate against certain content. Since then, the dominant trend in contemporary jurisprudence has been to protect the autonomy of the speaker and to reject speech regulation based on *content*. By the late 1970s, the Court, adhering to a principle of content-neutrality, had determined that "not even two of the most heinous, aggressive types of speech—the swastika and the burning cross" could be considered in the category of fighting words. These moves, honoring speakers' rights with little consideration of the fallout for vulnerable hearers and speech targets, culminated in the Court's striking down of a municipal hate speech ordinance because the ordinance was content-based (*R. A. V.* vs. *City of St. Paul, Minnesota*, 1992). Furthermore, issues of content-neutrality are not context-neutral. As we saw in Chapter Nine, the Court likewise rejects regulation based on *contextual* factors such as unequal distributions of power in civil relationships.

As Fish writes,

> "Free speech" always means for consequentialists "free speech so long as it furthers rather than subverts our core values"; and when an exception to a free-speech policy is made, it is not an anomaly or an afterthought but a continuation of the logic that has ruled the policy from the beginning. (Fish, 1994, p. 14)

Fish's challenge raises the implicit issue of how we reconcile speakers' rights with the rights of, and costs to, the rest of the community. With this in mind, jurisprudence might be guided by Justice John Paul Stevens, who cautioned against absolutism and encouraged the Court to "establish a more complex and subtle analysis, one that considers the content and context of the regulated speech, and the nature and scope of the restriction on speech" (O'Brien, 2010, pp. 12–13).

Cultivating symbolic speech

On the vaguely defined terrain between speech and action, cultivating symbolic space is of the highest priority in both the clinical setting and the public sphere. This priority should extend to First Amendment jurisprudential considerations in order to create a coherent, principled, and resilient free speech regime. In this way, psychoanalysis and democracy each practices faith in the possibilities of an often indeterminate and fuzzy line dividing freedom from tyranny, persuasion from coercion (Dunn, 2005, p. 132).

But the Court does not seem to entirely buy the idea that enabling "free speech" means enabling speech that is free. The sad irony is that the Court grants corporations and the wealthy the right to buy speech, creating a scenario in which, as Burt Neuborne (2015, p. 65) notes, "money literally 'talks.'" What's more, the Court has ruled that campaign spending is a form of "pure speech," accorded the highest level of free speech protection. Meanwhile, flag-burning (considered below) has been classified as pure speech, but burning a draft card as "'communicative conduct' entitled to only a watered down level of First Amendment protection" (ibid., p. 65). Further defying any internal logical consistency, the Court ruled that the casting of a write-in protest vote was not entitled to *any* First Amendment protection. In short, Neuborne says, "the Court's formula for distinguishing pure speech from communicative conduct [if it is granted any protection at all] is, to put it charitably, a shambles" (ibid., p. 123).

What if, in an effort to attain greater internal coherence, the Court drew guidance from psychoanalytic insights? It's not that psychoanalysis has been consistently articulate on this front either, so here I take some liberties: Free speech, understood psychoanalytically, would be the speech of free association and its movement of desire, towards symbolic life. Without that defined goal, the Court (and psychoanalytic practice, for that matter) is less internally consistent in its approach to jurisprudence than it might be. Fostering symbolic discourse requires an "open space" for speech, as I shall repeatedly emphasize hereafter. For now, let's note that such space is as essential to democracy as it is to psychoanalytic practice. While considering the goal of fostering symbolic speech and the space upon which it is founded, let's take a further look at a spectrum of issues facing the Court.

We begin with the Court's especially relevant but controversial and still contested decision, led by Justice Brennan, to uphold (rather than ban) the right to desecrate the American flag. Brennan, recognizing that "we do not consecrate the flag by punishing its desecration, for in doing so we dilute the freedom that this cherished emblem represents" (*Texas* vs. *Johnson*, 1989), distinguished between the United States government's legitimate interest in the flag as a symbol to be respected, and the function of the symbol to stand for the government and for the values which that government embodies. Likewise, from a psychoanalytic perspective, protecting the right to flag desecration or burning is vital to free speech. The entire psychoanalytic project is dedicated to our ability to create and to play with symbols, and even to symbolically destroy them. We need others to bear our destructiveness; they must (as per Winnicott) survive it in order to emerge as speaking subjects, capable of wielding symbols. This human developmental need is a central reason why it is so bewilderingly complex to identify and implement adequate "rules of thumb" for establishing pathways to free speech.

Consider the words of President Obama as he eulogized pastor Rev. Clementa Pinckney in the aftermath of his murder (along with eight others) by a white supremacist in Charleston, South Carolina. Speaking of the Confederate flag, Obama said,

> It's true a flag did not cause these murders.... But as people from all walks of life now acknowledge ... the flag has always represented more than just ancestral pride. For many, black and white, that flag was a reminder of systemic oppression and racial subjugation. (Obama, 2015)

The fate of the Confederate flag reminds us that a symbol can exhaust its last bit of open space and be reduced to an object that merely denotes, rather than connotes; there is no space for free play; the symbol is just the thing. Obama's speech, by aiming to bury the ossified racist symbol, attempts to resuscitate symbolic life.

Also relevant to these complex issues are current Supreme Court considerations of speech limits on social media. The question at hand is how to balance one person's freedom to express violent impulses with another person's freedom from threats of violence. As Emily Bazelon writes,

> For decades, the court has essentially said that "true threats" are an exception to the rule against criminalizing speech. These threats do not have to be carried out—or even be intended to be carried out—to be considered harmful. (Bazelon, 2014)

"The legal issue," Bazelon explains,

> is connected to a larger question: how to deal with the frequent claim that online speech is a special form of playacting, in which a

threat is as unreal as an attack on an avatar in World of Warcraft....
In the ongoing "GamerGate" campaign, a faction of video-game
enthusiasts tweeted death threats to women who had criticized
misogyny in video-game culture. When a few of the women felt
scared and left their homes, some gamers scoffed, dismissing the
threats as ephemeral. (Bazelon, 2014)

So far the tendency in such cases has been to interpret First Amendment
doctrine very broadly, such that absent an explicit communication of
the *intention* to harm, online threats are not prosecuted. As the *New York
Times* opined,

> Threats can terrify people and disrupt lives, but in a country devoted
> to broad speech protections, it is not too much to require the gov-
> ernment to prove that a speaker intended to make a threat before it
> can put him behind bars. (*New York Times* Editorial Board, 2014)

By the same line of reasoning, the analyst will reckon with "low value
speech" (including fighting words) not to prove she is willing to tolerate it, but because it is a conduit to her patient's "high value speech,"
to advance the patient's ownership of her intent. Much of what our
patients need us to bear is subversive speech, even revolutionary
speech—speech that threatens our "authority," speech that challenges
accepted norms or conflicted areas within us that, as analysts, we might
prefer to regard as "resolved." We seek to withstand the patient's efforts
at self-annihilation and/or annihilation of the other. Messy and fraught
as this terrain may get, it brings us a close-up view into the terrors and
longings linked to being truly alive to one's experience. It exposes the
emergent symbolization of what has previously been unconscious, as
yet unexperienced knowledge and agency. That experience requires an
act of surrender to a hearing, responsive Other. It also requires ventur-
ing from the illusory comforts of coercive and even threatening speech
onto an uncertain and yet untested terrain of free association and its
trade in symbolic thought and speech.

   These terrors and longings can, and often must, result in a patient's
provoking, demeaning, insulting, confronting the analyst, whose challenge, if we follow Winnicott, is to "survive"—which means to resist
retaliation or withdrawal. While they bring us into a mutual fray, they
also challenge us to locate lines between speech and action.

The analyst—faced with her patient's dare to step into the often inhumane, yet humanizing, thicket of the passions—needs to place some stakes in the ground. These stakes may look like and act as barriers in the path to "free" thought and free speech. But without them, coercive action and "low value" speech, rather than free speech, prevails. As Elliot Adler and Janet Bachant say, the priority is preserving "the integrity of the analytic situation" (1996, p. 1041), not in order to protect the analyst's authority, per se, but because that is the means by which we elicit the autonomy of the patient's freedom of association to which the analyst has "no rights of authority" (Kris, 1996, p. 22). Given the turbulence and destabilizing depths of the unconscious material that this discourse unearths, both parties are greatly tempted to avoid it.

For these reasons, in psychoanalysis as in jurisprudence, adjustments, discriminations, and decisions clearly matter. The question for the Court, from our psychoanalytic vantage point, is "how do we cultivate symbolic space?" All too often, both in the clinic and in political rhetoric, we confront a realm of brute, non-negotiable meaning, while the realm of interpretative and shared play with meaning seems a distant frontier. We observe quixotic quests to bypass the space for translation and mediation—quests that lead us into strategies that are at best fantastical; at worst, coercive, violating, and even violent.

The tendency toward polarization—for example to a discourse of violation and violated, or rigid orthodoxy and permissive laxness—points to the instability of spaces for dialogue, which are open and do not tyrannize by fear, repression, or neglect. The core values of psychoanalysis have always been freedom *and* responsibility. Not only responsibility for ourselves, as determined by an unconscious not of our own choosing, but also responsibility for our agency in choosing how to use this self-knowledge, how to fashion ourselves as moral beings in the face of desires that may plunder and destroy, just as they may lead to creative expression.

With each new treatment or new phase of treatment, the analyst is challenged to reexamine the boundaries that sustain free speech—and create the possibilities for symbolic expression. This requires improvisation, in what psychoanalyst Jim Fosshage calls "a moment-to-moment process level that is fluid and messy with fits and starts and changing contexts and not in accordance with a grand plan" (2010, p. 526). Such ad hoc adjustment is akin to the evolution of common law, through the lived experience of the Constitution. In both cases, the continual test-ing of terms and limits necessitates provisionality and flexibility. They are, as Justice Holmes said of the Constitution, "an experiment, as all life is an experiment" (*Abrams* vs. *United States*, 250 U.S. 616, at 630)—experiments in which uncertainty prevails. Uncertainty allows space for the testing of new ideas, without prejudging their merit.

But for both jurists and psychoanalysts alike, each new encounter is contextualized by previous encounters, that is, by precedent. Precedent is, as David Strauss says,

> the starting point, because it reflects the collective wisdom of previ-ous generations.... But precedent can be interpreted or modified (or even, in an extreme case, discarded) when the presumption of its soundness is overcome by a thorough conviction that it is wrong. (Strauss, 2002, p. 46)

In psychoanalysis, this grappling with precedent and received wisdom happens both in theoretical debates and in clinical practice; in Consti-tutional realms, at the level of legal theory and case law. This grappling is guided by a sense of ethics, rooted in a framework that lies in a space beyond the subjectivities of the analytic couple or the subjectivities of particular justices. For psychoanalysts, it is also founded in a third space where the ethical laws of speech channel the wisdom of unconscious processes. For legal theorists and jurists, this third realm lies between Constitutional jurisprudence and "the ancient landmarks of the com-mon law" (Amar, 1998, p. 154). For both, at least ideally, sustaining a space for free speech requires that it be bounded by a dedication both to others' values and to the fostering of mutual respect, equality, and self-determination. In the case of psychoanalysis, it requires a profound commitment to its own ethic of honoring the patient's growth, of cul-tivating a discourse of desire—one that requires and sustains an open-ness, even as it also poses inevitable encounters with "hate speech." Not all communication is equally (therapeutically) valid if the goal is to enable symbolic speech. Much of the art of clinical practice falls in the space between encouraging the uncensored discourse of the patient, and a kind of censorship that enables the free trade of symbolic life.

Psychoanalytic practice, therefore, exposes the illusory foundations of the libertarian free-enterprise fantasy. Freedom is always situated within constraint. We seek to foster Winnicott's "bounded formlessness" (Summers, 2013). This sort of boundedness is often referred to, in analytic parlance, as "holding the frame." It is not the same as withholding. Holding the frame creates the context for a dialectic between safety and risk, between familiarity and discovery, that is essential to the psychoanalytic process. Its elasticity and limits must allow for two people to develop trust, intimacy, and mutually respecting boundaries. When we bypass boundaries—or when we insist upon overly constrictive ones—we signal that we're afraid. We elude conflict and foreclose the space of desire. We also elide direct communication, making it hard to frankly discuss what is most challenging to say and to hear directly. Such direct communication requires a third dimension, which emerges from the boundaries we set to avoid devolving into fantasies of immediate presence, fantasies of a fusion with the analyst either through "angelic" telepathy, or demonic physical violation. Either attempt bypasses mediation, jeopardizing our very cherished quest for freedom, which requires a challenging and scary discourse with an Other who is also our own, disowned, desire.

In the clinical situation presented above, my patient's startle behavior stood as a form of speech. I came to understand it as a sign of protest against speech itself, the tool of psychoanalytic trade. Silence often serves a similar function in analysis, as I will explore in the following chapter. Though not yet a fully mediated symbol, my patient's startle, like any patient's sign, disrupted the accepted power arrangement that utilized words, and elicited in me a response that required interpretation. By sustaining discourse dedicated to meaning and interpretation, my patient's "resistance" was also conducive to enfranchisement in an evolving symbolic and shared community between us.

Let's remember that psychoanalysis began as a practice dedicated to articulating the patient's censored desire—more often a forbidden love than simply a stifled hate. Enlisting our patients' desire, so that they might claim free and erotic speech, paradoxically requires censorship. But our goal is not to censor, nor to place boundaries *where* our patient's free speech begins to matter to us. Rather, the goal is to create boundaries *so that* their speech may matter *to us*, and because we want to encourage them to *own* that their speech matters to them, that it is meaningful.

Psychoanalysts also set a very high bar for *limiting* free speech. The lines we draw are guided—aspirationally at least—by our intent to open up the symbolic space upon which free speech prospers. Although such clinical judgments may be personal and arbitrary, what cannot be arbitrary is the goal: to enlist the patient's "free" speech into meaningful, courageous discourse with an Other, challenging him to recognize a voice different from his own. Only then may "free" free association prevail.

CHAPTER ELEVEN

On having no thoughts: freedom in the context of feminine space

> There is no stronger evidence that we have been successful in our effort to uncover the unconscious than when the patient reacts to it with the words "I didn't think that," or "I didn't (ever) think of that."
>
> —Sigmund Freud (1925h, p. 239)

I explored in the last chapter the ways that setting limits on patients' speech (and communicative behavior generally) actually works *for* them, and *for* their ability to sustain genuine freedom of speech. For example, in the initial stages of assuming their own sense of power and privilege, their own self-respect, patients may emerge from obscurity and voicelessness by means of speech and behavior that is both too much and too little—it can be both intrusive and indirect. The analyst's active boundary setting can help enfranchise them in sustainable and meaningful symbolic communication.

Lest you get the impression that we spend most of our time reining patients in, more commonly we have to coax our patients out. Often in early stages of treatment—and almost always in heightened moments of conflicted desire—they are usually too reluctant, rather than too eager, to speak. Invited to free associate, a patient will respond with silence or by saying that he has nothing to say. Is his mind really blank? Is the problem that he has nothing to say, or *too much* to say, and that free association risks opening too much space—for fear, for desire? What does it mean to "have no thoughts"?

It takes two

It may seem that Freud himself, in establishing free association as the primary psychoanalytic technique, championed total freedom of thought and expression, without constraint or boundary ("Say *whatever* comes to mind ..."). But free association works not because it actually produces unbounded speech, but because it doesn't. It is the limits of the patient's free association, the sticking points and patterns and resistances, that reveal the outlines of deep unconscious landforms. Free association is in fact bounded and determined; its very point is to discover the limits and boundaries—and their causes—that escape a patient's awareness. The "free" in free association doesn't mean absolute freedom of choice, because when a patient surrenders to free association, what is revealed is not of his choosing. As Patrick Mahony puts it,

> the aim of saying all—however unimportant, irrelevant, indiscreet, nonsensical, or disagreeable it may be—rests on the substitution for conscious purposive ideas of concealed, purposive ones.... *Hence, free association is not free but determined.* (Mahony, 1979, p. 157; emphasis added)

The limited freedom in free association has changed both the way we think about it and the way we use it. In fact, we might not explicitly use the term with the patient at all, and if we do, it's not an injunction that they speak, but rather an invitation or recommendation to try. Even when the patient and analyst take up the shared challenge, truly *free* association is not ever fully achieved. Many analysts now concur that the goal is for the patient to grapple with this quest, and that when he is "*apt* to ... associate freely (in the analytic sense) his case is finished" (Meerloo, 1952, p. 21; emphasis added). Yes, *free* free association remains an ideal, but because it reveals its impossibility, it can't possibly be a requirement for cure; the aim is a *sufficient* achievement of expressive freedom. In other words, free association is a means to its own incompletely realized end. And in the course of striving for more freedom and openness, the psychoanalytic journey reveals the impediments to them. In fact, the impediments to freedom we find in our patients' struggles are not merely personal or localized; often, they give us insight into more general human tendencies and social tensions.

Because we spend most of our days listening intently as others struggle to express their most difficult feelings and most challenging thoughts, psychoanalysts are attuned to the many ways in which language inevitably fails. One fundamental reason that a patient may at best share *most* of what occurs to him, as he comes to experience the stream of his thoughts, is that he must content himself with symbols. He grasps at words to express himself, but he can never find enough of them. Even as he gains access to what may have been unconscious or unknown to him prior to speaking, he will always leave something out, something that words can't capture.

This realm that resists symbolization has been named and explored since the dawn of philosophy. It is Plato's realm of Ideal Forms, which can never be replicated in the corrupted material world that we inhabit. It is Kant's realm of the "thing in itself." The philosopher Walter Benjamin referred to a "paradisiacal language" as "one of perfect knowledge" (1916, p. 71). In psychoanalytic theory, this realm of the unsymbolizable, irreducible, and ultimately unknowable has been approached by way of Lacan's "register of the Real," Wilfred Bion's conception of "O" (or Absolute Reality),[1] and Christopher Bollas's "unthought known" (1987). In this limitless, infinite realm, as Lacan might say, there is no loss, no lack. But we do not inhabit this realm, and "the thing must be lost in order to be represented" (Dor, 1998, p. 135); we inevitably face our limits, and pay a price, as we enter into language, or symbolic communication generally. Even presuming "free thought," free speech never requites the angelological dream—it is never an unmediated window into free thought or into another's soul.

As the Lacanian analyst Bruce Fink reflects,

> the goal of analysis is not to exhaustively symbolize every last drop of the real, for that would make of analysis a truly infinite process, but rather to focus on those scraps of the real which can be considered to have been traumatic. (Fink, 1995, p. 26)

In the service of this goal, free association has natural limits, given the realistic scope of the terrain even a very lengthy analysis could possibly travel. Our aim, says Fink, is to help attach language to the "residual experience that has become a stumbling block to the patient." "By getting an analysand to dream, daydream, and talk, however incoherently" (ibid., p. 26), what has been previously unsymbolized is brought into relationship, "drawn into the dialectic or movement of the analysand's discourse and set in motion" (ibid., p. 26). What is important, and what is achievable, is the dialectic, and the motion, the aliveness; we seek a lived, experienced relationship to the unspoken.

Furthermore, as we have seen, neither party in an analysis is conversing with some neutral, passive "blank slate," but with an actual human being. Not only is the analyst incapable of reading minds; she is simply and necessarily an imperfect listener. Neither intuition nor interpretation ever gives us another's mind completely. Freud did challenge analysts to develop their skills as auditors of free associative discourse, to learn to listen with "evenly suspended attention" (Freud, 1912e, p. 111), with an ear sufficiently "undefended" as to be able to hear the gap between words, the unconscious dimensions of the patient's ideational flow. But even the most talented and available analyst (one unconstricted by his own defenses, and thus able to "hear" what is new or challenging or even hateful) will unconsciously tune out or selectively tune in to certain communications and bypass others, thus neutralizing some of the patient's free speech. The analyst's attention, however "optimally" evenly suspended, is not purely free, but determined by his commitment to the patient's associative chain. This point is underemphasized in psychoanalytic theory, though partly redeemed when we accentuate the intersubjective nature of unconscious communication.

Meanwhile, the patient is communicating with someone veiled to a degree in professional anonymity—whether because of the analyst's personal inclination to hide, her professional sense of what is useful to the patient, and/or the patient's need to not recognize her as a real human being. To this degree, what "looks like" free speech may actually be its doppelgänger, a window into an interminably solipsistic and thus confined and uncommunicative communication. Lacan, in highlighting this distinction, spoke of the shift from the relatively concrete but unrevealing discourse of "empty speech" to "full speech" through which the truth of the subject might be revealed. Walter Benjamin, following

Kierkegaard, believed that man was vulnerable to falling "into the abyss ... of the empty word, into the abyss of prattle" (1916, p. 72).

In short, to the degree that the patient cannot converse with the analyst as a realized human subject in a genuine relationship, his speech cannot be free because, paradoxically, he requires human context to bear his thinking and speaking at least some of what has previously remained unspeakable, even unthinkable. Wilfred Bion's aphorism, "it takes at least two people to think,"[2] captures this paradoxical conception that our deepest and most significant free speech or free association requires realizing the space between two minds. Just as we need air to breathe, and water to swim, we need relationship to think and to speak, or at least to bear certain otherwise unbearable thought and speech.

Inevitably, then, challenging patients to free associate asks them to surrender to a voice that they would not, for the life of them, make speakable. (Even if they realize, at some unconscious level, that their words could never fully capture their terrifying unspoken truths, they still avoid even approaching them, if they can help it.) Even where a patient has conscious access to his thought, he may often have no *conscious* desire to share. As psychoanalyst Philip Bromberg noted, implicit in the request to "speak everything that comes to mind" is also that "I will discover the person you wish to hide" (1994, p. 523). If and when they do finally surrender, what they share they have not chosen: their speech exposes a truth of their otherwise obscured desire and, often in analysis, of desires entangled in previously warded off trauma—and of desires entangled in and with the analyst's unspoken and unconscious desires.

The sounds of silence

Foreclosing free speech is thus, consciously and often unconsciously, purposeful—mental energy is being expended to sustain an endless loop that bypasses meaningful expression (Benjamin's "prattle") and thus transformation. Several authors have noted that "loquacity" is a more frequent form of defense than silence (Mahony, 2001, p. 33). That said, in interesting counterpoint to Bion's notion that it takes two people to think, Michael Balint emphasized that "silence is a phenomenon that occurs between two people" (Blos, 1972, p. 348; Balint, 1958). We (as patients, as citizens, as human beings) remain simultaneously motivated to "free associate" and motivated to sustain our own solipsistic control, warding off inquiry into the recesses of our fear, avoiding the exposure that is real relationship, perhaps also honoring a genuine human need for an inviolable realm of privacy. This psychic tug of war contributes to the length of many analyses. Of course, the analyst's rhetorical strategy of relative silence—the power of which, as Jacob Arlow noted, lies in its ambiguity (Mahony, 2001, p. 76)—anticipates the regularity of the patient's own defiant muteness.

Beyond this power dynamic, patients, at some level more aware of the losses than of the gains in self-knowledge and self-exposure, will hold back. They might for example keep entirely silent, as if to protest the futility of capturing what lies beyond the expressible, or to sustain a fealty to their inexpressible (if not fully conscious) knowledge. When we take a look at Freud's fundamental rule ("*Say* whatever comes to mind ..."), we discover that silence is not part of the contract. And yet patients often remain silent for protracted periods, reminding us that that silence has a power "indispensable to the effectiveness of speech ... human life needs at moments to steep itself in silence, from which it draws essential nourishment and in which it develops its deepest roots" (Nacht, 1964, p. 303).

Perhaps, if not consciously then on some deeply intuitive level, they perceive the potency of silence, as did Samuel Johnson: "You hesitate to stab me with a word, and know not—silence is the sharper sword" (Chandra Raj, 2012, p. 115). Walter Benjamin explained that in "all mourning, there is the deepest inclination to speechlessness"; and he granted special causal status to man's tendency towards "'overnaming'—the deepest linguistic reason for melancholy and ... for all deliberate muteness" (1916, p. 73). But muteness exacts its own heavy toll, one that Sylvia Plath captured evocatively: "The silence depressed me. It wasn't the silence of silence. It was my own silence" (1963, ch. 2). Muteness can be selective and highly communicative, a powerful statement of resistance to authority and/or a plea for recognition of an underground, obscured voice, too frightened and too melancholic to reveal itself but through silence. Silence, as Roland Barthes described it in *A Lover's Discourse*, is a powerful communication:

> [T]o suggest, delicately, that I am suffering, in order to hide without lying, I shall make use of a cunning preterition: I shall divide the economy of my signs. The task of the verbal signs will be to silence,

to mask, to deceive: I shall never account, *verbally,* for the excesses of my sentiment. Having said nothing of the ravages of this anxiety, I can always, once it has passed, reassure myself that no one has guessed anything. The power of language: with my language I can do everything: even and especially *say nothing.* (Barthes, 1978, pp. 43–44)

Silence is often used to remarkable emotional effect, as for example and probably most famously by John Cage in his experimental musical composition 4'33".

Speaking about silence is, perhaps not surprisingly, something that psychoanalysts do both in their practice and in their literature. After all, as Jacob Arlow reflected, the "magnificence of silence" is "its very ambiguity" (1961, p. 54), and to an analyst ambiguity is a sign begging for interpretation. Perhaps to begin imposing some order on its inherent ambiguity, Arlow divided silence into two broad categories: silences that function as defenses, and those that function as discharge or a communication (of desire and/or aggression). This effort calls to mind a still earlier study by Theodor Reik in which he noted the contradictory meanings of silence: "We can keep silence with another when we understand each other especially well, or when understanding is impossible" (Bergler, 1938, p. 171). Translated in the current psychoanalytic idiom of his time, he wrote, "the death instincts, find expression in silence, while love instincts, in speech" (ibid., p. 171). Freud (1917, p. 17) granted speech dominion: "By words, one person can make another blissfully happy or drive him to despair."

Some patients may share art, or music, or journal writing, bypassing direct verbal exposure while simultaneously performing an end-run around our communicative limits. They seek to go straight to Lacan's "Real," refusing to sacrifice the unmediated realm. There is no way to preserve the purity of the quest to express freely without ultimately conceding to limits imposed by language, editing, lost details, blurred memories, imperfect sketches; by the time limits of the session; by the analyst's imperfect attention, memory, defenses, and so forth. We may understand the psychoanalytic enchantment with dream life not only as a means of beguiling the unconscious to reveal itself, but as a collusive fantasy on the part of a patient and analyst (and human beings everywhere), as if, by eavesdropping on dream life, we may bypass these constraints on free speech. Dream interpretation, after all, was a mediated process that aimed to "transcribe" the unmediated: an essential route to the creation of free association, a means that reached for the unconscious by nearing its asymptote. Despite our angelological longings, there is no perfect communication. As Lacan might say, we need to sacrifice the "jouissance"—in one sense, orgasm, but also excessive pleasure³—associated with our attempts to find our way straight to the real. The symptom of hysterical repetition, as Lacan saw it, was "a trace, a kind of writing, that commemorates an 'irruption of jouissance'" (1969–1970, p. 89).

As compensation for our entry into the symbolic realm and our sacrifice of jouissance and its paradoxical satisfactions, we rediscover some of that jouissance in speech. The tradeoff is priceless—better, in fact, than perfect. Admittedly, jouissance has its masochistic aspects. But as Lacan sees it, it also sustains desire, keeping alive desire for its own sake. The structure and prohibitions imposed by language compel us to pursue an eternally unsatisfied interrogation of the truth of our desire. Speech is messy, interesting, alive, and incessant. In our concession to speech, we both sacrifice and sustain degrees of freedom—the freedom to appropriate the signifier (at least to some degree) for our own expressive purposes. That of which we make meaning is located in the gap, the spaces between. Sustaining the integrity of our acts of freedom, our allegiance to the truth of desire, requires that we honor this gap, essential to ethical communication. When we do so, we also stay close to the jouissance of the real—to what Lacan late in his career ventured to name: a feminine jouissance. This feminine jouissance, he suggested, is "'of the order of the infinite,' like mystical ecstacy" (Evans, 1996, p. 222; Lacan, 1972–1973, p. 103).

For Freud, silence speaks both to the patient's allegiance to unconscious desire (to an original jouissance, perhaps to this feminine jouissance) and as a resistance to it. In his early papers on technique, he inferred from silence a resistance both to "transference" (1912b) and to remembering (1914g). Of course, insofar as all roads in analysis lead eventually to conflicted realms of erotic desire, and insofar as analysis is a process of reading between the lines (however faintly drawn), in these ways silence is not simply an impediment to recalling or feeling unwanted feelings and desires. It is also a sign that helps lead us to them—a means, that is, of remembering. As Werner Bohleber (2007) observed, Freud's evolving conception of transference—the displacement of feelings from one person or object to another (usually less threatening) person or object, above all to the analyst—provided a kind of physical dimension to memory, because it involves repetitive behavior with embodied sensory-motor, affective and interactional dimensions. What's more, Freud, having once declared that "the most important sign" of a connection between two thoughts is the length of the patient's hesitation between them (1906c, pp. 109–110), went on to claim that "when the patient stubbornly insists that nothing comes to mind, he or she is in effect thinking of the transference" (Mahony, 1979, p. 180, referring to Freud, 1921c, p. 126fn).

In any case, whatever its aim, silence is never merely silence. It also speaks; in itself it is also a *sign* that is seeking to be interpreted. "Suffice it to say," wrote Lefebvre, "that silence is not the same thing as quietus" (1991, p. 116). As psychoanalyst Theodor Reik observed, one can have "meaningless speech and meaningful silence" (1968, p. 183). But what is meaningful in silence must be extracted, through translation "of the mute into the sonic ... of the nameless into name" (Benjamin, 1916, p. 70). As George Makari and Theodore Shapiro put it,

> A silence is "pregnant" only insofar as the semiotic elements that surround it have impregnated it with meaning. What are these other semiotic elements? When silence is broken, we hear sounds that are either signs or noise. ... One of psychoanalysis' accomplishments has been to rescue a whole host of such meanings from the aural meaninglessness, and redefine these noises as unconscious signs. (Makari & Shapiro, 1993, p. 1000)

That is to say, to create knowledge.

Silence, then, speaks loudly in psychoanalytic practice, and it often does so in defiance of the stated agenda and mechanism of the treatment: free association and self-revelation to a relatively obscured listener. Our patients supply numerous permutations on this theme. A selection from among them should give you a better idea of how in my practice silence speaks so insistently.

Even after spending the best part of many sessions talking about seemingly everything on their minds, most will ultimately claim that they have nothing to say. (Sometimes what follows is silence; sometimes they speak on nonetheless.) "I have no thoughts," says my 10:15 patient, Mr. T; "I have nothing new to say." Another patient, whom I see at 13:45, says to me, "That's it. I'm just repeating myself." My 14:30

patient, Ms. L, continues to steal dialogue's thunder: "My mind is blank. There's nothing going on." The story that goes nowhere, the plot line that doesn't develop, the deadness that expands to fill the space of the hour (and the day) endures. My 18:15, Mr. D, says to me, "I've hit the wall. It's a brick wall, but I can't even see it." The next morning, another patient voices a somewhat more interesting variant: "I've got nothing for you today. Nothing is in my mind."

"Nothing?" I sometimes challenge, inviting my patient to reflect on the activity implicit in their silencing—what may motivate their choice to share, and perhaps even to experience, "nothing." Sometimes, if I perceive in their claim a dynamic of giving and receiving that feels sufficiently accessible between us,[4] I may ask instead, "Nothing for me?" One patient responds with a look at once blank and penetrating, a look that conveys active disinterest in my question and skepticism that *saying* something (*to* me) is really *giving* something (is *for* me). I recognize the potential burden that my request may signify to my patient, but my goal is to signal that I am the addressee, and the recipient, of his silence and of his speech. I further aim to foster the patient's curiosity about his own agency in having no thoughts—at least in session, at least with me, in this context where the one explicit challenge indeed is *to share* one's thoughts, feelings, experiences. I'm asking him to consider how having no thoughts in our session relates to sharing or not sharing his thoughts with me. This particular patient is quick to tell me that our impasse is not about me or even about us. He often "goes blank," he says, when he is by himself, despite his ambitions to write, create, think, and be social. "Even my dream-life vanishes. There is nothing going on." He calls my attention to the immensity of our challenge, that he does not experience a sense of active conflict, let alone agency. Simply defeat, absence.

Interestingly, my patient does sometimes begin a session flooded with thoughts—thoughts that have an insistent, intrusive quality. In such sessions, he similarly experiences defeat and an absence of mental freedom, an inability to claim his mind as his own. Freud understood, of course, that in mounting a defense against certain thoughts, other thoughts will inevitably intrude upon our consciousness (or at least upon our dream life). "I can't get this thought out of my head. I keep obsessing about the same thing," another person tells me, and I find myself fascinated by the remarkable way that both having *no* thoughts and being *flooded* by thoughts create impasses. Either way, whether the mind is a vacuum or a din, there is no space available for curiosity or desire.

A voluminous psychoanalytic literature reckons with exactly this dilemma. We write of therapeutic stalemates, impasses, resistance. We explore the struggle between private self-retreat and public self-revelation—for the conflict between self-knowledge and self-deception is inevitably, intrinsically tied to trust, and to the courage to reveal oneself and to know and be known in a relational context. Psychoanalysis is increasingly framing these states of impasse as a foreclosure of space, a collapse of the space for mediation and interpretation. We speak of *shutting down* versus *opening up* a space for aliveness and growth. And we are led to consider the effective power of silence. But it's also a derailment of free association's journey (recall Freud's metaphor of free association as a train ride). Let us follow the tracks of associations to "having no thoughts" in the psychoanalytic literature.

Having no thoughts: the missing female genital

Freud remained committed to free association even as he came to appreciate its complexity, its interplay of verbal utterance with the involuntary language of a signifying body. In his clinic, women's bodies spoke when their tongues could not. Remember that Freud landed upon free association as a means "of making conscious what is unconscious, lifting the repressions, filling gaps in the memory" (1933a, p. 435)—a way of reclaiming links between hysterical symptoms (conduits of the body's memory and its repressed knowledge) and consciousness. As Bonnie Litowitz observes, "'Gap' freely associates to 'space' and then segues to 'analytic space'" (2006, p. 440). Referring to Freud's dreambook (1900a), she notes that "puns (hole, whole) dominate and opposites dissolve ('full' includes 'lack' or 'nothing' and therefore equals 'empty')." And, more interestingly, Roy Schafer (1968, pp. 57, 59) notes that Freud linked (by means of interpretation) gaps in dreams to representation of the vagina (which I will sometimes refer to here by the clinical designation "female genital"). Schafer takes this a bit further by suggesting that, more generally, "memory gaps in analysis may stand for associations to the female genital" (Kalinich, 1993, p. 208).

Bertram Lewin, in 1948, was perhaps the first to tie the statement "I am thinking of nothing" to the female genital. Lewin developed this insight during his work with a patient whom he describes as suffering from castration anxiety. One day, while discussing reality, "not in a dream but more abstractly," his patient "lamented that he had never been able to see it starkly. 'I have never faced reality,' he said sadly, 'I haven't faced reality since the day I was born'" (Lewin, 1948, p. 524). Lewin, pondering this equating of the female genital with free associations to the idea of "reality," observes among his patients' associative sequences corroborative support for this hypothesis. He further reports upon the link between the female genital and the sense of "a vagueness, a confusion." Taking an interpretive leap, he also links the inability to free associate (to have thoughts and associations) to the female genital and reports spelling out this interpretation explicitly to a patient. And this patient, a man, took the suggestion with good humor. "One day he began his analytic hour by telling me," writes Lewin, "'Well, doctor, I've been thinking of nothing all day'" (ibid., p. 525).

Many writers have since noted that female sexual experience is often characterized by abstraction and diffuseness. And there is a remarkable chain of associations in the psychoanalytic literature by which the hidden or absent (unsignified or invisible) female genital claims its power and presence paradoxically, through its very presence *as* omission and absence. If "genital silence … represents taboo against the expression of a direct sexual wish" (Meerloo, 1959, pp. 83–84), what does this have to do with reality? In the body politic, this paradox is reinforced by the denial of reality, and psychic life is forced underground with the female genital: one pretends genitals don't exist; no one knows anything; no one has any thoughts; reality is denied.

Sam Abrams elaborated on the ontogeny of this feminized "nothing" as a function of our experiences during various phases of early development. "'Everything' was the omnipotent mother, the valued feces, and the envied penis, while 'Nothing' was the helplessness of separateness, flatus, and the absent phallus" (1974, p. 115). Leonard Shengold (1989) riffs further on the meaning of "nothing," drawing from *King Lear*, throughout which the word resounds. Shengold refers to the all-or-nothing values of an early narcissistic phase, noting that while Lear asks his daughters for "everything," his favorite, Cordelia, says she has "nothing" for him. Her "nothing," Shengold suggests, means "not everything," and so it functions as the reality principle—as an attempt to speak and honor the truth. Where her sisters expertly gratify their father's narcissistic demands, with which they're intimately acquainted, Cordelia knows that feeding them will only sharpen them, and she's not going to pretend otherwise. To pretend to give everything is to give nothing real.

By the play's end, Lear of course does lose "everything"—his omnipotence, his kingdom, Cordelia. In the last scene, after repeating the word "nothing" five times when he realizes that Cordelia is finally gone (a fatal echo of her leaving him in the first scene), Lear's eyes are fixed on her, on her body:

> Do you see this? Look on her, look, her lips,
> Look there, look there! [*Dies*]
> > *King Lear,* V.iii.309–10 (Shakespeare, 1972, p. 205)

Shengold, provoking some scholarly controversy, associates these lips with the female genital. If we grant Shengold's premise, we can say that Shakespeare's explicit attention to a now visible female genital creates a genuine space for mourning Cordelia and for grounding Lear in genuine human meaning, between nothing and everything.[5]

Marjorie Barnett (1966, pp. 135ff.) questioned the "something" from which "nothing" is made and linked this vague sense of an absent presence to the *nonsphinctered* cavity/orifice/hole, which leaks and cannot be controlled, only plugged (Kalinich, 1993, pp. 214–215). Lila Kalinich sees in this the absence of a boundary, and it prompts her to think of a female patient who reports, "My mind is like a sieve" (ibid., p. 219). She notes the odd contradiction in Freud between his radical recognition that the "body ego" and bodily sensation served as the wellspring for all mental representation, only to then deny the central psychical and representational status of the vagina—an organ at the surface of inner and outer experience.

This brief tour through the psychoanalytic literature on "having no thoughts," on the inability to free associate, has converged on the female genital. Indeed, early on in Freud's writings, he came to the conclusion that, in hysteria, what is repressed are "the actual genital zones most of all" (1905d, p. 183), referring apparently to the lack of a signifier for the female genital. While this may seem just a bit too much of a caricature of psychoanalysis to be real, the abundance of citations, and the preoccupation with this theme are, well, sizable. An inability to free associate calls attention not only to the absence of *thought* but also to the missing *body* and, very specifically, *to the missing female genital*—to our disembodiment, to the disembodied, "unsexed" female. What does this mean in our conversation about free association and free speech?

CHAPTER TWELVE

Metaphors of space

Analogies, it is true, decide nothing, but they can make one feel more at home.

—Sigmund Freud (1933a, p. 72)

From retreat to relationship

Metaphors of space are becoming better appreciated, and more ubiquitous, in psychoanalytic thought, and this marks a quiet but radical transformation. Where we once focused on various psychopathologies (treating neuroses or character disorders), we now discuss the foreclosure and opening of "space" in the clinical and communicative encounter between patient and therapist, as well as the temporal dimensions of psychoanalytic space. This shift correlates with a greater understanding of psychoanalysis as a hermeneutic and semiotic process, dedicated more to *forms* of thinking and to the ways we organize our experience (Ogden, 2004a), than even to the *contents* of our thoughts.

Psychoanalysis is now seen as more than one person interpreting another's discourse. It is in the modern view a *shared* discourse. Even monologue involves multiple subjects; you could say that an ability to free associate requires the capacity to include, or even just

157

to heed, many conflicting voices inside one's own mind. We need to create an inner polis, an interior democratic space for our own experience; and perhaps paradoxically, we need language (which would seem to be fundamentally "external" and shared) to do this. This process also anchors us in a metaphoric, spatialized relation with each other—creating a polis between us, a space for shared, intersubjective discourse. This space, this polis, bridges that gap between the private and the public, between the psychoanalytic and the democratic. Ideally, this space allows us to transcend binaries, to become alive by animating deadened dimensions of living. We reach for the visible and the explicit by making contact at the border space with the less visible, the implicit—by touching the doorknob, turning the key, to the borderless unknown. In this tension, we grapple with new forms, new meaning, and new questions.

Freud's metapsychology turned on spatial metaphors. He depicted the individual psyche topographically, dividing it into unconscious, preconscious, and conscious zones. He also traced all symbolic life to the content of the familiar Oedipus complex—itself born in a triangular space, a relation among mother, father, and child.

Today we increasingly speak in terms of the topography between mind and body, and between self and other, sometimes between multiple selves and others (e.g., Bromberg, 1998; Davies, 1998)—and how they relate to a *third* space between (or among) them. And so along with a heightened recognition of psychoanalysis as a fundamentally relational enterprise, our use of spatial metaphors has expanded. This is partly because, as the philosopher Eva Brann has explained, we have no means of representing interiority "except metaphor, since in externalizing it, we are perforce spatializing it. The soul in utterance assumes a body" (Brann, 1999, p. 171).

Metaphors of space in psychoanalytical theory

As Freud came to intuit, the body was the recording instrument for what the soul cannot utter, cannot name. If free association signifies an emergent willingness to forge links between thoughts, to share (by naming) thoughts in the presence of an Other, to surrender to the serendipity of discovering the secrets of unconscious desire, then the body (and not only the mind) must speak. For the mind to hold the body, it requires space-holding metaphor, or to put it differently, if the soul in utterance assumes a body, that body (and its utterances) assume metaphoric shape.

This fact was essential to Freud's decoding of dream imagery and free association's symbolism. In particular, spatial metaphors were linked to the female genital. "The female genitals," he wrote in 1916,

> are symbolically represented by all such objects as share their characteristic of enclosing a hollow space which can take something into itself: by *pits, cavities,* and *hollows,* for instance, by *vessels* and *bottles,* by *receptacles, boxes, trunks, cases, chests, pockets,* and so on. *Ships,* too, fall into this category. Some symbols have more connection with the uterus than with the female genitals: thus, *cupboards, stoves* and, more especially, *rooms.* (Freud, 1916–1917, p. 156).[1]

Despite Freud's boldness in naming them, the material roots of such spatial metaphors remain largely unconscious and underexplored, again (as in the case of "nothing") relegating female anatomy to obscurity. His choice of metaphors—pits, hollows, chests—didn't exactly highlight the raw bodily, let alone erotic, tensions at play in the material realm. Let us try to recreate linkages between the sensate body and its spatial metaphors by listening to the voices of psychoanalysts who have voyaged into "space."

Psychoanalytic theorists, specialists in bridging mind and body, soul and utterance, frequently and unsurprisingly adopt spatial metaphors. Sabina Spielrein, remembered most often for her love triangle with Freud and Jung, put forth the idea that speech is located "in orality, in babbling, and in nursing: [in] the use of the mouth and lips for pleasure and contact" (Harris, 2014). Freud (1910i, p. 216) had recognized the mouth as a zone for oral pleasure such as "kissing as well as for eating and communication by speech." But while he recognized many spatial metaphors for the female genital, when it came to contemplating the "gap" in memory in the path of free association, his preferred metaphorical locus was the "uterus" and the "womb." He reached for and imposed such metaphors on the data, in a partly whimsical, partly "phallic" move. In speaking to Dora, for example, he famously deployed an evocative spatial metaphor, figuring the female genital as a "jewel-case" (1905e, p. 69).

Lacan likewise placed central emphasis on the idea of space, referring to it as a "gap," a "void," a "lack"; and he privileged the "space" of speech. Yet his recognition of space, of a void, was partly obscured by the almighty signifier. The Subject comes into bold relief only as she accepts the price of subjectivity: her symbolic castration—her fundamental lack. The female is signified by the inadequacy of her own signification—by the absence of a *space* for her in the symbolic register. One may read Lacan's work as reckoning with how this absence compels us to contend with it. We might accept the symbolic hand we're dealt, the terms and conditions that society imposes on discourse, hewing to reason, remaining mute in the face of a Real we swear is there but which resists symbolization. Or we can stop making sense and start free associating, entering the symbolic fray, appropriating the "agency of the signifier" for our own signs, symbols, and cultural participation, even as we concede to the limits of signification. This freedom, if and where it is even possible, requires an honest encounter not only with lack, but also with our uncultured desires, and so with our anxiety. As Tracy McNulty (by way of Freud, Lacan, and Canadian political philosopher, Peter Hallward) puts it,

> opening a space for the subject, a space that was not there before …
> gives rise to social change, without even aspiring to do so, because
> it is not guided by ideals or goals but by the desire of a subject.
> (McNulty, 2014, p. 122)

Wilfred Bion also invoked metaphors of space. We cannot by ourselves truly "think"; we cannot free associate alone. Our capacity to think depends on a capacity to bear connections between our thoughts, between associations. Yet often because we are terrified by the relations between our thoughts, we avoid or even attack these "linkages" (Bion, 1959). This terror begins at infancy, when we are bombarded by "raw sensory experience"—what Bion called "thoughts without a thinker," describing how we avoid and even attack "linkages" (Bion, 1959). Bion (1962a, 1962b) invoked the spatial metaphors of "container" and "contained" to capture the dialectic between the capacity for thinking (and dreaming); and the unconscious nascent thoughts (and dreams) derived from lived experience. Through (spatial) container-contained dynamics, infant and mother learn to communicate, in a language without (at first) speech, as singular though still largely interdependent subjects.

Bion recognized that a vital communicative capacity of the infant lies in his use of "projective identification,"[2] whereby he compels mother to make meaning of his "yet unthinkable thoughts and not yet tolerable feelings" (Ogden, 1994, p. 44). In turn, mother's capacity for "reverie" serves a vital maternal function, enabling her to bear the impact of her infant's unsymbolized communications, to in fact make meaning of her infant's early gestures and signs, his unconscious fears and desires. An early intersubjective space between infant and mother evolves. Without such reverie, the infant's "thinking" is tantamount to a "mental catastrophe." Lacking a conduit to the meaning-making mind of another, the infant remains psychically unborn, in a state of "nameless dread" (Bion, 1962a), deprived of a womb for the emergence of his very being.

Bion's ideas extended the scope of free association, reaching far beyond the interpretation of neurotic conflict to include the possibility of approaching what he referred to as "O." James Grotstein, grappling with the meaning of O, explains it as

> Bion's arbitrary iconic term for a third domain, yet really the first—the original and fundamental domain that is unknown and unknowable to us ... one that expresses the Absolute Truth about an Ultimate Reality. (Grotstein, 2007, p. 155)

Far beyond granting access to a strictly personal unconscious, Bion's model (not unlike Freud's) is a model for approaching what lies beyond knowing, in the sphere of the nameless, the "thing in itself," infinity, Ultimate Reality. Even as Bion sought to name a sphere beyond metaphor, he coined "O," a powerful and spacious metaphor. At the same time, O is barely a metaphor at all, as it never completes the act of symbolizing—it suggests more than it represents.

D. W. Winnicott (also a pediatrician) so powerfully invoked metaphors of "space" that they are inseparable, even coincident, with his intuitive theorizing. In one important essay, he described the fate of the infant who is deprived of the care of a "nonimpinging" mother (or other primary caretaker), one who, in the infant's earliest life, is dedicated to its needs, almost to the point of illness (1956). Such a mother risks losing herself as a separate subject (though she must not) in order to create a "holding environment," that is, a space for the infant's own experience of agency and his "spontaneous gesture"—what we might see as a personal imprint (1963b). In the absence of such caretaking and such an environment, the infant is robbed not only of *psyche* but also inevitably of *soma*. He is left in a state of precocious knowing (1949), relying on his mind, rather than on human relationship. He is left in a state of unthinkable anxiety, *with no metaphoric space* (no "third area of experiencing" (1971c)) for the place where we live, for playing, for creativity, and for embodied thought and experience. Winnicott referred to this third realm of experience as a "potential space": a "transitional" realm *between* fantasy and reality, *between* mother and infant, *between* private and public.

Jessica Benjamin, a psychoanalytic thinker with a strong foothold in feminist theory, also reflects on the significance of a reflective space of thirdness, in which we may create meaning beyond repetitive, power-based dynamics. But she also explores the gendered aspects of the spatial metaphor. Benjamin (2001, p. 54) considers "the maternal body container," which is inherent in Bion's thought, observing that

> the historical shift to maternal imagery in psychoanalysis has not only been associated with the idea of holding or containing rather than penetrating with insight but *more* specifically, this emphasis has been closely allied with another metaphor of analysis as creation of a space. (Benjamin, 1995, p. 160)

Winnicott draws a similar conclusion, that

> pure, distilled uncontaminated female elements leads us to Being, and this forms the only basis for self-discovery and a sense of existing (and then on the capacity to develop as inside, to have a container ...). (Winnicott, 1970, p. 82)

Thomas Ogden's spatial metaphors have expanded our psychoanalytic lexicon and our very thinking. Drawing from Winnicott's conception of "potential space," Ogden conceives an "analytic third" between the patient and the analyst, but also between the symbol and the symbolized. But sometimes symbol and symbolized become conflated, too tightly sealed, and so we need to "pry open" a third space. "[F]orever in the process of coming into being in the emotional force field generated by the interplay of the unconscious of patient and analyst" (Ogden, 2005, p. 6), this space is created asymmetrically between (and is vital to the emergence of) two subjects; it belongs to both and to neither. We need to create a space for non-reflexive living, for reflective thought and its dynamic tension. By means of this space, we are able to experience ourselves as authors of our own narratives, agents of our own desires. The patient reclaims, or claims for the first time, an ability "to dream one's experience, which is to dream oneself into existence" (ibid., p. 8).

Latin American analysts refer to *vínculo*, following Enrique Pichon-Riviére's effort to capture space "in between." *Vínculo*, metaphorized as a dialectical spiral, helped to inspire Madeleine and Willy Baranger's conception of the analytic field as a shared relational space that gives expression to unconscious elements (Bernardi & Bernardi, 2012). In a similar but distinctly American "relational" vein, Philip Bromberg, Jody Davies, Donnel Stern, and many others have written about the emergence of co-constructed psychical space. As Bromberg has described it, this space is

> uniquely relational and still uniquely individual; a space belonging to neither person alone, and yet, belonging to both and to each; a twilight space in which "the impossible" becomes possible; a space in which incompatible selves, each awake to its own "truth," can "dream" the reality of the other without risk to its own integrity. (Bromberg, 1998, p. 9)

"Health," in Bromberg's redolent phrasing, "is the ability to stand in the spaces between" (ibid., p. 274).

Towards a space between

Although antecedents of our multitudinous spatial metaphors can be traced to Freud (as noted above), Freud's theorizing is often regarded retrospectively as having had the unintended consequence of *flattening* the relational space we now believe to be so vital. For example, if we read his oeuvre, following philosopher Alfred Tauber, as a tribute to the human capacity for reason to master the irrational and entangled legacies of birth and early development, we find Freud tilting toward one pole, one understanding, one apex of the triangle. Tauber writes, "the entire psychoanalytic project rests upon the quiet authority of reason to understand and thus better to control the unconscious" (2010, p. 181).

Even if psychoanalysis did initially privilege (the analyst's) interpretation, and even if that is still a critical part of any treatment, Tauber's view that Freud granted primacy to reason and autonomy is *itself* an interpretation. He also recognized a third space—of interpretation itself—as an important feature of psychoanalytic inquiry from its very beginnings. In my reading, Freud locates psychoanalysis in a space *between*—between science and magic, between conscious and unconscious, between reason and passion, between civilization and its discontents, between analyst and patient, between id and superego, between past and present, between autonomy and surrender, between historical reality and constructed memory, between repression and free association.

However, Freud himself, so capable of envisioning that space between, was also prone to collapsing it into binary dualities. As Muriel Dimen and Adrienne Harris note in their edited volume reconsidering Freud and Breuer's *Studies on Hysteria*, a "set of binaries appears and reappears in the book: mind/body, psyche/society, dominance/submission, male/female, analyst/patient, soma/word, interpretation/suggestion, universal/local" (2001, pp. 29–30). But Freud does not merely oppose these categories, or divide the world neatly between them. Indeed, Aron and Starr observe, "Freud's genius and his capacity for maintaining complexity often enabled him to transcend the many dualities he created" (Aron & Starr, 2013, p. 31).

Jessica Benjamin captures the tensions of Freud's recognition of bodily and intersubjective space for the psychoanalytic project and his vulnerability to its erasure. She writes that Freud strove to make the "inarticulate articulate, to translate the symptomatic gestures of the body into language" (Benjamin, 2001, p. 40); and this required "the intersubjective space of a potential other" as "the very condition of symbolic activity" (ibid., p. 59). But, she observes,

> [f]eminists and psychoanalysts alike have pointed out the way in which Freud pursued the unlocking of meaning, the mining of secrets, the connecting of event and symptom in a seamless narrative—without gaps and holes, or other feminine metaphors of incomplete knowledge … —to the detriment of the analytic stance toward the patient. (Benjamin, 2001, p. 45, citing Moi, 1981)

It is fascinating and ironic that Freud's free association evolved as a means of bridging gaps in communication but eclipsed the space or gap *of* the female body—and so, as well, the space *for* the female body. Though he came to believe that speech presupposes a material gap and though he recognized symbols of the female genital orifice and cavity, Freud left the *actual* space between—vaginal space—under-represented and devalued in his theorizing. He both named female genitality and its symbols *and* missed their primal and metaphoric function in generating psychological tension. Yet his quest to fill in a perceived *and* real gap was also a quest to comprehend the mystery of sexual difference and to language the body. But he fashioned his method of free association in order to bridge space, aided by the analyst's interpretative (and penetrating) tools even as he obscured the feminine symbols, and their suscitating energy, that births free association. If women's bodies are both required and denied, true free association is in effect impossible, not only because it is in general an elusive ideal, but also because the process by which it might be achieved is trapped in a cynical conundrum.

Without the holding and meaning-generating function of the female body—the female genital—and its corresponding spatial metaphor, space becomes emptiness, an unbounded abyss. Elsewhere, André Green calls attention to the (unnamed) female genital as a location of wound and symptom:

> [E]verybody knows that Freud overheard Charcot saying to one of his pupils that it was always "the genital thing" that was the cause of the illness, not understanding why he did not state that loudly. (Green, 1995, p. 71)

Psychoanalysis was founded upon what Freud termed the hysteric's *reminiscences*, in which, he believed, the symptom behaves like a memory picture or reproduction of an encrypted thought. Freud proposed that there were two sources for such symptoms: "the traumatic event arising out of the subject's will and the pathogenic idea born in his imaginative mind" (ibid., p. 77). He thereby suggests a space in between history and imagination at the cusp of the symptoms. But these symptoms camouflaged both history and fantasy, even as they were simultaneously the key to secret memory, knowledge, and not yet revealed or formulated meanings.

Deciphering symptoms would require the opening of space for free association between body and mind, between symbol and symbolized— space itself. Spatial metaphors, grounded in physical actuality and its disruptive tensions, are essential to this process. The quest to claim space—for all of us, male or female or transgendered—inevitably extends Bion's evocation of the maternal body container and challenges us to recognize the female body and its vaginal receptivity and procreative capacity. And so we can begin to glimpse both the allure and mystery, the power and the vulnerability, that metaphors of "open space"—including a gendered dimension of Bion's "O"—hold for us as we tug at the threads of memory and legacy. We glimpse the possibility of moving beyond a vicious circularity of binaries by recognizing the porous, even fictitious, lines between what is accessible to human subjectivity and what lies in the inaccessible real.

Along these lines, a relatively new metaphor introduced by Bracha Ettinger's radical conception of a "prenatal symbolic space" relocates and renews the project of signifying femininity beyond phallic gendered binaries, beyond the impasses left to us by Freud and Lacan. Describing a "matriaxial borderspace," she offers us a new metaphor, a basis for conceiving subjectivity as "transsubjective," linked to the symbolic register but not confined "within the fortress of the phallic, rather than moving into open space" (Pollock, 2006, p. 13).

Contemporary psychoanalysis is awash in metaphors of space, but they remain unclassified and unnamed. If the female genital is largely missing, largely obscured, in psychoanalytic literature; if the female voice and female body are absent, surveilled, or overruled in the body politic; and if at the same time we find ourselves relying on metaphors of space to describe a path toward self-realization and mutual recognition; then our challenge, it seems, is to not only understand how these things are all correlated, but also, toward that end, to name what is hiding in plain sight. We must name what is present. More than that, we must name what is absent. Our metaphors of space and gaps are our ubiquitous feminine signifiers. *Knowledge of space requires that it be named.*

CHAPTER THIRTEEN

Phallic fantasy and vaginal primacy

> We know that they [artists] possess in their art a master key to
> open with ease all female hearts, whereas we [scientists] stand
> helpless at the strange design of the lock and have first to tor-
> ment ourselves to discover a suitable key to it.
>
> —Sigmund Freud, 1884, letter to Martha Bernays
> (Jones, 1953, p. 123)

Engagement, resistance, and genital configuration

Metaphors of space are everywhere, but their feminine foundation
remains obscured. In clinical practice as well as in the public sphere,
space eludes us. We avoid the revelatory, expressive—and ever violable
and fraught—pathways of free association and speech. All too often,
we take the easy route, preferring familiar, repetitive, and ultimately
power-based relationships, even non-relationships.

   The psychoanalytic literature on such clinical impasses, resistances,
and enactments is voluminous, and it has introduced another set of
spatial metaphors, figuring the *collapse* of space. These follow upon
the foundational work by C. S. Peirce on semiotics, the study of signs
and signification. Peirce distinguished between dyadic and triadic

167

(or thirdness) relations. Dyadic relations involve unmediated physical forces, such as those between pairs of particles, whereas triadic relations involve a third space of mediation. Ogden (1989) characterized dyadic unmediated immediacy and reactivity as emblematic of a "paranoid-schizoid mode of experience," in which there is no space for reflection or for the agency of an interpreting, historically situated subject. Without such agency or historicity, facts are mere facts, things just happen, there is nothing to reflect upon, and no meaning is made. Bion (1967) suggested that some thoughts may themselves attack the linkages necessary for thinking. Jessica Benjamin describes a "doer" and "done to" dynamic, evocatively capturing the experiential quality associated with this realm of finger pointing, blame games, power plays, and ethical quagmires (2004, p. 6).

In these perverse acts of agency, we sustain familiar, repetitive dynamics. We may, for example, re-enact our retaliatory, spiteful scripts against those who have hurt us, maintaining a loyalty and allegiance to the roles we've played (and the relationships we've had) with our perpetrators. What is lost is what is most threatening—and most healing: the pulse of aliveness; the animating sounds of unfamiliar, destabilizing voices and thoughts; the truths we most need but from which we recoil; the very space for mutual recognition. Captured in a state of semiotic collapse and experiential confinement—"close but no cigar"—we remain deprived of an essential *spatial* metaphor (Gentile, 2001). What is lost is often what is most desired—the space for interpenetration and play *between* our spatial metaphors and our more familiar and named *phallic* ones. Instead of genuine power and the therapeutic action of agency, we seek substitutes in the realm of power plays.

These debilitating dynamics are pervaded by what I shall call a "faux phallicism"—shows of dominance, the bluster of easy abuses of power. Many have investigated such social power dynamics: the Frankfurt School, Michel Foucault, feminists who seek to reform psychoanalytic theory but also to infuse psychoanalytic insights into feminist and social theory. By way of these analyses, we recognize phallic bluster as an effect of unchecked power arrangements that perpetuate an all too often gendered divide between (patriarchal) dominance and (female) subjugation.

Such exercises of negative power result in discourse that doesn't just lack space for mediation and interpretation; it also lacks *space itself*, above all feminine space—an opening for and recognition of the female body and its signification in language. This generative, vibrational space cannot be controlled, colonized, or fully "known," because it stands for the primal conditions of human subjectivity, just as it pre-exists human subjectivity. Because this space makes human symbolization and meaning possible, it represents feminine law, the principle of choiceful surrender ("yes") to the primacy of space, the lawful space of *no* rule. I'll expand considerably on this topic in the following chapters, because it's crucial in understanding how to open space for democracy and free speech. For now, let's limit the discussion to the spatial collapse that pervades not only many a psychoanalytic session, but also much public discourse.

Psychoanalysis, historically, has privileged the phallic signifier. By this I don't just mean that it has tended to favor the male sex organ per se, though it has. I also mean that it has granted the penis and its simulacra a large symbolic role in our imaginative and sexual development, and furthermore in our development as signifying creatures (see, for example, Lacan, 1956–1957). Because Freud did tend to assume the primacy of male experience and masculine symbols, he has been accused by many of "phallic monism" (Kristeva, 2001, ch. 4), a.k.a. "phallocentrism."[1] Not only are his assumptions the basis for much heated controversy within the field and beyond, they are a source of internal contradiction in his theories.

Later theorists challenged Freud's phallic monism and sought to balance his patriarchal inclinations by reclaiming the power of the clitoris and vagina as active signifiers of female experience, and furthermore as important symbols in all human experience. Some have focused on the elemental power of the maternal—and not just the mother as nourisher, but also the mother as an *erotic* figure, whose reproductive and specifically female generative potential is elementally forceful, but also potentially dangerous and therefore potent but fearsome. This is of course an empowering metaphor, but as the metonymic slide from "female" to "danger" suggests, its power may be too hot for some to handle. Potent as the metaphor is, it perpetuates the *suppression* of female sexual power, eliding the erotic and diverting focus from the actual female genitalia, in a move that inadvertently, at least in part, replicates Freud's. To privilege the procreative, generative functions of vaginal space is to downplay its undomesticated genital aspect; production supplants expression and pleasure. Only by recognizing the sexual presence—the sexual *somethingness*—of vaginal space do we appreciate how vital it is to phallic potency, both metaphorically and actually. An inability to face the ultimate carnality of sexual symbols has consequences—among them, consequences for free association and, by extension, for free speech in the public sphere.

Many serious thinkers have addressed the question of human motivation in the political sphere; few have grappled with its sexual dimensions without following Freud. Psychoanalysis, by embracing a "dark enlightenment" (Yovel, 1989, p. 136), situates itself at an invaluable juncture between despair and renewal: it is thereby the deepest and most encompassing theory of human motivation. In founding this theory, Freud built on the correlative recognitions that patients (no matter their symptom picture) will create impediments to free association, and that the path to free association and to free speech cannot bypass the body. And yet our body politic is all too often dominated by debates among "talking heads" that avoid reference to the physical body, to the gendered body, to the sexual body, to the sensate female body.

Tracing the role of patriarchy in subverting female voices and the voice of desire, authors such as Carol Gilligan and David Richards (2008) document the perversion of democratic values in history, and also in the evolution of Freud's thought. After his groundbreaking discovery of free association as a means of healing dissociation, Freud (as we have seen) infamously abandoned his seduction hypothesis (in which he recognized the truth value in his female patients' stories of incest) in favor of theory that the unconscious is pervaded by sexual fantasy. The cornerstone of this latter theory is a different story of incest: the legend of Oedipus.

Freud's reversal—understood by many as misconstruing and discounting the ubiquity of female sexual trauma—spawned an immensely generative feminist resistance. If Freud "assaulted" truth, as Jeffrey Moussaieff Masson (1984) notably contended, Gilligan and Richards hear the voice of consequent resistance as ethically grounded in a human desire for relational truth. Resistance speaks; and the free association that produces this speech is an essentially democratic enterprise, insofar as "its epistemological basis, the source of truth or knowledge, is evidence rather than authority" (Gilligan & Richards, 2008, p. 165).

Political resistance movements have increasingly focused on defending those marginalized, denied free speech, and excluded from constitutional protection (for example, women, blacks, gays, gay married people, and so forth). "Democracy's triumph," John Dunn observes, "has been the collapse of one exclusion after another, in ever-greater indignity, with the collapse of the exclusion of women, the most recent, hastiest, and most abashed of all" (2005, p. 136). But such optimism is belied by the widening of a real class divide in our neoliberal era. Not only has poverty been feminized, but it is women from lower socio-economic classes who have lost the most social protections (Harvey, 2005, p. 202). In the developing world, "the paths of women's liberation from traditional patriarchal controls ... lie either through degrading factory labour or through trading on sexuality" (ibid., p. 170). If democracy holds a continuing allure amid such gains and real losses, the appeal hangs in part on a nascent thread of personal agency—of having a say in one's own subjection. Psychoanalysts speak of the patient's voice of resistance as her emergent participation in the power arrangements that have, thus far, been mainly instantiated in the practice (and silence) of accepting the etiquette of a status quo that perpetuates inequality.

On a psychological level, then, emergent signs of resistance must be welcomed. Something is happening, and it is the patient who is the catalyst of action, action originally camouflaged as what Roy Schafer, writing in the psychoanalytic canon, described as "counteraction" (1976, p. 244). Resistance then is a sign of the patient's emergent status as agent, presaging her arrival by first revealing a conflict of agendas, in the emergent private-public sphere between patient and analyst. Such resistances, in giving rise to a shared sense of impasse, may temporarily subvert the analyst's (patriarchal) activity. It is the voice of resistance that trespasses upon forbidden knowledge, and that also constitutes itself on the margins of social intelligibility. Let me elaborate.

Psychoanalysis reveals that resistance is a powerful stepping stone for the patient to become an engaged participant in a discourse from which her voice has been marginalized and which she must appeal, contest, even scandalize. After all, resistant speech is grounded in a state of subjection and, as Foucault (2001) noted regarding political speech, its conventions are inevitably tied to power arrangements. Dina Al-Kassim located this poignant dilemma in the interstices between subjection and power, in the political "rant" (a "complex of address, entreaty, and attack"): The speaking subject materializes only as her "speech emerges or, more aptly, irrupts to contest the public space that abjects it" (2010, pp. 3, 9). By dint of injecting oneself "into a language that only belongs improperly to one," the rant "reaches within a social network of division and exclusion to participate in the power of the world" (ibid., p. 11).

What Al-Kassim is saying—at least as I see it through the frame of clinical phenomena—is that the power and the poignancy of resistant speech lies in its contradictory mixture of insecurity and boldness. Further, for therapeutic action to be transformative, more than resistance is required. This is so not only in the clinic, but also in the realm of political action. Material resistance may temporarily scramble status quo power dynamics, but only changing hearts and minds can alter the field of power itself. In psychoanalysis this involves transformative, messy moments (even "rants") in which the patient disrupts and destabilizes the analytic discourse, transforming her own potential to appropriate the signifying process by which she will claim her agency. Let's take a cue from Frantz Fanon, a psychiatrist renowned for his deep insights into the struggle for freedom of colonized peoples, and frame this more boldly: the reconstruction of humanity in the aftermath of psychic colonization may require the use of "every means available to reestablish your weight as a human being," including, at the individual level, possible acts of violence (1961, p. 221). Psychoanalytically speaking, this violence is sustained in the action of frank speech.

Beyond that liberating, even radical, expression, something more is necessary: psychoanalysis shows that the patient's battle to recapture, or capture for the first time, a personal sense of agency and self-determination also requires a positive assertion of desire and intent. This assertion will inevitably require acts of surrender (by both members of the analytic couple) that, as with democracy's ascent, entail "an uneven, reluctant, painful series of surrenders of an immense miscellany of other kinds of belief" (Dunn, 2014, p. 43). But the triumph of personal agency—and, I believe, of democracy as well—requires that surrender happen *on the terrain of the unconscious*, that it be a surrender to desire and to its voice, and that it be led not by defeat but by the determined claiming of desire and intent. Implicit in this process, but necessarily explicit for this discussion—and for a generative inclusive psychoanalytic *and* democratic discourse—is that asserting this voice of desire insists upon sexual agency and the cultural and linguistic signification of the female body.

It is a commonplace, and not only within psychoanalysis, that the censorship, and sometimes the sequestration, of women has been historically ubiquitous. The legal and feminist scholar Eva Cantarella (see Chapter Five) has shown that, from the dawning days of democracy in the ancient Greek polis, women's excision from political life and the distribution of her possible social positions ("as wives, concubines, heterae, or prostitutes") were "regulated by a series of laws that established her inferiority and permanent subordination to a man" (1987, pp. 50–51). In short, democracy was founded in a social space that excluded women from any form of political participation, suppressed women's voices, and practically imprisoned their bodies. In our own more advanced and enlightened times, we celebrate our equal freedoms and equal opportunities while the representatives of a great number continue to seek legislation aimed at controlling women's bodies and their use. Some want to make sure that we cannot even refer to women's genitalia in public debates.

In June 2012, for example, Democratic state representative Lisa Brown attempted to debate a retirement bill on the floor of the Michigan House of Representatives. But her Republican colleagues shut her down because she had dared, while discussing women's health in the previous session, to utter aloud the word "vagina"—a word "so offensive" that, in the words of representative Mike Calton, "I don't want to say it in front of women." As Brown herself noted, if members of a democratic body are to legislate what women may or may not do with their bodies, then they should be obliged to allow, in a body of publicly elected representatives, free speech and full debate on the issue.

Of course, the term "vagina" is not unspeakable simply because it's involved in conception and childbirth, or because it's a metonymy for the female body as potentially reproductive—topics all too frequently subject to political debate and regulation.[2] What is this preoccupation, even fixation, with silencing the female body, and, specifically, discrediting her vagina, about? The problem with "vagina" is that it opens the symbolic space to sex and its evocations; it's mostly used to symbolize a medium for sexual pleasure and intimate communication, whose mystery to men seems to figure powerfully in their cries of offense. The vagina, so puzzling and so unspeakable, is nonetheless as foundational to male experience as to female; and so it assumes the role of ultimate symbol of Woman as "other": elusive, enigmatic, *uncontrollable*—and therefore coded as subordinate, and ultimately invisible. And, unsurprisingly, such thinking (or lack thereof), becomes for women a problem of identity as well.

In Lila Kalinich's view, a woman, because of her "genital configuration," the hiddenness of her sex, is "predisposed to a sense of invisibility" that can be overcome only when she is recognized by "the Other," in particular the father. Without this recognition, she is "dead as a subject," she is only an "object to be consumed by another's desire." In this dynamic, where subjectivity requires not only seeing but being seen, and not only symbolizing but being symbolized, the "female genital, in that place between perception and consciousness, unseen and often unnamed, excluded from symbolization, becomes the blind spot" (Kalinich, 2007, p. 44). So even beyond its significance for sexual communication, the vagina signifies what lies beyond the visible, in the terrain of the unknown; and so it signifies the mysteries of female power *and* of intuitive, untamed, unconscious knowledge.

The vagina speaks

Regardless of the horror occasioned in Michigan, we of course live in a society where women do occasionally dare speak the names of their genital configurations. But such a thing was practically unheard of in *fin-de-siècle* Vienna. And it was there that Freud founded psychoanalysis by taking to task the basic censorship imposed on his mostly female hysterical patients. What he discovered in the course of treating them is that this group of women, lacking means or opportunity to speak of their experiences, had rechanneled their suppressed speech into physical symptoms. They often made dramatic gestures, and these spoke volumes to him and his fellow practitioners. Not satisfied to observe and attempt to decode what women did with their bodies (and at the behest of his patient Emmy von N., who struggled to teach him), he eventually discovered the power of women's speech. In the process, he learned quite a bit about female desire, women's suppression of their fantasies, and the repression of their actual histories of traumatic sexual abuse. The vagina spoke, and Freud recognized its language. Consequently— and contrary to how we typically narrate the story—he granted it a prominent (but not a potent) role in psychic life. But that is only part of a far more complex story.

As perplexing, and even infuriating, as Freud's contradictory and often antifeminist impulses were, it's possible to try to understand and even empathize with him. He did, as a man of his era, or rather as a man of any era, grant primacy to the phallus. His theory of "penis envy" presumed *a priori* the inferiority of the female sexual organ. But his discovery and promotion of the power of free association, including its inevitable ties to bodily expression, led him in a different direction. In his studies of hysteria, he both silences female voices *and also* privileges them (in tandem with dissociated physical expressions) as avenues to truth and enlightenment. These dueling tendencies prevented Freud from fully appreciating the implications of his intuitive and startling discoveries. Instead of acknowledging and contending with the metaphorical (and visceral) powers of the female body, he clamped space shut just as he opened it; he imposed his own voice on the patient's discourse and he thus tightened the vise on the female genital as a signifier.

Freud did perceive, if dimly, the power of the (excised or suppressed) female body to signify; he believed in the material (including bodily) foundations of psychic life; and he saw that the pathway through psychic blockages might be found through somatic symptoms and "memories." Thus the female body was and remains always *present* as a basis for psychoanalytic thought. However, Freud was also attached to a view of sexual development that assumed female castration. He believed that his female patients ultimately had to make peace with their native state, *not* of knowledge or power, but of *lack* (of a penis, of phallic power). For him, presence and potency were male properties.

In *Inhibitions, Symptoms, and Anxiety* (1926), for example, Freud equates the genital with the phallic. Extrapolating from this premise, he would assert that a "castration complex"—an outgrowth of discovering her "lack" of the valued penis—is the central organizer of a girl's psychic life. As Doris Bernstein notes, "He considered her own genitals inert, inactive, unknown, not to be discovered until their maturation in puberty" (1990, p. 192). A girl's discovery of her genital difference from boys, instead of setting her on the path of psychological maturation, leads instead to repression, to a denial of "the unwelcome fact of [her] castration" (Freud, 1927e, p. 156).

This is just false, of course. But there is no denying that in the realms of culture and imagination, women have indeed been deprived, and so in this sense symbolically "castrated." Men's persistent dominion in politics, the arts, and most social domains may indeed provide some basis for Freud's insights, even if Freud found them in the wrong place. Few psychoanalysts now take literally the idea of actual "penis envy"; instead, it functions as a metaphor for the envy or resentment that some women harbor in a world of patriarchal power dynamics. Or, as Dana Birksted-Breen has asserted, it is more properly understood as "phallus envy" insofar as, for both sexes, the phallus represents an "illusory wholeness, a state free of desire" (1996, p. 650). And so,

> it is this phantasy or the penis as phallus which confers to masculinity's coveted position, and if we think of this phantasy as ubiquitous, it goes some way towards explaining social phenomena which have given men greater power and status. (Birksted-Breen, 1996, p. 651)

Feelings of resentment or despair that emerge from this kind of "phallus envy" are indeed prevalent in many analyses; but they're not really what Freud was talking about.

Many feminist psychoanalysts have challenged and discredited Freud's phallocentric conceptions that regarded all libido as masculine. Even Freud conceded that little girls display an awareness of their clitoris and recognized this as their "leading erotogenic zone ... homologous to the masculine genital zone of the glans penis" (Freud, 1905d, p. 220). He also believed that the excitatin of the clitoris in adolescence was so intense that it ushered in a second wave of repression—and that it was this very repression that enabled men, in striving to overcome it, to experience the full force of their own excitation. His theory that male orgasm depended on female "frigidity" basically ruled out mutual orgasm, or any mutual sexual engagement, which was reduced to a tug of war.

Freud did however acknowledge that women could have orgasms. He even admitted that clitoral orgasms were common. But he ascribed primacy (health and maturity) to the vaginal orgasm, crediting the clitoris with the minor role of providing its kindling. So one hand gave and the other took away. The vagina was the ultimate pleasure center but not the power center, as the clitoris was seen as the female phallus. But he saw it as an "inferior" equivalent of the penis, a mere trigger for the true or mature vaginal orgasm.[3] Even that fractured achievement rested on a complicated developmental arc that, if we follow his line of thinking, required finding a missing organ—one that served reproductive rather than explicitly sexual functions.

Many have argued persuasively that a little girl has knowledge of her vagina, and that she even experiences vaginal arousal. But, as we saw in the previous chapter and as Lila Kalinich notes, despite years of discussion of the vagina as a "something" with its own internal sense, psychoanalytic literature has tended to treat the vagina as the "no thing" or "nothing" of the castrated genital. Marita Torsti, for example, finds it "astounding that the significance of the vagina has been ignored by theorists in outlining the development of femininity in classic psychoanalytic theory" (Torsti, 1994, p. 473; Elise, 1998, p. 435). My argument here isn't so much about how wrong such ideas are; it is rather that they invert the significance of female biology and the female experience of both physical *and* metaphorical space.

Rosemary Balsam calls upon psychoanalysts to return to the material body, to the physical. "The body, being common to all of us," she writes, "is a good place to look for anchorage when we seem to drift too far into abstractions and lose touch with our animal and even libidinal and mortal selves" (2012, p. 189). It is only when we link psychical fantasy with material reality, including the matter of our physical bodies, that we can possibly assume our status as desiring subjects—subjects who share their desire with each other (Gentile, 2007, 2010, & 2014). We not only share in space and time, but we gain an experience of physical and metaphoric space when we acknowledge the actuality of bodily experience, the spatial primacy of vaginal experience.

Between absence and presence: the somethingness of feminine space

Space—whether regarded as absence or as presence, deprivation or provision—is the linchpin between psychoanalysis (specifically, clinical discoveries about human experience) and democracy. There is a powerful relationship between free association and personal agency, as well as between free speech and political agency. What's more, this powerful relationship is sustained by the space or "nothingness" exemplified by material female experience.

If the female body itself represents not the *lack* of some positive or phallic reality, how do we understand this presence of "nothing"? Let's examine the struggle to claim female space *as both metaphoric and real* by exploring further insights from the clinic. The female genitalia, more complexly organized and structured than are the male, are defined by a kind of interiority (rather than evident protrusion, though the clitoris also offers that) and a diffuseness of sensation (difficult to describe or contain in language). Doris Bernstein has noted that, in response to genital stimulation, women's minds "blur, they get 'fuzzy,' they experience an inability to articulate.... [A]fter an initial 'blank,' they are surprised to find how much they really 'know'" (1990, p. 194). Kalinich too reflects on how commonly a woman will refer to her subjective experience as "spacey" or forgetful; "details fade into an impressionistic canvas ... she feels cognitively impaired" (2007, p. 207). Her bodily diffuseness is mirrored in her cognitive diffuseness. What bypasses language remains inarticulate.

The ubiquitous presence of *absence* in psychoanalytic investigations into female genital experience—marked by diffuse and fragmented memories, vagueness, and mental inhibitions—suggests that what "is" (the real) becomes present only by way of what "is not." Implicit in the professional literature is a tension between genital absence and presence (in experience and as a sign), between the hiding (or repression) of the real and its exposure. From the mid-1920s onward, Freud focused on girls' sense of missing a body part—the penis; he also believed vaginal sensation to be dormant until adolescence. And just as early, Karen Horney (1924) disputed this, arguing that the vagina's presence was sensed early. Melanie Klein, too (1932), asserted that there is always unconscious knowledge of the vagina and womb. The vagina, fundamentally constituted between absence and presence, announces itself *silently*, but that silence structures the spoken discourse; that absence claims its presence. Without it, free association and free speech remain elusive.

Nonetheless, Freud sustained his conviction, his phallic fallacy perhaps, that the phallus is primary, and that "the vagina stays terra incognita for the child" (Verhaeghe, 1997, p. 164). He also remained convinced that the pursuit of knowledge was set into motion by the child's curiosity, his quest to answer the mysteries sparked by the earliest markers of infantile sexuality. As we will examine in the following chapters, the child cannot "know" the vagina, because it (along with the female gender) remains unsignified, in the realm of the unknowable and unknown, Lacan's Real. But the vagina, though both utterly material and utterly immaterial, occupies a third space and can't be reduced to either pole. Thus, it is not actually situated strictly in the Real: that placement *defies its physical actuality* as a space between, and it deprives patients, psychoanalysis, and the culture of an essential spatial metaphor. The vagina marks the space between non-metaphorical reality and metaphor, between what is accessible and what lies beyond reach. It does not only inspire mystery; it is also what spurs the child's fantasy life, the quest to bridge the gap between what is knowable and shareable, and what lies beyond knowing and naming.

That is, the study of missing female genital experience ultimately reveals far more than absence. We begin to glean the presence of "space." Space is not emptiness, it is not deprivation, it is not absence. Jacqueline Rose, writing from a feminist and Lacanian perspective, notes that the space of desire "functions much as the zero unit in the numerical chain— its place is both constitutive and empty" (1982, p. 32). It is, like the void, like the Biblical "face of the deep," a generative opening. (It was not exactly an accident that the mystic psychoanalyst W. F. Bion used the symbol O to signify Absolute Knowledge.) Without space, without some emptiness and incompleteness in our discourse, there is not only no need to speak, but no possibility. When all is said, nothing more can be.

Speech is never entirely private or entirely public; it occupies the space between. And the female genital is at once the reality and the symbol of an opening up, a creation, of space between private and public. The private becomes public in the symbol, which is really neither public nor private but a property of both. These ideas, which reveal the function and power of women's bodies, have historically remained submerged beneath a faux phallicism that collapses and hides the very space upon which a genuine phallic power rests. When the signifier of the reverberant female genital cavity remains missing, so too is its inherent space, between limit and excess, of and for receptivity, penetration, pleasure, mystery, excitement, tension, and sharing.

Donna Bassin calls for new metaphors to describe female experience, beyond traditional roles and reproductive functioning—a bodily schema of a productive inner space that will allow for "representations of woman's interiority, and not her inferiority" (1982, p. 200). Dianne Elise insists on a distinction between "being depressed over being a female and being a female who is depressed" and stresses "the impact of object loss on subsequent mental representation of the genitals and on the experience of anxiety and depressive affect intertwined" (1998, pp. 430–31). By "object loss," she is referring not to the debilitating sense, inculcated in girls the world over, of coming into being as girls by virtue of lacking what boys have and what everyone wants. Rather, she is referring to an anticipated or experienced loss of relationship, to the girl's perception of being unfulfilled or unwanted by an unresponsive father. It is not a penis she wants, but a relationship with her father. The vagina remains the site of unrequited, "unfulfilled desire" (ibid., p. 427), and the girl closes down her own space as an act of self-protection. Girls remain unseen as providers of something essential, of space, but instead are seen as "painfully lacking" (ibid., p. 431).

Without a real and metaphorical conception of space, the entire psychoanalytic project founders. And without a real and metaphorical space, the democratic polis also fails. So it did in ancient Greece, where female bodily representation was denied in the public sphere; and so, too, the polis often continues to fail in our own self-styled democratic society. When psychoanalysis negates female bodily space and knowledge, it forecloses its own power, averting an openness to the emergent unconscious. Likewise, free speech requires that the body politic maintain space, both literal and metaphorical; that it embrace this "feminine" principle while inviting all to speak openly.

To assert the problem directly: the realization of potency in psychoanalysis, or in democracy, is not founded on "phallocentric" expression, on the hegemonic effort to *occupy* and control all discursive space. Such efforts leave us ever vulnerable to the collapse of space, to exercises of negative power—to discourse that lacks not only space for mediation and interpretation but that also lacks *space itself*. *Above all, what is missing is feminine space*—an opening for and recognition of the female body and of female genital experience, and for their signification in language. Without a feminine metaphor, what also is missing is a space between vaginal and phallic symbols and for their free trade, for their mutual labor. True phallic achievement is predicated on a foundation both real and metaphorical: vaginal space. *Knowledge of this space requires that it be named.*

CHAPTER FOURTEEN

Laws of lack and feminine law

The cave you fear to enter holds the treasure you seek.
—attributed to Joseph Campbell

Between a masculine and a feminine law

If conceiving (thinking) the female genital is essential to free association, and if free association is both the mechanism and goal of psychoanalysis, then we must recognize the female genital's status as essential to "cure." If a cure is ever achieved in psychoanalysis, it is a talking cure. Such a cure involves a sense of directionality, a telos toward emancipation that comes as we gain status as speaking agents, beyond the confines of merely circular or repetitive discourse. Repetition's confinement also produces moments, intonations and accents of, difference—nascent glimpses of open space and its motion. This space, a conduit between unknown and known, material and mental, private and public, is intimately linked to the body's experiences, somatic sensations, physical pains and pleasures—and to female genital experience.

And yet psychoanalysis, which claims to pursue free discourse for mind and body, has historically been little better than society as a whole at holding open this feminized space for free speech and meaningful

181

discourse. Analysts, like everyone else, have avoided talking much about, or even naming, let alone hearing, the vagina, that gendered signifier of space. Even today we live in a culture pervaded by traditional "phallocentric" perspectives, which assume that sexual and social life are organized around male attributes and male power, and which thus close down female space (and space for females). They do so by erasing, or at the very least denigrating and/or obscuring, the female genital, as a physical object, as a topic, and as a representation of female presence and self-possession. They do so by shutting down, rather than cultivating, an open space for the liberatory pulse of desire's discourse.

Freud's own phallocentrism was very much on the surface, and he never felt the need to apologize for his notions of female castration and penis envy. Later analysts did attempt to correct analytic theory to some degree by routing around these foundational concepts, downplaying the prominent role of the phallus in Freud's thought. But the influential French analyst Jacques Lacan made a more interesting, and for our purposes more productive, move. Instead of scaling back the role of the phallus, he inflated it; but at the same time, he almost completely negated its material link to the male sex organ, and by doing so he turned it from a symbol that filled space into a symbol (or rather signifier) that created space. Lacan feminized the phallus.

Lacan's thinking is challenging and largely beyond the scope of this book. But a few of his ideas do open a path to better understanding the bases for free speech. In fact, Lacan, perhaps more than any other psychoanalytic theorist, understood that to be human is to be enmeshed in language, to be a signifying being, on the surface and in depth. "The unconscious," he often said (in 1957, e.g.), "is structured like a language." And in his view, our immersion in a world of signification is a marker of lack; we signify something because we are unable to experience it in an unmediated way. Mari Ruti expresses with an admirable, deceptive simplicity the incessant, elusive, nature of this quest: "Language generates lack. Lack in turn generates desire" (2008, p. 488).

This lack, this space for desire, Lacan claims, is marked off—even created—by the phallus. Because in Lacan's terminology, the phallus is not the penis, nor any material representation of male potency. Rather, it is the signifier of difference itself, and thus of desire: we cannot want what we already are. Lacan speaks of the function of the phallic signifier or "Name of the Father" (*le nom du père*) as the key third term in an otherwise undifferentiated tie between infant and mother. The father's name, if not his words, if not his presence, if not his actual penis, causes the first separation or rupture, and that helps the child find a foothold in the world of shared meaning (language). For Lacan, language brings things into subjective existence and makes them part of human shareable reality.

Freud, like Lacan, attributed to the father our introduction to the symbolic order, in particular to a primordial father figure, whose implicit or explicit "No" marks transgression, both creating and limiting desire. Examples from Freud's writing include Laius, murdered by his son Oedipus in myth, and the father of the primordial horde from his mythological tome, *Totem and Taboo* (1912–1913). In death, or especially in death, the father transcends biological relation and takes on the role of a symbol—as an all-powerful imago of authority—even beyond his role as executor of castration. Freud continues advancing this formulation in *Moses and Monotheism*, while also developing a more fully symbolic template for law. The Mosaic narrative, he implies, creates a space for desire and for its sublimation. Why? In Tracy McNulty's interpretation (2014, pp. 79–85), God is absent: His name can't be spoken, He can't be represented in physical form, His earthly dwelling (Jerusalem's "Holy of Holies") cannot be directly approached and remains off limits to human encounter. Where there once was *presence*, now an unbridgeable chasm, a *gap*, is revealed.

Lacan's "paternal law" or metaphor both marks an exit from totemic law and instantiates Mosaic law—the entrance into the symbolic realm and its lawful processes of signification. Father's injunction instigates the loss of our impressionistic, unnamed, maternal world, leading us to grapple not only with boundaries but also with space, with the emptiness that our fall from totemic law exposes. Lacan's introduction of the phallic signifier (the Name of the Father) serves to mark a *space-creating* boundary that stands in contrast to the obliteration of lawful boundaries associated with what I earlier described as a faux phallic discourse. In that sense, the phallic function introduces limit and alienation. For Lacan, this limit is introduced by the father's most characteristic utterance: "No." This is Lacan's paternal law or metaphor: the rule of "no," understood as a symbolic function that instantiates the subject's desire.

Lacan conceived the phallus, because it forbids and separates and introduces lack, as *desire's* signifier, as the *name* of desire, and in this sense, the phallus belongs to neither gender but is available to be claimed by all. Insofar as desire itself is ineffable and unspeakable, and because the phallus is never anything more than a signifier, it, like desire, is always associated with lack, with the impossibility of complete fulfillment. And so it is also associated with castration. In this way, Lacan contravenes Freud: it is the phallus (because it represents unfulfillable desire, for an illusory state of wholeness) rather than the female signifier that is associated with castration and lack. And yet the phallic signifier is at the same time that which constitutes the subject, because it is by entering into language that she takes a leap towards symbolization, relinquishing her tie to the Real, which has now been lost.

So Lacan's ideas of the relationship between the phallus, the father's "No," and boundary setting are essential not only to psychoanalysis's pursuit of free association, but to all democratic discourse. Here we see the rhetorical resonance among Lacan's paternal law, its incantation of the Father's "no," his "Name-of-the-Father," the "no rule" implicit in Freud's fundamental rule, and the Founding Fathers' brilliantly evocative assertion of a negative, "Congress shall make no law."

The primacy of no law is feminine law. The father's (rule of) "no" provides the boundary setting opening to feminine law, which acknowledges (and releases us to) the primacy of "no rule," of a genuine space for free speech and its erotic discourse. Feminine law is not prohibitive like totemic law; but neither is it inscribed, like the laws of Moses, the laws of the father. Instead, it is *found*, embedded in the Real, not capable of being fully symbolized, as it names what is a principle of representation and thus beyond representation. This is Lacan's dilemma, as it had been Freud's dilemma. This is why neither man could represent Woman—though (as I shall explore in the next chapter) Lacan found an indelible, iconographic solution: ~~Woman~~.

In her book *Wrestling with the Angel*, Tracy McNulty wrestles with these very issues. She arrives at an understanding of the limits of traditional paternal laws or "laws of lack"—limits that inspire an "urgent need to theorize a paternal function beyond the law" (2014, p. 59). Seeking "a symbolic life 'after' the patriarchy," McNulty perceptively exposes "a groundlessness that is a structural condition of the symbolic" (ibid., p. 60). Where McNulty emphasizes the "'unfoundedness' of the symbolic [that] is key to its true function," I prefer a subtly different conception. Simply put, what is unfounded is *found* in the Real. In my view, rather than seeking a paternal function beyond the law, we can look beyond the paternal altogether—towards a *feminine* law.

By privileging the phallic signifier, at least as I interpret him, Lacan obscures the very gap that he seeks to open. What about the possibility of recognizing the status of the phallic signifier in marking a boundary that opens space and, at the same time, recognizing the status of the feminine, vaginal signifier, as affirming that open space, as signifying space itself? A feminine law, on this account, would "enshrine" the ambiguous presence of open space and exist in paradoxical tension with a paternal (for my purpose here, masculine) law, which wields the *phallus* in confronting the subject not only with castration but also with the birth—and constraints—of her desire.[1]

Beyond obscuration, boundary setting

We say that nature abhors a vacuum. Certainly *human* nature does. Despite ourselves, we feel compelled to fill in space (and time): to absorb, to take in, to violate our own empty wanting. We fill open space so that we have no thoughts. We rue our lack of space, including our lack of temporal space, for thinking, experiencing, being: the "no space" that conceals the nothing that we both seek and fear. Perhaps we occupy open spaces because they trigger an ominous foreboding; perhaps they provoke, on some level, what Winnicott called a "fear of breakdown." Winnicott's use of "breakdown" is purposefully vague. He refers to a general fear of breakdown of defensive organization but then asks,

> a defence against what? And this leads us to the deeper meaning of the term, since we need to use the word "breakdown" to describe the unthinkable state of affairs that underlies the defence organization.... I contend that clinical fear of breakdown is *the fear of a breakdown that has already been experienced*. It is a fear of the original agony. (Winnicott, 1974, pp. 103–104)

If we accept Winnicott's hypothesis (and its reverberations with Lacan's) that opening space requires us to face an original loss or emptiness, we can contemplate on a deeper level (beyond castration fears) Freud's conception of symptom formation as a defense against remembering and conscious knowing. To open that space we must not only sustain a dialectic between boundary-setting constraint and space-creating boundary. We must also be willing to endure lack, to experience desire (and its insatiety), but also to encounter our "unthinkable" thoughts—thoughts that require the presence of another mind so that we might at last bear thinking them. We must be willing to experience what Winnicott called our "original agony" and Bion our "nameless dread." Beyond that, as Lacan and others have argued, these two minds and this agony require language to become speakable: they must also be held by (and accountable to) a Third, "the semiotic field, the field of the unconscious resonances of history and culture" (Muller, 1996, p. 189). To the degree that those unconscious resonances inculcate an experience of emptiness as "a form of female perdition" (Erikson, 1963, p. 374), it may be no wonder that psychoanalysis and the culture at large has failed to appreciate and "hold," let alone traverse the tensions of an empty, wanting, brimming-with-desire, open space that is hidden in plain sight.

In our early negotiation of a dialectic between boundary and freedom—before we are willing (or brave enough) to bear our dread, let alone name our desire—we must first assert a negative. Freud recognized early on (1900a) that there is no "No" in the unconscious. And once he observed how regularly patients will contradict what they have already said, and what they have always known—presumably to circumvent repression, while also remaining loyal to it—he went on to draft an entire paper on negation (1925h). Bonnie Litowitz, elaborating upon Freud's thinking, suggests a developmental line of negation, noting that "more is involved in negation than opposition to affirmation: 'nothing' entails a thing or category; 'no' indicates a relationship to another; 'not' requires a proposition; while zero is a placeholder, a space" (Litowitz, 2006, p. 439).

The entire psychoanalytic project, beginning with Freud's earliest studies of hysteria, has wrestled with the dialectic between knowing and not-knowing. The core purpose of negation is to counter a corresponding affirmation, but also to mark a boundary. The entry to a space of desire requires saying "no." The developmental psychologist Rene Spitz (1957), who studied the evolution of negation in normal infancy, recognized that before the child can say "yes," he negates what the adult presents to him, as if by so doing he creates a stepping-stone to a positive assertion his own desire. (At the very least, we are all familiar with the often fierce and exuberant quest of young children to claim "mine"—implicitly, "not yours!")

The philosopher Eva Brann has observed, "'no' seems to mean something more even than a declaration of independence: an aboriginal delight in negativity." She relates this achievement to the recognition "that something absent can be depicted as present, that something bygone can be now recalled, and that what is not can be meant and uttered as well as or even better than what is" (1999, p. 165). This "No" emanates from the child's authority; it is her boundary, not one imposed upon her from above by a paternal (masculine) authority. It sets in motion a dialectical tension, a reverberating gap, between no and yes, boundary and space, limit and desire, masculine and feminine (lawful) signifiers.

Winnicott well described the patient's paradoxical achievement in arriving at a position in which "*the only real thing is the gap*; that is to say, the death or the absence or the amnesia … that this blank could be the only fact and the only thing that was real" (1953, p. 22, emphasis added). In adult life, we encounter more quotidian incursions that only hint at this phenomenological signpost in which the "the real thing is the thing that is not there" (ibid., p. 23). For example, we often experience stereotypical gender behavior: the man in a couple insists on his need for "space"; the woman in a relationship, working outside the home, clamors for more "time" (which we might understand as space in a temporal dimension). The ability to claim space—and the ability to say "mine"—also requires wrestling with what is "not mine," but ours or yours. The opening up of space (time) requires wrestling with limits and boundaries, and an encounter with what lies illimitably beyond us, with a world—a universe—that we cannot control or possess.

How does this space become real, visible—not merely inferred through its (apparent) absence or lack of signification, but achieved through the assertion of boundaries? To get a feel for the possibilities, let's return once more to the clinic.

A baggage claim dream

One of my patients described a recurring dream in which she was at a baggage claim, besieged by other people's luggage, as she waited to reclaim her own. During the wait she experienced a quality of despair and mounting desperation, until she glimpsed or (in some versions of the dream) wrested her luggage free from the others toppled upon it. Based on that emblematic dream, I've come to signify other dreams with a similar theme (wresting "mine" from the onslaught of "theirs") as "baggage claim dreams." Another patient, for example, dreamed that toxic waste had been dumped in her yard. The problem was now hers to dispense with; but she felt, quite naturally, exploited and victimized.

In such dreams—and truly commonplace experiential quandaries of patients—we see the colonizing weight of the signifying baggage of others (parents, teachers, peers, society) that deadens the individual's own experience of aliveness and agential, singular expression. The traditions of a culture, the toll of social hegemony, the tyranny of the Other's discourse operate in repressive and oppressive ways. The patient may become paralyzed and despairing, may retreat to private aspects of meaning-making, not legible to the social world. But the quest in psychoanalysis is to liberate the subject, to challenge her to surrender to participating in a social fabric without yielding her agency, her proto-efforts at creating her own signs and symbols, her capacity for a resignification now allied with the truth of her desire. This resignification lies in the power to claim the signifier, and to animate it (through its fidelity to desire) with what Mari Ruti describes as "the immortal vitality of the real" (2012, p. 126).

Returning to my patient's toxic waste dream, decoding it revealed the challenge that lay ahead, ensnared as her meaning-making abilities remained in others' narratives. In this dream, her private property was besmirched, and she felt violated. She also resented the fact that taking on active agency and asserting her rights would involve an uphill social and bureaucratic battle that would cost her dearly. Meanwhile, she had to struggle with the diffusion of the waste, whose seepage was both laborious to contain and threatening to her neighbors. Allowing herself to feel justified in asserting a sense of violation, she then took all the toxic waste, packaged it up, and pushed it back onto the presumed violators of her property and her purity. "It's yours, not mine!" she exclaimed.

Upon waking from this dream, my patient enjoyed a fleeting experience of power. She had fought for and claimed the difference between what belonged to her and what belonged to others, refusing to bear responsibility for what was not hers. For years she'd wrestled with a vague but persistent despair and an overwhelming sense of futility. But now, in her dream, she'd "concretized" an insidious plague while establishing a boundary. That boundary fostered a sense of interiority. Subsequent to this dream, she took palpable pride in drawing this line, claiming it in a series of interactions that had been previously characterized by the diffusion of responsibility and agency between her and her family, between her and her friends. I believe that her newfound pride derived in part from the newly created line in itself, and her ability to assert herself to achieve it.

What was most thrilling for her was that she now experienced a sense of space, and in that space an openness to initiate experience based on desire and curiosity. This was, however, a mixed achievement. She soon came to realize that the price of victory in establishing a boundary (marking what is "mine") was high. The previous diffusion of boundary and the lack of establishing her personal property rights, so to speak, had spared her a certain measure of real conflict. As her sense of agency now shifted, she came to experience this price as potentially greater than that of stirring conflict with the other (violating) party. In drawing her line in the sand, she also devised a new solution: she claimed for herself a morally "pure" experience. Not only did she reclaim her sense of space and interiority, but she claimed a space of *me versus other* (or at least, versus "not-me") that became joined in her mind with moral oppositions: good against evil, pure against impure.

This was not a fully ethical solution for her, nor was it sustainable. Insofar as it raised barriers against mutual recognition and respect— against the opening of "democratic" space—her achievement came at the expense of knowing herself and real others. Her mind and body had claimed their initial victory, but that victory entailed simplification and self-deception. Living in a world in which right was on her side, in which evil and impurity were projected onto external malefactors, she could not recognize, let alone comprehend, parts of herself that were messy and far more complicated than the easy dichotomies she fantasized. Her victory also came at the expense of knowing the other, equally complicated and messy and real, neither pure nor impure, and not a flat, black-and-white caricature.

My patient's step was absolutely necessary if she was ever to claim an experience of personal agency and the freedom to speak and to know. But this enlightenment was just a first step along a darkened path, one along which we must discover heretofore unacknowledged impulses and desires and take responsibility for desire that will sometimes shame, frighten, or overwhelm us. All the while, we must sustain a tension between "the degradation of a closed systematization" (as above) and "the anarchy of intuitive processes" (LeClaire, 1998, p. 16). This path is treacherous and there is no road map, except that provided by the illuminating signposts of desire in concert with the boundary setting function of ethics.

By locating these signposts, and by better understanding the ways the phallic signifier figures in establishing boundaries, we can begin to appreciate the larger reverberations of my patients' experiences. We can also encourage their (and our) capacity for empowering participation in intimate relationships and in cultural and political life. At the same time, when we follow the articulation of the far more obscured female genital signifier—the vagina—we can begin to unravel its mysteries and its space-creating potential in personal and democratic relationships.

In fact, understanding the dialectical and dynamically driven relationship between the articulated phallic signifier and the obscured spatial feminine one will illuminate matters that are central to this book: the expansion of freedom and agency in the public sphere as well as the private. Both the Supreme Court and psychoanalysis contend regularly with the tension between the opening and closing of space that is essential to the preservation of free association and free speech. Rather than a one-time achievement, this sustaining of an open space—and this challenging of our tendencies to collapse it—is a perpetual quest, through which the possibilities and the promise of the First Amendment and the fundamental rule are kept alive.

My patient, at her transitional juncture, revealed an emergent capacity to mark a boundary "between tyranny and slavery" (Farrar, 1992, p. 18), staking a claim to her private, personal space. Through such boundary setting, she would also enlist herself as a participant in open, shared, and symbolic space. This is as essential to personal self-sovereignty as to the sovereignty of a people, of citizens in a democracy. The struggle for democracy is inseparable from that of claiming a gendered voice and body, and from our need to contend with difference and otherness, including sexual difference but extending to racial, ethnic, cultural, religious, gendered differences.

The psychosomatic frontier and our democratic project

Freud, of course, was no stranger to the paradoxes of the human quest for freedom and the inevitability of constraint, if not impediment. He, famously and endlessly controversially, deemed that "anatomy is destiny"—setting off a number of contradictory interpretations that nonetheless mainly assume sexual (anatomical) difference may be a matter of destiny just as it is a matter of constructing meaning. That is to say, our earliest encounters with otherness—beginning with other bodies—challenge us to interpret difference. Our lives begin with this encounter, in our earliest explorations between our minds and bodies, and between the minds and bodies of those who are different from us, even as they are family/familiar to us. That conversation, in Freud's terms, was initiated by the child's startling discovery of genital difference.

The child's psychosomatic frontier—that third space between mind and matter—was also Freud's own frontier. Locating and sustaining this space is also, whether Freud knew it or not, a project for sustaining a democratic and inclusive vision. If we fail to maintain the dialectic between psyche and soma, we inhabit a collapsed world in which the physical assumes too much weight, and the mental endures too much strain. We must engage our minds with the material world and wrestle with it,

> not only in the situation of desperate and all-pervading oppression ... but in a human condition common to us all, however infinitely more fortunate we may be ... [because] everything we choose and value in life for its lightness soon reveals its true, unbearable weight. (Calvino, 1988, p. 7, on Milan Kundera)

Reclaiming one's own signs and meanings from the weight of culturally imposed signifying "baggage" that has colonized our psychical and bodily space is essential to our constitution as subjects. The project before us is also between us: Grounding desire's unbounded discourse between mind and body, between imagination and memory, in a dialogue with another complicated human subject, is both fundamental to the claiming of a democratic relationship and absolutely terrifying.

My patients tell me they can't think; they have no thoughts. They also tell me they have no space. I conclude they are telling me as much about their bodies as they are about their psyches. But they are also telling me about their access to words, to metaphor. Psychosomatic space depends upon our capacity as a symbolic species to grant destiny to anatomy, to dare to name what is unnamed and obscured. Without it, free association remains elusive and the entire psychoanalytic project—the human and humanizing, democratic and democratizing—project of symbolization—falters. But we still know that by so doing we cannot capture space, we cannot master freedom. We approach, by naming, what must remain elusive and "inappropriable" (Nancy, 1988, p. 169).

CHAPTER FIFTEEN

Naming the vagina: on the feminine dimension of truth

> After all that, Lonzi returned to talk of this essential female part, and it turned out he was speaking specifically of a woman's vulva. A good example of how it was Lonzi had come to be leader. He was willing to think to extremes and name them.
>
> —Rachel Kushner (2013, p. 76)[1]

As it explores the means by which the unnamed is named and the inconceivable is conceived, psychoanalysis awakens us to the presence of absence. We eventually discover the key role, albeit a *shrouded* role, of female sexuality—and specifically of female genital experience and the female genital itself. As we explore the ways in which we may bring the submerged to light, we better appreciate why free speech is such an alluring, indeed uniquely privileged, value in both psychoanalytic literature and in the U.S. Constitution.

Now we must go a step further. My "prescription" for democracy involves not only pondering what some will see as the outlandish interpretations of psychoanalysis. It also involves signifying, acts of *naming*, that which refutes naming. In this chapter I will try to explain what I mean by "naming," why it is so important, and what actual effect naming a hidden body part can have. I hope to show that once we are able to name and speak of the female genital, then it also becomes metaphorically approachable. Furthermore, with this knowledge will come a fuller capacity to materialize the space required for truly free and equal speech. Further, by metaphorizing the female genital, we also name *the woman*. No longer subjugated as a condition of the unsignifiable, she gains status in the symbolic realm of shared discourse.

Signs and names

We will begin by taking a tour of semiotics (the study of signs), which I introduced in Chapter One. Recall that its founder, Charles Sanders Peirce, distinguished between dyadic and triadic relations: the former involve unmediated physical forces, the latter a third space of mediation. The signal-response behavioristic communication of animals (and sometimes of human beings) is dyadic: signal triggers action without any intervening concept or representation. In the sphere of triadic relations, we do not merely signal; we use *symbols*. (Symbolizing also marks our difference from the angels, who at least in our fantasies communicate instantly and without mediation.)

The author and occasional philosopher Walker Percy claims (somewhat hyperbolically) that "dyadic relations account for 98% of natural phenomena like Newtonian mechanics," while "the phenomenon of talking-and-listening falls in the remaining 2%" (1975, p. 162). Of course, the "triadic" activities of talking and listening are the bedrock of both psychoanalytic free association and democratic free speech. So what do Percy and Peirce offer to our understanding?

Percy first distinguishes between the confusing terms *symbol* and *sign*, which are practically interchangeable in everyday speech. But for Percy (who draws freely here from Peirce),[2] a *sign* is a simple pointer or indicator. It might be an animal's cry of distress, which points to (*signals*) a dangerous intruder; or it might be a clap of thunder, which points to an imminent downpour. Signs are thus not uniquely human. A *symbol*, on the other hand, doesn't just point; it "means."

In Percy's account, a name is capable of being both a sign and a symbol; for example, the word "ball" does not necessarily cause a human being to look around for a ball, though it might cause a dog to do so. Partly by virtue of this duality, naming is powerful because it conjures up something we call "meaning," and to make meaning we must experience a division from what is signified, and thus a gap in consciousness. "Naming is unique in natural history because for the first time a being in the universe stands apart from the universe and affirms some other being to be what it is" (ibid., pp. 153–155).

Without naming—without the entire signifying system that naming engenders and that engenders naming—there is no way to conceive or represent predicates about what is real or true. Thus there is no shared realm of meaning. As Percy says, What is required is that the thing be both sanctioned and yet allowed freedom to be what it is" (1975, p. 75). Without naming, there is no world of co-intention, no world to make meaning about, a world (and word) inconceivable. As Jacques Lacan puts it, "Naming constitutes a pact whereby two subjects in the same moment agree to recognize the same object" (1954–1955, p. 202).

Democracy is such a pact on a large scale, a total social compact, and it requires that we open a space in which potential knowledge and meaning can be cultivated and shared. Building a democracy involves extending the realm of meaning, the linguistic community, so that everyone may share in and contribute to collective knowledge. We make a semiotic pact. Lacking such bonds, we have no way to share, or to put a space between us and the otherwise excessive impact of our experiences. Francoise Davoine and Jean-Max Gaudilliere explain that what makes something traumatic or catastrophic is that "it occurred originally in the presence of another who simply registered it without responding, without naming it. The patient in turn registers it in an unsymbolized mode" (Muller, 1996, p. 98). What cannot be symbolized cannot be metabolized. What is not named remains a ghost.

What's more, in order to assume full humanity, we ourselves need to become subjects who can be known; we need to be named. As Lacanian analyst Mavis Himes puts it while reviewing *La Force du Nom*, a book on the proper name and its impact on human subjectivity,

> it is only through an act of nomination that we become an "I," and to say "I" is to occupy a space in the world.... To live without a name is to live on the margins of life. It is to belong to the kingdom of animals that roam through their world nameless and anonymous. (Himes, 2012, p. 15).

Winnicott intuitively recognized this condition, distilling early maternal care of the infant to a few essentials: "an infant is kept warm, handled and bathed and rocked and *named*" (1945, p. 150; emphasis added).

Lacan is not concerned simply with the effects of naming; he also points to what resists naming: the woman. Or rather, he locates the female sign, "woman" (sometimes signified with a strikethrough), in the register of the unsymbolized Real. There, its link with trauma, with what lies beyond knowability, is suspended in a kind of eternal purgatory, beyond the redemptions of symbolic life. The return of the repressed—along with illuminating shards of a boundless unrepressed unconscious—requires this sign to be enfranchised by speech, by means of naming. "In name," said Walter Benjamin, "appears the essential law of language" (1916, p. 65). Yes, we have all kinds of slang words and epithets to refer to the vagina and vulva; but these are mere analogies for the thing in itself, not fully rendered symbols. Likewise, while signifiers that are "gendered" as female (pink, lipstick, lace, etc.) proliferate, they orbit around a void, a missing center, which is the sign of the void itself, of space, the sign I have nominated as the quintessential and definitive sign of the female. The word "vagina" may not be unspoken, but it is almost always localized, almost always just a sign in Percy's sense. Bereft of symbolic access, it flies under the radar of law.[4] Not only does Lacan's "Woman" (as unconscious subject) remain unnamed (W̶o̶m̶a̶n̶), but there is a larger principle that remains unnamed, and unacknowledged, a principle that is even more fundamental than a phallic principle. To this point I shall return.

Naming the gap: the feminine metaphor

It is no surprise that psychoanalysis, dedicated as it is to *terra incognita*, has generated many signifiers for what cannot be named and what cannot be (consciously) known. Freud described the repressed unconscious and that which we experience as the "uncanny" (1919h). Wilfred Bion spoke of "unthinkable anxiety" and "nameless dread." Christopher Bollas wrote of the "unthought known." More recently, Philip Bromberg (1998) and Donnel Stern (1997) have discussed the realm of dissociated, "not-me" experience. The entire psychoanalytic project, that of making meaning in the face of that which remains nameless, unknown, unsymbolized, takes place against and in tension with this abyss.

Naming, as Percy suggests, is an "aboriginal" act that both defines us as human and sets us on a path of metaphor. By naming things, we enjoy the fruits of a certain kind of knowledge ("not as angels know and not as dogs know but as men, who must know one thing through the mirror of another," 1975, p. 82). Furthermore, in naming things we liken one kind of object to another. Through naming, he says, "A perfectly definite something is pointed at and given a name, a sound or a gesture to which it bears only the most tenuous analogical similarities" (ibid., pp. 78–79). That is to say, as metaphorical beings, as namers, we equip ourselves to create an illusorily continuous world picture. As Percy contends—in a very Freudian phrase that highlights the inseparability of psychoanalysis and semiotics—"Gaps that cannot be closed by perception and reason are closed by magic and myth" (ibid., p. 203).

How does this idea of the symbol as gap-bridger account for the female sign's consignment to the nameless Real? And how does this idea fit with my argument for the importance of naming and symbolizing female space? Recall our earlier discussion of Lacan's twist on the phallic signifier. For Lacan, who disposes with the materialism of Freud's "penis envy" and his assumption of female genital lack, the phallus is not the penis. Nor is it any other material representation of male potency. Rather, it is a signifier (or in Percy's terms, a "symbol") of difference itself, and thus of desire. It marks a boundary for an open space in which the subject will come to be—where the infant emerges from his unmediated, phantasmagoric tie with mother, in which the gap between need and satisfaction is barely discernible, into a world of "castrated" others. These others are, psychoanalytically speaking, no longer mythical but human. They are subject to consensual laws even if, somewhere in fantasy, the ideal of limitlessness lives on. In this sense, desire is always correlated with lack, thereby impelling "more speech."

The phallus is for Lacan "the *name* of desire" (my italics), and "castration" comes to be understood as a symbolic representation of lack, rather than physical deprivation. It also marks the distinction between what is accessible and what is off limits. Lacan's point is that castration draws a lawful limit (as "No") that marks our entry into language and the symbolic order. In crossing this line, we leave behind the unmediated world, and the boundless vistas of our infantile omnipotence. We mourn. In compensation for our losses, we gain status as symbolizing agents. We acquire tools for claiming (or reclaiming) knowledge of our repressed desires, now equipped with a mediating third term between wish and action—between, to put it plainly, stimulus and response. The advent of symbolization grants us a third option between repression and naked, raw drive. We become subjects of the law.

But what of a feminine signifier? As Lacan saw it, women are luckier in one way than men: they *are* able to sustain a foothold in the register of the Real, in the limitless, because they are not completely bounded by the symbolic order. The woman remains to some degree "uncastrated." This privilege is also however a detriment: it compromises her status in the cultural realm in which mediation (symbolization) is essential. She cannot be truly represented. Lacan concludes: "Woman does not exist." In the words of Bruce Fink, "there is no signifier for, or essence of Woman as such. Woman can thus only be written under erasure: ~~Woman~~" (Fink, 1995, p. 115). She is there and not there, present and absent. Just as she cannot be fully symbolized, she cannot fully engage in the mediation that is so essential to dialogue, to free speech, to genuine democracy.

This duality of presence/absence in Lacan's thought captures the essential void at the center of symbolic life. The masculine signifier— the phallus—negates but also marks the entry to our lack. This dualistic function inaugurates the symbolic realm and lawful processes of signification, exposing to us what is hiding in plain sight: the feminine metaphor. It is the feminine metaphor that marks the ineffable border to the unknown, the as-yet-to-be-signified and also the unsignifiable. Only by naming a feminine law—desire's law—do we glimpse the primacy of space: the space that free speech requires. Taken together, "masculine" and "feminine" laws create the essential Escher-like dialectic between the boundary setting function of the masculine signifier and the space-creating function of the feminine signifier—space itself, always both immaterial and actual, which resists and elusively invites naming.

Naming desire, naming truth

The laws of "No"—the Founding Fathers' "Congress shall make no law," Freud's fundamental rule, Lacan's "No"—set in motion this essential tension between law and lawlessness at the heart (and body) of free speech. They beckon us nearer to an encounter with desire's primordial and restless wellspring—to what naming in fact once denied us: Bion's "O," Lacan's Real. Together, they challenge us to cultivate a space for democracy, a space for equal access and for the exposure of (previously unthinkable) truths. For Lacan, naming is "a murder of the thing," just as the "thing" *eludes* naming; so we must continually grapple with the desire and the limits that give rise to our field of symbols. Paradoxically then, naming *is* a way to escape Lacan's economy of death, by way of more naming, specifically the naming of what resists naming.

Even more is at stake. Psychoanalysis's mission is to name desire— often forbidden, unnamed desire. To the degree that we are better able to name our desire, we are also better equipped to preserve ourselves from being intoxicated or subsumed by what the psychoanalyst Jean Laplanche (1989) referred to as enigmatic signifiers. Instead, we are free to translate, interpret, play with them. Akin the patient who remains faithful to Freud's fundamental rule is the "subject of truth" as depicted by philosopher Alain Badiou. This subject, who like our patient has the fortitude to sustain fidelity to desire, is, in Mari Ruti's words, "inhabited by a truth that is 'immortal' in the sense of being eternally valid" (2012, p. 88). He must "name" this desire, according to Badiou, a naming act that, by definition, can only be partial, a piece of an infinite process.

Badiou bids us to take a step further, to name a kernel of the nameable within the unnamable. He speaks of "truth-events," moments of epiphany that shatter our commonplace experience of the world. Such events release new, transformative, even transcendent energy that can revitalize our collective humanity and its signifying mission in a territory between mysticism and enlightenment. In Badiou's conception (Badiou & Tarby, 2010), truth is the subjective reckoning with such events that carry the charge of revelation. The event, a rupture of the normal order, is not itself subjective, and while it might appear to come out of nowhere, it must emerge from somewhere; it originates in a realm equivalent to Freud's receptive unconscious, to Lacan's Real, to Bion's O. The event exposes a gap or void between us and this realm; what had been invisible is now revealed and reckoned with. What had remained inaccessible and taboo is now at least in part accessible. What had lain dormant and seemingly lacked form, now (in the truth event) exposes its formidable and indelible inevitability both as a keystone of the previous arrangement and as the catalyst of a new, even revolutionary, upheaval.

Badiou's subject is challenged to name the void exposed by the event, to name the unnamable. This impossible project contains a seed of possibility, and vice versa, "the possibility of the impossible" in Badiou's koan-like phrase (Badiou & Tarby, 2010, p. 39). Our efforts to name the void are always also resisted by the unnamable kernel of truth, the real, what cannot be known or named.

To my knowledge, Badiou doesn't link the void specifically to female anatomy or its signifier, and yet, perpetually unnamed, the female genital preserves its status as that which *resists* naming and being known. And so why name it, or try? Because the vagina is the *quintessential* representation of and symbol for space—the space for generation, the space for intercourse, the space for discourse, Winnicott's "potential space" for play, for an emergence of what he called the "spontaneous gesture." As long as that (vaginal) space—metaphorical and literal— remains unspeakable, it remains diffuse, and it remains *inconceivable*. We remain caught between our fantasies of immaculate conception and those of brute colonization and imposition. This is at once a failure to know and a defense against knowing, a rejection of mutual recognition and of genuine mystery. It is an evasion of our essential natures. For naming the female genital is the foundational act of signifying *space,* and it is this space that frees speech and that differentiates not only female from male, but ultimately human from animal.

It is not just in abstruse psychoanalytic theorizing, but in Western culture at large, that masculine categories, masculine interests, and masculine imagery dominate the organization of our symbolic life. Everyone knows and has seen the many phallic symbols that represent cultural power. But who speaks of of a "vaginal symbol"?And without that symbol, how can we acknowledge the necessity of open, receptive space not only for the phallic thrust and for penetrating discourse but for novel, emergent "unthought knowns" (Bollas, 1987, p. 4)? Without this acknowledgment, we cannot foster an environment in which there is space, and a level ground, for all to find a voice that speaks of their experience.

Perhaps this is one way in which psychoanalysis can help pave the way to a better democracy. Donna Bassin expresses this hope:

> If psychoanalysis is in part an opportunity actively to construct a new world view, women should be provided with the means to acknowledge and gain mastery over their own body imagery rather than having to look to phallic and castrated metaphors for bodily organization. (Bassin, 1982, p. 197)

Luce Irigaray advocates for

> a feminine language (*écriture féminine*) that can locate sexuality
> at the site of origin—a return to the maternal body and to the
> autoerotic. For her, naming the unnamable, the inscription of the
> female body and female difference in language and text, is itself a
> cure. (Atlas, 2012, pp. 228–229).

But this revolution does not appear imminent. Rosemary Balsam (2012)
laments the continuing paucity of references in the psychoanalytic
canon to female exhibitionism and female bodily pleasure, while Galit
Atlas calls into question whether "psychoanalysis has ever adequately
theorized healthy genital exhibitionism for girls" (2012, p. 230). And
it naturally should. Recognizing the material female body, and by
implication naming it, advances the project of creating space for female
symbolization, female representation, female memory. By representing
vaginal sensations and experiences of inner space, we can create embodied structures for psychical processes, ones rooted in the
female body and not derivative of phallic representations, but rather
available to intermingle with them as equals.

Creating such vaginal space will not swallow up the phallus; the
goal is a more inclusive consciousness—achieving the richness and
possibility that follow from claiming both genital metaphors. The goal is
to enable us to equitably distribute our trade in gendered signifiers and
to create a healthy interchange, a free trade and conversation between
them. It is to find a balance between shaping the world through our
words and actions, and being shaped by the world by cultivating space,
the very space (and void) that sustains our proximity and fidelity to a
truthful, vitalizing, interruptive discourse that is also an encounter with
what perpetually eludes familiarity, capture, and conscious knowing.

On metaphors and gaps: naming the vaginal void

For Freud, the antithesis of truth was not falsity, but rather oblivious-
ness (Mieli, 2001). His goal for psychoanalysis was to empower the
patient (by way of free association, and through the inevitable transference relationship) to uncover, access, and recognize her unacknowledged
truths, her voice of desire. Our truth experience depends on truth's
articulation; what is subjective, but not arbitrary, must be represented,

symbolized in inevitably *partly* arbitrary ways that also allow an infinity of possibility. Keeping true to seeking truth—be it to Lacan's Real, Bion's O, Badiou's truth-event—both enables us as subjects capable of self-determination and requires that we concede to the otherness and limitations of speech. And this recalls our introduction to language, when we were infants no more. Just as we become severed from "truth," we stay near to it, reuniting with it as we infuse it with symbolic life and as our symbolic life transfuses it.

As the philosopher Robert Sokolowski has observed, "Things can be said about an object only when it is so held by a name" (1978, p. 4). By daring to name Badiou's void, here conceived as the unnamed or absent or obscured female genital—"vagina"—we allow it to be known, to have things said about it, to be actually *thought about*. By endowing our otherwise primordial landscape with words, says Percy, "we are dealing with natural existents, the object and the vocable, the sound which actually trembles in the air" (1975, p. 261).

Let us pause to consider the sounds and etymology of the words *vagina* and *vulva*. The term *vagina* was first used in seventeenth century medical Latin, deriving from the classical Latin for "sheath, scabbard, covering; sheath of an ear of grain, hull, husk" and thereby ultimately from the proto–Indo-European root *wag*, "to break, split, bite."[3] The earlier and more inclusive term *vulva* (by which today we encompass the external female genitalia, including the labia, clitoris, and vaginal orifice) dates to fourteenth century Latin, where it referred to the womb, and where it may have derived from the sense "wrapper" embedded in the verb root *volvere* (proto–Indo-European *wel*), "to turn, roll" (and also "to turn over in one's mind"). Therefore, the very words that have come to designate the female genital contain, while concealing and shrouding, the opening or the gap that splits consciousness and the subject. More to the point, these etymologies sharpen the boundaries of that space, accentuating their openness, while simultaneously designating the vagina and vulva as holders, "wrappers," *of* space, but also of the penis. *Penis* itself, another term that entered English in the seventeenth century, derives either from the French *pénis*, or directly from its Latin ancestor *penis*, which before designating the male genital meant "tail." The word *phallus*, first attested in English in 1610, refers to an *image* of the penis; its Greek ancestor *phallos* more particularly referred to an image of an *erect* penis. So we have a denuded penis, and its erect phallic representation, which provides some (symbolic) cover for the penis (it is a different word). But we discover that the vagina is defined, perhaps apocalyptically,[5] by contradiction: it is exposed in hiding. As a bare analogy, the vaginal lacks symbolic camouflage.

Naming the vagina and the vulva uncovers what lies concealed and whose revelation requires turning it over in our minds. The etymology of "vagina" not only exposes its primal metaphorical sheathing function; it also suggests that space itself requires a frame, that we cannot conceive of space or a gap absent a sense of boundedness, limit, constraint. In particular, interior space must be approached metaphorically, and we gain metaphorical access by naming woman, naming her body, her vagina, her vulva. And at last, because we now have space-creating and receiving symbols, we also have a foundation for symbols that emanate, fill, protrude, and penetrate. We call them by a name. We pronounce them, without hesitation of fear and censorship: Phallic symbols.

Of course phallic symbols and discourse interpellate us even prior to our own acts of naming. Naming what is *visible* creates a shareable reality, which is fundamental to our constitution as subjects. Naming what is *obscured* or taboo, furthermore, is essential both to psychoanalysis and to democracy. As Lacan puts it, "through the word, which is already a presence made of absence, absence itself comes to be named" (Lacan, 1957, p. 65; translation as modified by Dor, 1998, p. 135). In this same passage, as Rosine Perelberg notes, a "journey that started *then and there* … is being transformed *here and now*, opening up the future" (2013, p. 568). Linking past and present, we move beyond the traumatic repetitions by turning nameless dread into named truths, and thus knowledge. Symbolization enables us to create a present society that is rooted in history, even as it anticipates (by creating cultural footprints) a sense of future.

Fixed narratives or coercive subliminal messages that infiltrate the cultural landscape masquerade as this process: they bypass the gaps and crevices that interpenetrate social hegemony and that challenge us to create meaning at the crossroads of what is unknowable and what can be known, discovered. Substituting illusory projections for shared meaning may nonetheless have real consequences, authorizing oppressive solutions that jeopardize social well-being. We can't ignore the gaps any more than physicists can discount the space that surrounds and engulfs the atoms of our seemingly solid world.

From this new vantage point, the female genital (in name and as metaphor), far from signifying lack or inferiority per se, as is so often suggested in the psychoanalytic literature, gains status as that primordial signifier for the entire project of human symbolization. Lacan's masculine "no" inaugurates the lawful processes of symbolization; beyond that, naming the unnamable (the feminine "yes") enables us to approach Badiou's "possibility of the impossible." In essence, naming the female genital *names the (idea of) gap*. To name the gap is to conceive of the gap, and that creates the possibility for knowledge, just as it also impels our insatiety.

In the moment we name the female genital, we take a step beyond the boundary setting (and hegemonic) function of the phallic signifier: we create a limitless metaphoric space. In this space we claim our status as a symbolic species—a species that, because it is capable of creating words and symbols, is also capable of transcending mere stimulus-response behavior. To close the gap literally would also close the gap between us as speaking, symbol-creating creatures, and those organisms that only operate in terms of stimulus-response behavior. *But to "close" the gap symbolically is to open the gap to the infinite spectrum of the human imagination*—in Percy's words, "by magic and myth."

And by so doing, we replenish our discourse with the animating eternal energies of desire's truth. We create the possibility—between private and public, between fantasy and reality, between feminine and masculine signifiers, between space and penetration—for all that is vital and creative in free expression. To close the gap is to foreclose desire. Or, more poetically, to close the gap "is to write the epitaph of desire" (Malater, 2014a). By refusing to close the gap, we keep the pulse of desire alive. Free association lives in this breathing space, between ordering (naming) and the singularity of desire. It lives between the phallic dominance of the signifier and the unfettered jouissance of the "thing in itself," the Lacanian Real. It lives in the space that conditions symbolic discourse, that open, enigmatic space bounded by physicality, the gendered dimension of Bion's "O" and of Winnicott's "potential space"—that feminine space, "the *space between*."

The unnamed, the poetic, the traumatic

Freud traced the metaphorical significance of hysterical "conversion" symptoms, setting psychoanalysis and us on an ongoing semiotic mystery tour. I have remarked (many times) on the degree to which, when following this semiotic trail of what is unspoken, unnamed, or unknown, psychoanalytic literature points to the female genital as its marker. Psychoanalysis also reminds us that what is unnamed lies in unconscious regions, in the realm of trauma—its silence, its terror, and its guilt. As it remains unsymbolized, trauma produces repetition in the form of (somatic) symptoms, what Lacan would describe as the insistence of the Real.

Lacan, interestingly, used the French *béance*—a term meaning "large hole or opening," but also the scientific term for the opening of the larynx—to signify gap, the opening to speech (Evans, 1996, p. 72). By contrast, Freud originally had named a body part, a body opening to mark the gap between the known and the unknown: the navel. In his *Interpretation of Dreams,* he concluded, "There is at least one spot in every dream at which it is unplumbable—a navel, as it were, that is its point of contact with the unknown" (Freud, 1900a, p. 111). But navel-gazing seemed to point only to another mystery that continually compelled Freud's attention, and that has compelled psychoanalytic theory ever since.

This quest to name and to know corresponds, in Lacan's thinking, to a kind of hysteria. Or rather, it is the hysteric who finds herself compulsively, almost erotically, driven to connect with a submerged and perhaps irretrievable state of prior innocence and prior truth, seeking an encounter with it, and so also eroticizing her pursuit of knowledge. In the words of Bruce Fink, "the truth of the hysteric's discourse, its hidden motor force, is the real" (1995, p. 134).

At the same time, the hysterics that guided Freud also revealed the self-contradictory nature of this desire (to know and to name) itself. It is perhaps not an accident that one of Freud's earliest case studies, with his famous "hysterical" patient Dora, involved a certain suggestive object that she initially fails to name. Paul Verhaeghe traces the way Freud traverses an obstacle course, seeking an (his) answer (the location of female sexuality within the Oedipal constellation) to Dora's question, while actually never pondering the real question. He turns to one association after another, tracing a "symbolic geography of sex" (Freud, 1900a, p. 99), exposing what Verhaeghe calls "a drawn-out search for a signifier which simply wasn't there" (1997, p. 63).

As Freud probes again and again for more detail regarding the attentions of her would-be lover Herr K., Dora finally reveals that he gave her a jewel-case, and then that she offered no "return-present." "Perhaps," Freud leads on, "you do not know that 'jewel-case' ... is a favorite expression … for the female genitals" (1905e, p. 69). When we dare to name, when (as Freud attempts here) we take "a leap towards the word," to symbolize the female genital, something remarkable becomes possible. We create an irrepressible space between the "thing" and the analogy, a space between truth and error, between reality and poetry. Moreover, when we dare to name, to symbolize, the female genital, something else remarkable becomes possible. The woman, too, is named: She gains an embodied, cultural location between private and public, she becomes visible, and equal. Thus the interplay between the act of naming the vaginal and the act of naming the Woman reveal themselves to be inextricably linked, the former so essential to the latter as to be its defining essence.

In his late seminar on what he called the *sinthome* (symptom), Lacan draws attention to the vulnerability we share to the oppressive, domesticating effects of language, but also to the ways in which we claim our unique subjectivity through "giving a little nudge" to the language that we speak—staying close, says Mari Ruti, to the "unruly energies of the real," to its transmission of jouissance to the signifier—without falling into its abyss (2012, pp. 121, 119). Perhaps it is because we lack faith in our poetic nature that we remain so vulnerable to the abyss. Perhaps because we doubt the durability of our metaphoric and real space, that we seek to dominate, to capture the ineffable "territory" that eludes us and that marks the frontier of sexual mystery/ knowledge—the frontier of "O."

Certainly there remains a widespread resistance to naming the female body, and to acknowledging what is particular to female sexual experience, negative or positive. This resistance and neglect serves to delegitimize what Dianne Elise (2000), adapting Freud's phrasing, calls women's "psychic geography," their way of understanding how their particular anatomy and biology position them in the world. This resistance is evident even within psychoanalysis, despite its dedication to exposing truths that have become camouflaged in symptoms that so often call attention to the body's muted knowledge. The same resistance is only greater and more comprehensive in our larger society, where it is not only women's sexual differences that are ignored (or subject to patriarchal surveillance), but their overall narratives. As one may imagine, this problem is particularly acute in repressive patriarchal societies, even when, in the wake of some sustained atrocity, they establish "truth commissions" to speak the hidden violence.

A major study of truth commissions and gender, as Priscilla Hayner details, revealed that many of them

> have failed women—the crimes they have suffered are under-reported, their voices are rendered inaudible, their depiction in commission reports is one-dimensional, and their needs and goals are deprioritized in recommendations for reparations, reform, and prosecutions. (Hayner, 2011, p. 86)

This failure reflects not only the psychological toll on women who share their stories, but a historical bias of truth commissions towards discounting the political motivations and dimensions of sexual abuse and crimes against women. Although progress has been made to expand the mandate of truth commissions to document women's stories, the challenge to do so remains daunting. And these are *truth commissions,* not corporate boardrooms or town hall meetings. When women's stories remain shrouded in silence, they are effectively wiped out from history, and when their voices are silenced and their bodies erased, they are thereby deprived of political and personal agency.

If psychoanalytic and democratic realization require placing the most private marker of the unknown into the sphere of knowability, how do we understand the resistance to naming? Winnicott, perhaps psychoanalysis's premier theorist of "space," had this to say late in his career:

> there is no getting round the fact that each man and woman *came out of a woman*. Attempts are made to get out of this awkward predicament.... We find that the trouble is ... that at first everyone was *absolutely* dependent on a woman, and then relatively dependent. (Winnicott, 1964, p. 191)

He goes on in his analysis to conclude that "somehow a hatred of this has to be transformed into a kind of gratitude if full maturity of the personality is to be reached" (ibid., p. 193).

Earlier (and even more boldly), Winnicott, insisting on the psychologist's responsibility to draw attention to unconscious factors, links our deep-rooted fears of the female with "democracy":

> [I]t is found that all individuals (men and women) have in reserve a certain fear of WOMAN.... This fear of WOMAN is

a powerful agent in society structure ... it is also responsible for the immense amount of cruelty to women, which can be found in customs that are accepted by almost all civilizations.... There is a debt to a woman. The original dependence is not remembered, and therefore the debt is not acknowledged.... As an offshoot of this consideration, one can consider the psychology of the dictator, who is at the opposite pole to anything that the word "democracy" can mean. *One of the roots of the need to be a dictator can be a compulsion to deal with this fear of woman by encompassing her and acting for her.* ... The dictator can be overthrown, and must eventually die; but the woman figure of primitive unconscious fantasy has no limits to her existence or power. (Winnicott, 1950, pp. 252–253)

Freud, for all his indicting of women and his hubristic proclamations of their genital inferiority, ultimately humbled himself, conceding to the elusive, enigmatic mystery of women—of their bodies, of their desire. (And at least in his imagination, he foresaw his ultimate surrender to the feminine, as it was the "silent Goddess of Death [that] will take [an old man] into her arms," 1913f, p. 301.) Furthermore, if, as he claimed, all psychological and political conflict was ultimately rooted in sexual repression, he came to believe that it was the repudiation of the feminine that constituted, for both sexes, psychological bedrock. I think that Freud and Winnicott would have both concurred with Justice Brandeis's remarks in *Whitney* vs. *California* (274 U.S. 357 (1927), at 376): "Men feared witches and burned women. It is the function of [free] speech to free men from the bondage of irrational fears."

CHAPTER SIXTEEN

Clinical interlude: the body announces itself

To free ourselves from fear, we must first learn to claim space. Claiming space—summoning space—is a critical stepping-stone to shared knowledge and to genuine discourse, which rest on the dialectic between female and male signifiers, between receptivity and potency, between interiority and penetration. But how do we make this claim? How do we begin to dismantle the defenses and resist the negations? Signposts illuminating this pathway emerge from our work in the clinic. Here, I offer anecdotes from my practice.

For many of us, the body will tenaciously resist before it will speak. As my patients fight (indeed, it is often a fight) to claim their desires and voices, their bodies protest, hurling back against the door that's beginning to open onto interior space, blocked by embarrassment, fury, and shame. One woman tells me of her torn cuticles; a man tells me of his deformed penis; a woman tells me of intrusive herpes symptoms.

The body emerges ingloriously, stripped of pride, discouraged. It is as if it were separating and dissociating from its own vitality. The mind announces its presence in a similarly dissociated fashion. Patients relate intrusive sexual fantasies, often experienced as not of their own making. One man tells me he is bombarded by images of performing oral sex upon demand. A woman tells me that she cannot masturbate without impinging images of her father insisting that she please him. A man cannot expose his desire without suffering episodic rashes that exceed mere blushing, diminishing his potential pride, reminding him and me of his vulnerability to shame.

At this stage of emergence, my patients are still very much in the throes of having *no* thoughts, of having *nothing* to say, except perhaps by covering once more the redundant, restrictive, circumscribed terrain that they've often traveled and shared with me. But, in tandem with having no thoughts, it appears that they are also revealing that they have *no body* that they can "own." That is, the inability to free associate is correlated, metaphorically and in actuality, with an inability to own bodily desire. They are describing a battle for their own agency as much as for mind and body. But as yet, they experience a relative sense of defeat as they try to claim their desire, with its wants and needs and insistence.

Some retreat into the silence of unmarked and unnamed territory, an interior abyss from which they cannot escape and into which they cannot delve and explore, describing an experience characterized far more by mystifying confusion than by intriguing mystery. Others seek to skip a step, becoming preoccupied with the phallic signifier they are as yet unable to wield—predicated as it is on first claiming a sense of interiority and space, naming that void, noting the presence of absence, that unknown but present space that marks the entry to wonder, and to knowledge. Sometimes they tell me of their relationships with phallic objects and their pursuit of phallic fantasies, their toying with guns, knives, cars, penis enlargement. Women, too, concretize phallic signifiers, sometimes as penis substitutes, sometimes as totems of female sexual power: clothing, hair, dildos.

One of my patients felt defined and burdened by the label of "ADD," the signifier of an identity he did not choose but that had been imposed upon him as a child. Several years into treatment, he finally drew his line in the sand. He refused to lie on my couch or use the chair in my office, insisting on sitting on the floor, positioning himself in nonconformist postures, sometimes leaning backwards, sometimes performing a headstand. "It's my body," he insisted, "and I'll do what I want with it." The claiming of his bodily boundary, this claiming of ownership, also marked an emergent space for sharing, without unwanted intrusion. While he would of course eventually have to deal with social limits on this avowed freedom, at this point in his development he could claim a profound, decisive victory in the battle for psychesoma—for personal agency.

A child in my practice takes his sketch pad and sprawls out on the floor between us. He draws, not telling me his intentions, and erases so quickly that it's hard for me to decipher his sketches. I begin to glimpse a pattern, as he becomes more brave, allowing the image to linger between us before he feels the need to erase. I wonder with him about the erasing. We talk about something missing, expunged—about his agenda in negating his own intentions and communication. We talk about what is at stake. These conversations have the quality of musings, *as if* something is at stake, but also as if interpreting, musing about his erasing, is what matters. Does he experience it as a requirement (of his perfectionism, of his need to keep control over exposing his desire, of what it means to share and to trust)? There is a space for him to erase, to modify, to decide to leave an indelible mark.

What becomes obvious to me is that he is dissatisfied with the images that he is drawing. A series of, well, perhaps mountains, perhaps breasts, concave and convex shapes that he seems to need to draw even as he can't quite allow them to take up space on his page. Finally, he produces a series of quite lovely mountainous shapes. He doesn't erase them. The next session, he opens his sketch pad. He looks at his images. He turns the page. He now has a new shape that he draws. Is it a triangle? It looks like the curvy breast-shaped, rounded figure from before. But now it is pointy. It looks more like a jagged mountain.

He erases. His next drawing is more elongated, a compressed mountainous shape, with an edge somewhere between being pointy and rounded. He is delighted, giddy. He tells me he has drawn a rocket! A projectile that is so powerful it enters far into *space*.

An adult male patient concedes that he feels like a fraud, an emperor with no clothes, acknowledging the limits of his faux phallic control. Throughout our work to date, he has sought to assert his dominance over me. But he now tells me he is shooting blanks, that he feels he can no longer have an impact this way. But at the same time, he is telling me of the silver lining that he now appreciates: that although they are blanks, he is able to "shoot" and begin to play with his power, even reveal his felt lack of power. He experiences an emergent sense of authentic agency now, no longer a faux potency or a defeated castration. Having located a (yet unclaimed, demeaned) capacity for "nothing," he is demonstrating the power of his mind to open space, to create meaning, and to begin to shoot "something" other than blanks. Without this capacity, we keep obscured not only the female metaphor, the vagina, but its powerful contribution to psychical life, for both genders, for the transgendered.

A woman in my practice mimes drawing a vase, a receptacle, describing it as vaginal space. She then talks about wanting to receive and to take. She tells me that her *vagina* exists; it is the first time that she has spoken the word between us, the space between us becoming more palpable even as the space within her becomes more real. She tells me that she breathes more deeply these days, that she doesn't experience digestive cramping as in the past. Soon, she tells me more about her experience of vaginal, interior space; that she is ready to receive a penis; that she desires impact; that she longs for an interpenetration of ideas and bodily communication; but that she had felt far too fragile before to desire this. She grows sad, pondering the losses that have accumulated from so many years in the "fog," while she was unable to articulate her own bodily experience. Unable to draw a boundary around her bodily space, she had remained unable to claim her private property, and thus unable to participate in the give and take of intimate and shared verbal and physical discourse—intercourse in all its senses.

This achievement, this capacity for shared exchange, so fundamental to the most intimate of relationships and to the most public, hinges on democratic discourse just as democratic discourse hinges on it. It unfolds in that "space between" angelological, telepathic, fusion-based longings, and in its mirror image: the realm of dissociated, disembodied, even brute physicality. We must create that space in between, one that always requires letting go of longings for unmediated direct contact, perfect union. We must also surrender our longings for a sacred, omnipotent, private sphere, where we may rule "incommunicado" (cf. Winnicott, 1963b). As John Durham Peters observed, "Communication involves a permanent kink in the human condition" (1999, p. 29). We can never communicate like the angels; this is a tragedy and a blessing. Peters cites Adorno's comment on our inescapable alienation from each other but our equally inescapable longing to bridge it: "The ideal of communication ... would be a condition in which the only thing that survives the disgraceful fact of our difference is the delight that that difference makes possible" (ibid., p. 31).

A man with whom I have worked for years, and who has insisted on making me his "angel" or "mother," now decides that his fantasies have cost him a real relationship with me. As long as I was cast in these roles, he had no real opportunity to "know" me, or to engage in a real relationship, or to know *himself* as an authentic man with his own desires and power. He tells me, "You're too abstract. I need you to be more real. I want to know you. Angels have no genitals. I want to make love not to my therapist or to a doctor or to an angel, but to *you.*" He no longer sees me as an icon; he buries the plaster figure and resurrects me as a human being, as a *woman.* He begins a new conversation by telling me of his curiosity about the vagina, the mysteries of private and interior space. In this conversation, his "I" is touchingly linked with his penis. But in contrast to the way society often mocks men for being ruled by their anatomy, he tells me of the vulnerability he experiences when his penis is erect. He tells me of his wish to penetrate but, what's more, his longing to be held, shrouded, to be longed for and to be "belonged" by a (my) vagina. He is excited, and we're both poised, and precariously unpoised, between fear and desire.

A dialogue has begun. It is the very human dialogue between fear and desire, between disembodiment and embodiment, between dissociation and free association. We've created a platform between the mystical and the knowable, between the psychical and the material, and between each other, for intimacy, challenge, and, yes, inclusivity and sharing—democratic relatedness.

CHAPTER SEVENTEEN

Free speech on the playground of desire

Knowing and not knowing

We previously explored how naming is related to knowing, and how metaphor is related to the ever-elusive real. We saw that as symbolizing creatures, human beings may have lost access to things in themselves, which are unspeakable and ultimately unknowable. In describing how human beings develop as *speaking* creatures, we focused on our experiences as *infants*—creatures "unable to speak." We considered how the primal, immersive, sensation-dominated, and wordless world of infants and mothers is disrupted as we become aware of our separateness and limited power.

This primal loss initiates a lifelong experience of negotiating the gap between the immediate and the mediated; of longing for (re)union and emancipation. Freud understood as the origin of the maturational challenge the necessity both to surrender to what is (unconsciously) determined, and to exercise choice and self-determination. In this space between the given and the gained, the determined and the free, we must realize our power to speak, to emerge from symbolic infancy. With words and symbols, we bridge that gap between mute, subterranean desires and spoken narratives.

Let us explore how this dialectic emerges in our earliest attachments with our primary caregivers and later with others who surround us. Psychoanalytic theory is based on the understanding that what happened in the past gives us insight into our adult relationships with families, lovers, peer groups, and society. Put differently, as we repeat ourselves in words, reactions and transference, *the present* reveals a portrait of what happened in the past, before we had words and means to name our experience and claim this knowledge. This insight helps us understand why free association is so difficult to practice; why free speech is so hard to maintain, even when afforded social and legal protections; why, even when we attempt to name, we also long to *bypass* naming.

Freud encountered this tendency to avoid naming and knowing early in his career. In *Studies on Hysteria* (1895), written with his colleague Josef Breuer, he noted that the buried knowledge he sought to expose through free association was knowledge that the patient was hiding not only from Freud, but also from herself. As a consequence, when free association does bring to light hidden experiences, feelings, and ideas, they seem to the patient both *familiar* and *strange*. In "this strange state of mind … one knows and does not know a thing at the same time" (Freud & Breuer, 1895d, p. 117fn).

Freud, pondering this paradox, which would practically define psychoanalysis, landed upon the concept of the "uncanny." After closely studying the history and current usage of the word, *unheimlich* in German, he concluded that it signifies objects and experiences that are both frightening *and* familiar (1919h, p. 220). The uncanny is paradoxically something beyond our familiar knowledge, yet linked— through free association and free speech—to what is most familiar: our origins and home (*heimlich* denotes "homely" in the sense of "homelike"). This paradox raises a central psychoanalytic question: Why do patients seek out "strangers" to engage in the most intimate conversation of their lives? Perhaps by exploring the mechanisms of early attachments we will be able to answer this question and shed light on challenges presented by psychoanalytic and democratic ambitions.

Attachment, courage, and agency

Attachment theory is an area of psychology devoted to studying early patterns of attachment, and it is a theory with which psychoanalysis has had an ambivalent relationship. Originally developed by John

Bowlby in the 1960s and 1970s, this theory addresses the early need for security through attachment to another. It describes and classifies mother-infant attachment patterns on a scale from relatively secure to relatively insecure. Through empirical studies attachment theory demonstrates the lasting effects of early attachment patterns on a host of lifelong developmental phenomena.

Bowlby's original understanding (1969) was grounded in biology and ethology (the study of animal behavior). At that time he saw attachment as a *behavioral* system involving "proximity seeking." In the face of frightening experiences, the child instinctively seeks the physical closeness of a protective figure. But over time Bowlby and his followers' ideas became more psychological, eventually interesting those who pursued intersubjective and relational approaches within psychoanalysis. Paul Wachtel (2010)[1] illuminates how both contemporary attachment theory and relational psychoanalysis share a similar "two-person" perspective. This dovetailing creates an opportunity for these two fields to explore how the odd bedfellows intimacy and strangeness speak to each other. In tandem, the two fields may help us better understand how we experience a wide range of relationships that depend on the familiarity of comfort and security as well as the strangeness that leads to excitement and a sense of freedom.

Attachment research is based on observations of infants' interactions with their caregivers (typically mothers) in the context of a "separation and reunion" research paradigm. The classification of a child's attachment as secure or insecure has proven to be an important and highly reliable predictor of functioning later in life (see, e.g., Cassidy & Shaver, 1999). Secure attachment relationships are directly related to the confidence needed to explore and sustain curiosity in one's environment and independent desire. Therefore, "secure" attachment classifications predict not only internal security but also the ability to freely explore and engage with the world in adulthood.

By dint of our human design, according to Bowlby, we seek strong attachments to help us survive, as they provide emotional shelter from external threats. In turn, this "secure base" fosters initiative and exploratory behavior. It is but a short leap to infer that it also fosters free association. Attachment relationships allow personal agency and intentionality through which we gain the ability to wander into serendipitous discovery. Far beyond a narrowed conception of our need for protection from external threat, seeking attachment is an expression of our *intent*, our *agenda*.

Contemporary psychoanalysis suggests that we seek attachment not only for security *needs*, but because we are inherently relational beings: our sense of self is constituted *in relationship*. Further, it suggests that personal desire and mutual recognition emerge in tandem. We need and want to be wanted. We desire and want to be desired, to express ourselves through mutual desire. Along this pathway of desire, we become knowable to ourselves and to others, and we come to know others. Through owning our intentions and taking the responsibility and the risk to signal our truthful desires to a personal but also symbolic other (with her own independent desire), we gain a "subjectified" status. We become *personal* subjects (Slavin, 2010) but also *transitional* subjects, with a foothold in private but also symbolic life (Gentile, 2007, 2008). This step advances our quest for both self-knowledge and intimacy. It is only when the patient dares to expose her thoughts and desires within a *specific* attachment relationship, one in which the analyst assumes personal significance even as he *also* comes to assume *symbolic* status as Other for her, that attachment security or free association—or for that matter, transference love—becomes possible. And this involves *naming* desire.

Needing to name desire complicates our achieving the twinned goals of personal agency and free and open social discourse and assembly (free "association"). Exposing desire renders us both powerful *and* vulnerable. We tend to mind the vulnerability more than we enjoy the power; therefore we hide our desire even from ourselves. Thus we avoid self-knowledge, the source of much of our power in the world, defeating our impulses to know and be known through desire and curiosity. As we free associate and speak freely with those who matter to us, we release our voice from repressive constraints—we discover agency and of courage. And in this release, we relinquish our fantasied control over the Other's desire, and we launch our discovery of a new frontier, between the familiar and the strange.

Attachment theory, semiotic agency, and the talking cure

As we explore the relationship between democracy and the "talking cure," free speech and free association, we better appreciate how, as *homo sapiens*, we are born as *signing* creatures. Semiotics, the theory of communication systems, offers us a bridging lens to clarify the complex connections among signs and symbols, naming and knowledge, and the capacity to form attachments, communicate, and share desire.

Empirical studies have demonstrated clear links between maternal sensitivity and the capacity for reflective functioning, which is a kind of *semiotic* signaling ("I can 'read' your feelings"), and attachment security, including a child's acquired capacity to signal his own needs and desires and to, in effect, manage his own feelings through such semiotic capability. John Muller, who has interpreted Lacanian thought from a semiotic perspective (Muller, 1996), argues that it is the grounding of mother[2] and infant (as well as analyst and patient) in a semiotic code that enables them to transcend their dyadic relationship, therefore grounding them in the cultural, linguistic, social world beyond them.

As we have seen, this code grounds the dyad in its creation of space, the space of *thirdness*. By naming the female signifier, we acknowledge the gendered, unnamed dimensions of this space, thereby advancing our quest to symbolize what exceeds our grasp, what continually eludes the sphere of naming and knowing. Mother embarks on this pursuit as she interprets her infant's gesture and finds herself and her experience in a layering of "between-ness"—between her material body and her "immaterial" mind, between her and the infant, between her and the physical-social-cultural world, and between her own inner representations of her attachment figures. These personal figures are also metaphoric conduits between presymbolic and symbolic worlds. What Lacan referred to as the *Name-of-the-Father* marks the child's initiation into the realm of shared culture and speech, extending beyond the mother-infant relationship. In the language of semiotics, the developing child (or patient, respectively) becomes capable of using signs and symbols to effectively communicate intent and desire. This developmental advance fosters an evolving *space* (in his mind, and between his mind and body) to play with ideas, without resorting to brute force imposition of speech acts and without paralysis of thought and imagination.

Through this communicative process, mother facilitates for child what has become known as a capacity for "mentalization" (Fonagy, Gergely, Jurist, & Target, 2002)—a capacity to reflect, interpret reality, play with meaning, and experience mental freedom. Mother's dedication to her infant's capacity to signify intent and desire not only empowers her infant as a semiotically capable agent, but also facilitates his attachment security. Both semiotic agency and attachment security may be understood as requiring a space *between*—between separation and reunion, between proximity seeking and exploration.

How dissociation becomes free association

Moving on from this we may begin to answer the question that began this chapter. A sense of personal agency, for desire and for leaving a mark on the world, requires a lifelong pursuit of discovering the familiar in the strange, and the strange in the familiar. In analysis, the analyst offers through transference an opportunity in which desire and curiosity might be experienced rather than repressed or disavowed. Within this relationship the stranger/analyst becomes a substitute for someone familiar while at the same time emblematizing the strange, the unknown, the "other" in the familiar.

This achievement requires as much talking as listening, and both require a courage and discipline that we avoid in everyday conversation. It is in this conversation, between a freely associating patient and an analyst's free-floating attention, that something authentic and "truthful" materializes and becomes the basis for a mutual, secure, and ultimately ethical attachment. Typically, free association and attachment theory have not been considered together, nor do we think about free association as signifying an attachment relationship even if we nod to its status as a form of address. But what do we seek when we ask for free association? We ask for exploration and authenticity in the presence of another. We are asking for personal and moral agency and a willingness to surrender control that is *enabled* by secure attachment and also *promotes* secure attachment. We ask for a sustained, honest, truth-telling conversation that guides self-determined agency and collective action.

This is a great deal to ask, and a great deal to offer. As we have seen, free association is a means of both discovering and experimenting with revelation and retreat, exposure and hiding. In this respect, it shares elements of Enlightenment ideals of scientific experimentation while fostering something like play. D. W. Winnicott, arguably psychoanalysis's premier theorist of play (and of space), recognized that, for many patients and analysts, considerable psychic work must be done before play can begin. What this "work" yields is a capacity to sustain a dialectic, a "potential space"—between mother and child, between fantasy and reality, between constraint and imagination, between the familiar and the strange.

This *space between* becomes the *sine qua non* for our play and for our own subjective freedom—our capacity to freely associate, and to associate freely, beyond our familiar attachments. We begin to discover attachment security and to trust an Other who lies beyond our control, one who survives the play even when it gets rough, threatening to violate the rules of the game. These benefits of free association are often unrecognized, because we tend to highlight the workings of one's own mind and body, or to highlight the mutual co-construction of analytic dialogue that both downplays the agency of the distinctive subjects who construct that dialogue and disregards "free association" as a legacy of an outdated intrapsychic model. We forget that the capacity to free associate is achieved (if ever) through the transference, that is, in the presence of someone else—someone who remains present and listens and keeps playing, even when we show our darkest, unruly, shamefully violent and eroticized sides, someone who is paradoxically situated between past and present, familiar and stranger.

Winnicott's understanding of the extraordinary liberating power of being alone in someone else's presence—a means of "coming into being" (1958b; 1960, p. 43; 1963a, p. 75)—sets the stage for free association founded on a secure primary attachment relationship. And contrary to common views, Freud's therapeutic philosophy also allowed for play in the treatment relationship. He conceived of transference as "a playground in which it is allowed to expand in *almost* complete freedom" (1914g, p. 154, emphasis added). "Almost" is key: it marks constraint that creates the possibility for play rather than pandemonium. Jacques Derrida's conception of language as *freeplay*—as a "field of infinite substitutions only because it is finite, because there is something missing from it" (1978, p. 260)—homes in on this essential tension.

This evolution both enables and requires the analyst to invest in the relationship on a deeply personal level, while sustaining a professional commitment to it. This reciprocity is located between two strangers who become familiar, and between two who are familiar yet become strangers. The hallmark of mutual recognition is an encounter between two subjects, each of whom resists assimilation and insists instead upon his alterity, which therefore facilitates a secure attachment.

Erotics and attachment: towards a third space

I have discussed attachment as a matter of security and means to mutual recognition, but this is not where the story ends. For once a space is open for the free expression of one's desires, one is playing in an arena of meaning that Freud identified as psychologically fundamental, and that is rarely associated with feelings of security—namely, sexual meaning and the realm of the inaccessible taboo. Adam Phillips, rendering the implicitly unsettling nature of Freud's conjecture, reminds us that "because sexuality begins in incestuous fantasy, it always smacks of the forbidden" (1993, p. 16). When we venture to freely associate, to expose our desires in relationships that involve both the familiar and the strange, we also expose, in some fashion, our formerly taboo erotic desires.

This hints at the stakes of reconciling attachment theory with a psychological picture of the emergence of mutual recognition between freely associating subjects of desire. It suggests a possible reunion of contemporary psychoanalysis with attachment theory. Moreover, it connects to its own ancestry and origins in infantile sexuality. It also puts in context and humanizes the psychoanalytically compelling metaphor from non-linear dynamic systems theory of the "strange attractor." Jean-Michel Quinodoz (1977, p. 702) calls attention to how the strangeness of the attractor reflects antagonistic tendencies—attraction toward and divergence from it.

The concept of strange attractor relates to Freud's hypothesis of forbidden desire. As subjects of desire, and as sexually-driven creatures, we must begin coping with strange feelings before we can name them. For the "strange" of desire is part of our most familiar world from the moment we first feel that our overwhelming need for reunion with mother will never again be fully requited. From the very start, Freud marked his discovery of the erotic impulses of childhood as Other, describing them as "strange," as "alien" to the psyche (Verhaeghe, 1997, p. 28), and the primal familiar/strange—"uncanny"—relationship in our lives is the family triangle. This triangle has been a fundamental subject of classical psychoanalysis almost since its origin. Freudian theory posits that incestuous, "Oedipal" fantasy is a universal human experience, and that because of that fact, such fantasies are taboo. This taboo on desire and forbidding of acknowledgment (knowledge) result in repression and defensive solutions that compromise free association and free speech. To attain free association, we must reclaim our forbidden desires in relationships with others. These others who were familiar now become *defamiliarized and erotically reconceived.*

Put another way: To be in the world, we must contend with others not just as personalities or voices, but also as material bodies, intellectually, emotionally, and physically charged. We must contend not only with others' thoughts and wishes, but also with their physical needs and drives. This, in turn, means we must contend with our *own* physical needs and drives, which Lacan calls jouissance. For without the body, there is no medium for expression or communication. As John Durham Peters says, "The body is not a vehicle to cast off; it is the homeland to which we are traveling" (1999, p. 65). At the same time, we should resist the reductive materialism so often attributed to Freud's claim that "anatomy is destiny" (1912d, p. 189). Our physical characteristics and differences may indeed contribute to how we "fit" in, or differ from, others. But the challenge of fulfilling our status as gendered subjects begins with Freud's proposition, which requires us to *interpret* difference.

Along this path, as we accept and interpret the body, we begin to glimpse an opening. This opening is a third space between the silenced, repressed, and taboo, and what is freely spoken, symbolized, embodied. Such a third space is implicit in Freud's original concept of the Oedipal family configuration—a relation of three, mother/father/child. As Paul Verhaeghe explains:

> The child must evolve from a dualistic relationship and has to make later and elsewhere a choice to create something, namely an identity of its own in relation both to the Other and to its own drive. If this succeeds, the oedipal structure has carried out its function. (Verhaeghe, 2009, p. 88)

This conception locates desire in a space between the family and the erotic other, between our early attachment figures and those to whom we later become erotically attached.

But there is an intermediary step. Andrea Celenza (2010) reflected, "all treatments must revolve, at some level, around the question, 'Why can't we be lovers?'" (p. 66)—a conversation, of course, usually reserved for when a sexual relationship is realistically possible. Because psycho-analysis's special province consists of, and insists on, a verbal discourse on desire, this distinctly (quintessentially) psychoanalytic conversation of the unspoken taboo becomes possible in sustained analyses. Guided by the revelation of hitherto inaccessible longings, it compels us to rec-ognize and *to reconceive* our attachment figures as eroticized others. We come to recognize them as subjects of their own desires, as we contend with the presence of our lack, and our inability to fulfill their desire.

This lack challenges us to grapple with the messy animating presence of our own longings, essential to our destiny as desiring and alienated subjects. Since our parents were both primary attachment figures *and* Oedipal partners and rivals, we follow a singular trajectory of desire, conditioned by these familial "lovers" and their inevitable loss as romantic partners. But in that space between longing and re-finding, we search for traces of what Lacan called "the Thing," the primordial deprivation and loss of an "originary (lost) object of desire" (Evans, 1996, p. 207).

If we are lucky, in our travails along the trail of desire, we find such inspiration. We find others who compel our vulnerability and our awe. We experience passion and quandary. Our sense of completion and joy is precariously coincident with our utter sense that what we seek remains elusive, that we long for what is "beyond" our posses-sion and our comprehension. We discover previously inaccessible and undiscovered, if oddly familiar, dimensions in ourselves and in others. We become subjects, then, because we are subject to the impact of the strange familiar Other on, and for, the very constitution of our strangely familiar desire.

Through this journey, we find "something strange to me, although it is at the heart of me" (Lacan, 1959–1960, p. 71). Longings, rooted in our primal origins, insinuate us into relationship, just as they insinuate us into a discourse on desire. We finally begin to find a path to relation-ships of equality, mutual recognition, democracy. We can now see that the talking cure—constituted as it is by talking, listening, translating, interpreting—is a discourse grounded in triangular space. This talking admits to a sphere of impossibility, a jouissance that cannot be named or regulated. When the triangular space that defines the Oedipus complex is joined with the triangular space inherent in dialogue, we begin to recognize that the dialectic between security of attach-ment and associative freedom—that is, an ethical space of speech—is fundamental to the achievement of attachment security, free association, and the playground of desire. This ethical space carries a price and is priceless. It is an inherently disruptive, incessant discourse of desire and revelation that guides self-determined action.

We are compelled by the prospect of discovering something new through freedom, of speech, assembly, and association. But our instincts also draw us to that which is familiar, or even *too* familiar. We cling to what we know just as we cling to what we refuse to know (the taboo). We repeat ourselves and flatten our public and private discourse. What looks like free speech sometimes forbids new interpretation and ideas. We domesticate desire and we domesticate democracy.

Both psychoanalysis and democracy promise freedom from inner and outer forms of tyranny, promising personal and collective sovereignty, while admitting an inevitable measure of subjection. But both have suffered a shift away from ideals of sovereignty and towards the *institutionalization* of the very practices aimed to advance it. As John Dunn observes,

> Representative democracy is democracy made safe for the modern state: democracy converted from unruly and incoherent master to docile and dependent servant. To an Athenian eye this version of democracy would seem not so much tamed ... as *neutered*—denatured, and deprived of all generative energy and force of its own. (1993, p. 248)

Within the history of psychoanalysis, it is almost commonplace to observe the conservative, if not neutering and denaturing, impact of institutional practices and their means of judging legitimacy of individual members (or of sets of ideas) on an otherwise inherently radicalizing and subversive theory and practice (e.g., Kirsner, 2000).

When we contemplate the core of democracy as "a political system of citizen self-rule," and the core of psychoanalysis as a psychological theory and practice of the patient's capacity for self-rule, we discern what is missing. Namely, the *lack* in the subjects' or citizens' powers of self-agency. We simply cannot *own* our, or anyone else's, freedom. Without a conception of surrender to what lies beyond law, our possibilities for lawful personal or collective agency diminish to the vanishing point. But when we return to the founding rules—the First Amendment, the fundamental rule, Lacan's paternal law—we discover that they all simultaneously obscure and privilege the primacy of space. We discover an elusive, but nonetheless potent, feminine law. This law, or metaphor, honors an ethical *space between* us, between our desires and actions, between softness and firmness.

When we borrow psychoanalytic insights and create a bridge, a third space, we enable forbidden erotic desire and provide an outlet for ideas that are creative, challenging, and nearer to "truth." Free associations enable and are enabled by our freedom of assembly: we create new associations and shared alliances, not least of all with truthful discourse. What we assimilate and what remains abject or unknown shifts; naming and knowledge expand, but limits remain. We discover that we no longer need to live in reactive fear and repression; we can rather sustain a sense of purpose, collective solidarity and meaning-creation through speech.

Safety, much like freedom, is at best a relative, and perhaps entirely illusory, phenomenon, and fear, as Dunn notes (1993, pp. 265–266), "is just as democratic (and just as important) an emotion as hope." But experiments in democracy, beginning with those in Classical Greece, also give "long and enduring lesson[s] in reasonable hope" that "as long as there continue to be human beings," the "voice of democracy" will not be silenced. Psychoanalytic practice too shows that people, when reasonably enabled, will seek personal and collective agency rather than subjugation by repressive authority. As sufficient confidence in the foundational (third) space of free speech emerges—in the microculture of the clinic or the macroculture of civic society—emancipatory personal, political, and communal acts of ethical agency become possible. As we, analysands and citizens, come to experience security *and* freedom necessary to give us the courage to speak truth in a space between private and public, we come nearer to a practice of enhanced free association, which broadens our freedom of assembly, our *freedom of association* (Kris, 1996, p. 3).

CHAPTER EIGHTEEN

Coda: homeland security and the secure home base

> I sensed that there was a beyond, to which I did not have access, an unlimited place … a desire was seeking its home.
>
> —Hélène Cixous (1991, p. 1)

The transference of faith and freedom

Alexis de Tocqueville observed that democracy is a faith-based regime, founded upon and secured by not a god or gods, not princes or a king, but "the people" (Meaney & Mounk, 2014). We transfer our faith from father figures to our brothers and sisters—and to ourselves. Psychoanalytic practice also requires faith, and *transference* of faith to that liminal relationship between past and present, between repetition and recreation. Freud, early in his career, believed that "every patient is in a state of expectation colored by faith" (1905a, p. 258). Despite his qualms that faith merely leads us into illusion, he well understood that it was precisely by this faithful transference that psychoanalysis works its magic. In this book I have attempted to reclaim that space between truth and illusion, between naming and what resists knowing, between the magical and the material. Only in this space may psychoanalysis prosper.

We began our tale in a world still suffused with magic. Freud dabbled in that world, but soon launched his revolutionary attack on magical thinking, to build a science that would expose false idols and rescue us from superstition. His quest for the natural laws—the secret truths—of human nature led him onto the field of speech. There, in transference, he found the path by which memory takes on a physical dimension where it is articulated not just in speech but also in repetitive behavior (Bohleber, 2007, p. 329). A fidelity to transference, despite ourselves, would keep us honest, lead us toward truth.

The pathways of association are not only private; they join public thoroughfares. Free association finds its public echo in the practice of democracy, whose odyssey has been "unprecedented in the history of human speech" (Dunn, 2014, p. 91). Both democracy and psychoanalysis evolved as rebukes to repression and tyranny. They both established imaginative sets of ideas and practices for helping people claim the power of self-rule. Both aspired to principles of inclusive and participatory self-governance. Both claimed a progressive enlightenment born of truth-seeking (reason and truth) and soul-searching (passion and faith).

Yet both were also predicated upon, and reinforced, various exclusions. Freud discerned that "the hypnotic spell" a doctor casts upon his patients might lead to anesthesia and accommodation rather than self-authorization. His rebellion against mesmerism and its subjugating power fit nicely into democratic and egalitarian traditions, but it also pulled us off the neat, domesticated Enlightenment path straightened by reason's rule over the passions. Freud would not have been surprised to discover that, for all of democracy's achievements in promoting individual will, it too tends to cast a "hypnotic spell"; it too raises and worships false idols (Dunn, 2014, p. 91).

Arriving at the seemingly contradictory conclusion that "If [man] has no faith, he must serve and if he is free, he must have faith" (Tocqueville, 1835, p. 419), Tocqueville anticipated the "area of faith" (Eigen, 1981) central to Winnicott's intermediary or transitional space—the *sine qua non* "space between"—where we also may get lost, or fall under a spell. In fact, its viability and endurance requires that we allow it to remain unbroken. But it's not a hypnotic or anaesthetizing spell. Far from it. In this third space, it is faith as "a scientific state of mind" as Bion puts it (1977, p. 32): a faith in "O," a "faith that there is an ultimate reality and truth. Michael Eigen (psychoanalyst *qua* mystic) explains,

> One cannot "regulate" the movement of truth.... To try to control where truth will lead is to put oneself above truth, and so, in part, shut out the potentially reorienting effects of the latter. To maximize the possibility of contact with what is most important for becoming at one with oneself, the subject must relate to truth with faith. (Eigen, 1981, pp. 424–425)

This faithful dimension—what Tocqueville described as a "disinterested love of truth" (Mansfield, 2010, p. 650)—coexists peacefully with at least notional scientific aims. Joined by their fidelity to a space between, and by their ever-evolving, experientially expansive, imperfect pursuits and practices, psychoanalytic and democratic missions also inevitably inspire turbulent, awakening, dislocating, illuminating, and even practical, cultural and symbolic effects.

Jacques Derrida wrote of democracy what psychoanalysts learn time and again in the consulting room: that "a future worth having is a future that is experienced as yet to come" (Glendinning, 2011, p. 95). Psychoanalysts would add that this future will include an experience of a past never fully consciously experienced and therefore never mourned but also never known. We approach a future "worth having" by striving—guided by our wanting—towards a "we don't know what" (ibid., p. 92) that belongs as much to the past as to the future.

More poetically, dramatically, and even psychoanalytically, novelist Rachel Kushner puts it this way: "We want and our want kills doom. This is how we take the future and occupy it like an empty warehouse" (2013, p. 74).

Detours from desire's enlightenment

Many seek psychoanalytic treatment because they've been raised in families and within contexts and cultures that practice bad faith, exploiting (if often unwittingly) the naïve and tempestuous longings of childhood. Contemporary America, broadly speaking, is such a culture. Our sacrifices to the neoliberal idol have yielded little, and for most of us yield *nothing* of the space *between*. We too seldom sense the reverberations of O, that "spacing essence of freedom" (Nancy, 1988, p. 145). Our democratic faith, our system of belief, has consequently suffered. Today's disenchanting gaps in wealth and in access to power signal a crisis of democratic faith.

If we are inured to these depressing developments, then my hope is that psychoanalysis may help. Psychoanalysis is perpetually unsettled but inevitably secured by its fidelity to desire and to the transference to which desire speaks. It is positioned in the space, between law and transgression, where the unconscious voices its desire, the space opened by and for speech and symbolization, with all their constraints and impediments. For these reasons, it may help foster the conditions not only for libidinous desire to break forth, but also for democratic desire to blossom, for truth to be spoken, and for novel ideas to find fertile soil.

Of course, there is now a proliferation of virtual platforms and outlets for ordinary American citizens to voice their opinions (to claim self-representation) with little fear of harsh repercussions. But it's also true that a "digital divide," paralleling inequality on other speech platforms, marks the inability of economically disadvantaged households to acquire broadband access and thus to truly engage in contemporary debate. Meanwhile, as the population shifts and clusters, and as voting districts are locked down ideologically, the American landscape is, like the Webscape, breaking into increasingly homogeneous and polarized blocs. We're finding it easier and easier to avoid alien views; many of us preach only to our own choirs. Even then, we hold back lest we reveal any conspicuous difference from those Tocqueville called our "semblables." Thus we miss chances for a broader understanding and for mutual impact, and most of us, most of the time lack direct access to government institutions, officials, or assemblies. Instead we entrust representatives to hear *both* the voice of our (individual) speech *and* that of the collective. But when our voices are inaudible to that Other, or that Other betrays our trust, free association and free speech suffer in silence and in symptom.

Just as psychoanalytic patients must surrender their omnipotent fantasies in order to claim their singular voice and a sense of meaningful belonging to society, "self-styled emancipators of the market" (Wordsworth, 1818, p. 254) must recognize the inescapability of our global (capital) interdependence. It is naturally well beyond this book—or my expertise—to map this story, but catastrophe (or redemption) hinges on matters central to both democracy and psychoanalysis: free speech and freedom of assembly.

Free speech, be it democratic or psychoanalytic, is the lever that redistributes voice. Of course, this can't be true when moneyed speech, which skews any plausibly representative democracy, is equated with individual voice. If the movement of unconscious elements, of desire, of libido, characterizes free association, then impediments to free association (and speech) spell trapped desire and blocked insight. Desire that can't sustain its fluid motion in speech, because it is congealed, gives rise to symptoms. And it takes no great leap of logic to suggest that the flow of desire (speech), when disrupted by inequities in the accumulation and blockages in the circulation of capital, creates societal symptoms. Such resistance bypasses the triadic space of democratic speech and instead operate in a brute force, dyadic realm of power, dividing the culture into haves and have-nots. The victory of moneyed speech, then, is a failure of democratic speech, because democratic speech requires surrender, and this surrender is, I've suggested, to the feminine signifier that marks its fertile open space.

The "content" of speech in a grossly unequal system is, as clinical experience reveals, inevitably replete with bitterness, fury, resentment, humiliation, shame, and despair. These are the experiential companions of discourse that is sequestered in semiotic (and structural) confinement. If money is ever to act as a genuine proxy for free speech, then it too must be released from the labyrinths built to protect privilege and power, and to frustrate practical freedom. We truly exercise freedom only within the constraints that open a space for the agile flow of desire and its symbols. That is, genuinely freely speaking capital would animate passions beyond those of resentment and hate and greed. Democratic cures, like psychoanalytic ones, require speaking truth to power, enlisting the voice of the marginalized in the franchise of speech, surviving destruction, liberating desire. The content of *that* conversation, however sentimental, naïve, and idealized it may sound to say, is one of freedom and truth—but also of hope, compassion, generosity, excitement, courage, love, and a striving toward equality, despite actual and inevitable compromises with inequality.

Having and having not

My central aim has been to explore the unchartered terrain linking the psychoanalytic project with our Constitutional project. I have argued that as it matured in theory and in practice, psychoanalysis discovered

ways of opening spaces for the silenced to speak. Even as it remains prob-
lematically an "elite technique," as Walker Percy dubbed it, it provides
a method of cure springing from a *common* human design—the talking
cure—to which "the patient can, by reason of his own gifts, also aspire"
(1975, p. 213). In this sense, psychoanalysis is not only a practice of transitional subjectification as I've elsewhere argued (Gentile, 2007, 2008,
2010, 2013); it is also a practice of transitional *democracy*.

Psychoanalysis has tended to frustrate its own aspirations to communicate its relevance; so its destiny as a democratizing force may seem
improbable. When it comes to theory, or even broader claims to social
power, we have after all talked mostly to each other; and even then,
our speech practices are hardly free of polarizing political and theoretical *partis pris*. But I also believe our reach is limited because we have
undertheorized, until very recently, the means whereby patients cross
the divide between symptomatic solipsism and the larger realm of free
and public discourse. Cultivating the space essential to democratic and
analytic freedom is an especially critical goal when the subject's speaking abilities (and thus sense of agency) have been most undermined. But
it is this nascent state—where the collapse of the very space upon which
free speech is founded has become a deeply embedded, felt reality—
that we most need to articulate a robust model of how to emancipate
free speech, how to liberate personal and collective sovereignty.

Freud's practice of free association combined two signature
freedoms: free speech and freedom of assembly. The freedom to speak
raw, emergent desire arose in the context as well as under the constraints
of relationship (transference). Psychoanalytic speech, like democratic
speech, introduces the familiar to the stranger, the stranger to the familiar.
Individual and collective destinies meet in this opening for unconscious
emergence, wherein (self-)sovereignty admits its own limits, because
it arises in relational encounter and is perpetually defined by its roots
in the triangular space between freedom and constraint, knowledge
and the unnamed. Nonetheless, through speaking the patient names
and shares unspoken desires and forbidden knowledge. She gains a
capacity mutually resonant with the exercise of what is granted (in the
U.S.) as her First Amendment privilege. She assumes her status at the
interstices between a marginalized and an empowered semiotic agent,
gradually learning to claim what the framers of the Constitution implicitly understood as an inalienable right (at least for white men). And as
she does so, she not only assumes a measure of self-determination but
also a capacity for ethical action and democratic self-government in the

collective sphere. There, "being-in-common" arises from the sharing of being (Nancy, 1988, p. 73).

But there remains a significant and widening gap between those who do and those who don't have access to speech and the means for being heard. I have accentuated the gender inequities perpetuated by psychoanalysis, in the process regrettably neglecting other discriminatory barriers to inclusiveness: class, race, ethnicity, disability, sexual orientation, etc. These barriers continue to disgrace psychoanalytic and democratic projects, but gender, constructed or innate, is also metaphorical, and as such stands for other conditions and identities that suffer discrimination (Dunn, 2005, p. 170). However valid and substantive, it is merely one point of pressure that reminds us that our Constitutional project remains unfulfilled not only because it is a necessarily remote ideal, but also because we have yet to find a way to honor all voices, the quiet as well as the loud, the disadvantaged as well as the privileged. Achieving universal access to free speech requires ongoing and mutually reinforcing collective—*and* judicial and legislative—action.

For the Constitution's framers, free speech (including freedom of thought and religion) was bound to "the right of the people to peaceably assemble." Fulfilling these First Amendment guarantees requires acts of courage, as we have been reminded from the Civil Rights era to the present—courage to express our ideas, regardless of how provocative or offensive, and the attendant courage to listen and hear, even when others' ideas are disturbing or wounding.

From both democratic and psychoanalytic perspectives, freedom from repression makes way for free speaking and free thinking. Those who take on the challenge of free association's odyssey, daring to name untold truths, surrendering to the guidance of desire's law, are more able to claim their voices in innovative ways. We become able to participate in, without becoming subservient to, hegemonic discourse—promoting more active, vibrant, and efficacious initiative. What is good for the health of the individual is also good for the health of the polis.

Encouraging courage

The mutual requirement of expression and hearing, secured and even strengthened by difference and change, embeds in our political order something very like attachment security. In debates over the Civil Rights Act of 1866, John Bingham made a passionate case for equal protection of both "the citizen and stranger within your gates" (Amar, 1998, p. 172). Bingham, witnessing the brutalities of slavery and the tragedies of civil war, recognized that when we reduce each other to the unnamed and unnameable, we miss opportunities for mutual recognition and shared exploration. Such defensive solutions bring illusory comforts but fail to yield *genuine* security.

A refusal to speak and to respect the freedom to speak "the thought that we hate" deprives us of the open space for meaningful discourse. This is true of political desire as well as personal desire, on the global scale as well as on the local. Without the exertion and tolerance *of space* demanded by true free speech, we slide into an all-too-familiar estrangement from shared and mutually constitutive global agendas. We find ourselves reduced to *the* familiar and *the* strange. "Reduced to becoming omnipotent" (Grotstein, 2007, p. 33, quoting Bion) and "grounded" in fantasy projections, we sacrifice the recognition of both true difference and true equality: such solutions place us at actual peril.

The lessons of attachment theory echo this point. Deprived of the natural advantages of secure attachment relationships, which are the basis for free imagination and genuine discourse, our ventures into the world—like those of the developing child—are compromised. When mothers signal fear of their infants' explorations, infants become anxiously preoccupied with their "home base." Likewise, when our government addresses us in the language of fear, we are more apt to feel anxious in general and especially about our "homeland security." Instead of feeling curious to explore, we fall back on projections and stereotype. These feed back on themselves, leading to a kind of cultural solipsism.

David Harvey so compellingly dials in on what is at stake that I shall quote him at length:

> The fear is of foreigners and of immigrants, of outside agitators and now, of course, of terrorists. This leads to the internal circling of wagons and to the closing down of civil liberties and freedoms ... the tendency to characterize all critics of administration policies as aiding and abetting the enemy. This kind of nationalism easily fuses with racism (most particularly now toward Arabs), the restriction of civil liberties (the Patriot Act), the curbing of press freedoms (the gaoling of journalists for not revealing their sources), and the embrace of incarceration and the death penalty to deal with

malfeasance. Externally this nationalism leads to covert action and now to preemptive wars to eradicate anything that seems like the remotest threat to the hegemony of US values and the dominance of US interests. (Harvey, 2005, p. 196)

Genuine knowing always requires a real encounter with an Other, who lies not within our comforting (or alarming) fantasy of control or annihilation, but beyond our exclusive possession and fantasy projections. This encounter requires humility but also bravery.

While curiosity and exploration call for courage, courage itself can be encouraged. Mothers (and caretakers) can foster attachment security through sensitivity to their infants' communication, thereby facilitating the ability to effectively signify (and interpret) intent and desire. Furthermore, we find in the principles instantiated in the First Amendment the basis for engagement and grounding in a sphere of dialogue that extends beyond the narrow, self-interested, and ultimately solipsistic terms in which power is often seized through a brute-force use of language. In psychoanalysis, this dialogue requires that the patient engage with a real, alive, and personal analyst—not a blank screen—who is also more than real; she is a metaphor. In public discourse, this dialogue requires that citizens engage with real, alive Others, who are personal and specific, but who are also metaphors for the collective. In both cases, free speech is strengthened when we recognize its alliance with social interests.

Both a means toward, and a consequence of, achieving attachment security, such semiotic agency is the natural byproduct of a commitment to free thought and free speech. It takes no great leap to imagine that what promotes a secure home base (in Bowlby's terms) also promotes "homeland security." Recall (from Chapter Three) the "uncanny etymology" of *freedom.* Its hidden origins in "return to mother" will surprise neither attachment theorists nor psychoanalysts. But the Constitution's framers, while they certainly did look to their mother Britain and its legal system for guidance, would probably have been more "at home," at least on a conscious level with a different derivation.

Free is also related to the word *frank,* from the twelfth century Old French *franc,* meaning "free (not servile), sincere, genuine, open, gracious; worthy."[1] As the word's meaning evolves, so do linkages between ideas of freedom and truth. For example, *candid* (meaning "white; pure;

sincere; honest; upright" from *candere* "to shine") by metaphoric extension became associated with the word "frank" by the 1670s. *Franchise*
emerged from an Old French word meaning "freedom, exemption,
right, privilege."

We now begin to glimpse how frank, free speech—speech that is
liberated by boundaries—becomes a boundless tool in our natural and
national arsenal.[2] The power of free speech, as Freud and our Founding
Fathers dared to dream, lies in the possibilities it unleashes for candid,
truthful discourse, for social and political *enfranchisement*, and for self-
determination beyond conditions of servility. Free speech is a call to
translate our native desires, both familiar and strange, into speech. We
create signs that inspire new signs, creating the possibilities of an associative chain that aspires to freedom, just as it also recursively joins us
with our points of origin, our home base.

The cases for intervention

Freud observed that impediments to free association were not merely
commonplace but inevitable and invaluable. All roads, all freedom
of association, lead back to our points of origin, to our most familiar
(namely, our familial) assemblies. Yet precisely because desire,
understood psychoanalytically as incestuous, lies so close to home, it
is also taboo. It is the source of much unrest and animating passion
but also, potentially, of the means by which we may win peaceful
coexistence. Minimally, our incestuous desires expose the mythology
behind our angelologic longings for unmediated communication (see
Chapter One), and they expose what we must mourn if we are to
advance toward the telos, the destiny, of psychoanalytic and democratic practices. As we traverse our fantasies at the frontier of speaking
by naming and knowing the stranger of desire, we irretrievably dislo-
cate familiar (familial) power and social hierarchies. But we also forge
renewed and strengthened alliances.

Perils to the analytic dyad, and to the society at large, also contain
seeds of hope. Tocqueville, in a far more optimistic conclusion than
Freud ever reached, believed the people to be "insatiable and restive"
(Mansfield, 2010, p. 11) in their desire for freedom, and that "the passions
of the people 'have no lasting obstacles'" (ibid., p. 38). Having recognized the power of the *demos* to get what it wants, he also recognized
the inevitability of power (class) struggle, between "the democratic

instinct for extending power to the people and the aristocratic desire to restrain them" (ibid., p. 39). That psychoanalysis sets in motion exactly these conflicted (and class-based) desires is a story that each patient and analyst frequently visits and revisits over the course of their work together.

In psychoanalysis and in American history, neither the fundamental rule nor the First Amendment has assured any easy victory against repression or exclusion, let alone for free speech. Both narratives, time and again, document an uphill battle between constraint and liberty. Both narratives include cycles of repression and fear-driven collapses of expressive freedom. As Justice Brandeis (joined by Holmes) argued in the *Whitney* dissent (274 U.S. 357 (1927), at 376), "The wide difference between advocacy and incitement, between preparation and attempt, between assembly and conspiracy, must be borne in mind" if we are to sustain courage and faith in the advantages of free speech and free assembly in the face of our vulnerability to paranoid fantasy, let alone our merely all too human and very valid fears.

Psychoanalysis, early on, recognized the patient's resistance to her own self-knowledge on top of her resistance to the analyst's authority. Furthermore, it came to recognize that resistance itself is a form of speech mandating translation and respect. For Freud, that which the patient did not choose to speak—the slips of tongue, dream processes, the matter of jokes, unintentional thoughts that bubble up and emerge from us in garbled or confused form—revealed an intent, an unconscious agency that had a logic, even an impassioned logic, worthy of interpretation and attention. It was this logic of the unconscious that he set forth to describe, convinced of its revelatory and truthful lessons—*its* authority.

By the same token, beginning at least as early as John Stuart Mill's essay "On Liberty" in 1859, the social interest in freedom of thought has been linked with the idea that suppressed knowledge or ideas may contain a truth that society needs. The history of First Amendment interpretation reveals a progressive recognition of the cleansing power of the truth and transparency (sunshine being the best disinfectant). And over time it has become increasingly clear that truth is more likely to emerge in an atmosphere promoting what Justice Holmes, in 1919, referred to as a "free trade in ideas."

Just as a patient's defenses protect her and others from "knowing," they simultaneously fate her to become symptomatic and less potent. Deprived of a forbidden self-knowledge, she operates with an invisible handicap and cannot be on equal footing in a society that claims to be democratic but actually privileges certain sorts of knowledge. In a similar vein, patriarchal methods of squelching civil liberties, inculcating fear, and vanquishing dissonant thought deprive both patients and citizens of their most potent (and most humane) natural resources: the freedom to think and to communicate.

Psychoanalysis was designed to help patients gain a foothold in their own discourse, agency in their own lives. It came to recognize that it had to reach beyond narrowly defined, so-called "neurotic" maladies and the people they afflicted. Its purview has expanded to include, for example, patients who suffer from developmental deprivations and environmental trauma, and it has abandoned misguided and prejudicial presumptions about gender and sexual orientation. Innovative and affirmative technical reforms also expanded the franchise of psychoanalysis and free association beyond former exclusions. By a similar token, collective action to *actively provide* positive incentives for greater inclusion is essential to fulfill the promise of the First Amendment. Public sentiment might nudge the Court to formally recognize a nontextual First Amendment right to voting—what Burt Neuborne (2015, p. 77) describes as "the ultimate act of political expression and association." What's more, the Court's ambiguous lines for granting some speech favored status ("pure speech," including moneyed speech) relative to other disfavored speech ("communicative conduct," which includes free assemblies) sorely need jurisprudential, and ethical, coherence. Further, the inequities entailed by the *Citizen's United* decision underscore the necessity of activist government intervention in the economic sphere (e.g., limitations on media ownership) to foster freer speech, and to strengthen the reciprocal relationship between individual and community. Beyond that, citizen action is also essential. If we want greater popular sovereignty (as opposed to sovereignty of positive law), we must introduce formal mechanisms to increase citizen participation— say, in the courts and in other less-than-democratic institutions.

Yet even when encouraged and protected, free association and free speech remain elusive and ambitious quests. Freud recognized that resistance, born at the cusp between symptom and direct communication, carried both camouflaged *and* (potentially) accessible meaning. He came to regard "all the forces that oppose the work of recovery as the patient's 'resistances'" (Freud, 1926e, p. 223). But somewhere, in the infancy of his theory, Freud dared to recognize himself as implicated; "How does it come about that the transference is so admirably suited to be a means of resistance?" (1912b, p. 104). To which he answered, "transference, which seems ordained to be the greatest obstacle to psychoanalysis, becomes it most powerful ally, if its presence can be detected each time and explained to the patient" (1905e, p. 117).

Further etymological excursions on the journey home

Free association and its obstacles led Freud into a conflicted relationship with an Other, a patient who dared to have her own voice and agency, as well as knowledge that he (and society) might have deemed taboo. Uncanny knowledge. Knowledge on the margins of the familiar, of the stranger who is beyond, but also within. Knowledge that requires both free speech and free assembly. Knowledge that exposes our wanting and our needing each other.

Free association that exposes serendipitous, surprising knowledge, and that transforms us from mute (*infans*) into enfranchised agents, relies on our exploratory meanderings, our embrace of an ethic of *vandals*. Let's wander the etymological path once more, in the spirit of free association. It takes us back to the end of antiquity, where we find a Germanic tribe, dubbed "Vandals," who sacked Rome in 455 C.E. We might now associate their name, metonymically, with willful destruction; but its origin reveals a different side of their character. The original Old English rendering, *Wendlas*, derives from the proto-Germanic *wadljaz*, meaning "wanderer." Here we find ourselves on a risky path: the path of wandering, which requires daring, which embodies freedom—and equal footing—and which perhaps even leads to a vandalizing of knowledge. Courage is required when we wander upon forbidden knowledge, knowledge we both do and don't want to loot.

If we attend once more to the uncanny etymology linking freedom to a "return to mother," we hear resistance speaking through the female body. Here resistance meets assertion, subjugation meets authorization. Still, a translational process guides us towards coherence, a space in which free association meets its ally in relationship, and where free speech and freedom of assembly are not only paired property rights of the people, but mutually constituted privileges. As Patrick Mahony (1987, p. 41) points out, hewing close to etymology, not only does *freedom* bring us back to mother, but *association* (rooted in the Latin *socius*) attaches us.

As we have seen, there is no straightforward path to free speech and free association, which are intimately bound to our social, even primal, attachments. The struggle to liberate unconscious forces, to bring them onto the symbolic field of communication, begins and (potentially) ends in a dialectic between boundary setting and space-creating discourse, restraint and liberty; it is inevitably *conditional*. Anyone who has tried to "get there," to genuinely free associate, knows that any victory on that playing field (or battlefield) implicates body and gender dynamics, masculine but also feminine genital signifiers. Free association, like free speech, is achieved only through the material and metaphoric conduit of the body, especially the female body, a primal condition.

We claim greater voice as we grow freer to create and to use symbols, space-filling symbols—phallic symbols—ubiquitous features of both psychoanalytic and democratic confidence and aspiration. But these will also always require their counterpart: real and metaphoric *space*. And so the polis cannot succeed with silenced voices nor with excised bodies.

Freud remained stymied at the end of his career by the question, "What does a woman want?" (Jones, 1955, p. 468)—a question, as Dianne Elise noted, he bequeathed "to female colleagues and future colleagues" (2000, p. 125). When we recognize, as Jessica Benjamin (1988) has, that women want to want (that is, to possess a sense of agency and desire), we glimpse cultural and political implications. We intuitively recognize the profound psychological empowerment that flows from women's claiming their bodies, including their vaginal responsiveness and experience of "space." When we extend the power of this metaphoric space as essential for all of us to claim—regardless of our genital anatomy—we come closer to appreciating its fully democratizing function.

In an essay inspired by the *Duino Elegies*, Benjamin invokes Rilke's image of the Angel. Benjamin considers the patient's creation of the analyst as Angel in an eroticized transference. She notes the paradox at the heart of psychoanalysis: that our "slavish love of power" (1994, p. 152) both blinds and enlightens us. Worthy of the genre that is psychoanalysis, the patient abandons her familiar speech and her familiar autonomy, accepting tutelage, for the sake of her knowledge. She will journey along a path through erotic transference and through love that exposes a truth that both imprisons her and holds the key to her liberation (Slavin, 2007). But in exchange the analyst, no longer magical, nor angelic, becomes accessible, and the patient gains what is of "inestimable importance to her"—her mental freedom (Benjamin, 1994, p. 152, citing Freud, 1915a, p. 169). Paradoxically perhaps, it is by means of our angels—from the Greek *angelos*, "messenger"—that we come to inhabit embodied knowledge, the conduit to our symbolic freedom.

Towards a feminine law

We began our journey with Freud's radical discovery and daring pursuit: to locate that space between the angelic and the material, between our longings for unmediated psychical knowing and for unmediated physical touch. Beyond the "use of magical formulas and purificatory baths," Freud landed upon the "magic of words" (1890a, p. 292)—the third of speech, a mediating bridge that challenged us to bear (sometimes unbearable) losses and to conceive (sometimes inconceivable) knowledge. That path required a journey through the erotics of desire and transference, our forbidden longing for unmediated love with our attachment figures. As a patient whom we met earlier realized, he needed to relinquish his transference attachment to his therapist as angel. He had to ground her in her body, with actual genitals, in order to reconceive her—as a particular woman with her own personal subjectivity and humanity, and as a symbolic embodied other—but also to claim his own genitals and embodied speech, located as they were between a receptive and penetrating intercourse/discourse, between the actual and the symbolic. Our relationship matured, grounded now between body and mind, between adult sexual desire and (previously foreclosed) childhood Oedipal fantasy, between present and past. New possibilities for equality, personal and political agency, and for mutual recognition as members with shared ownership in symbolic life, could now be glimpsed, and even gradually realized.

Freud set us on the path to these discoveries. But he had a blind spot: his inability to acknowledge the significance of the female genital for all of us, whatever gender one might claim. This blindness created (and itself was a symptom of) a troubling legacy. For all that Freud granted to civilization, even if by also exposing its discontents, he remained mystified by the question of female desire. Late in his career, he was still clinging to his theory of penis envy, and to the view that a woman's alleged refusal to "abandon her wish for a penis," her "repudiation of femininity," was both psychological "bedrock" and "a biological fact, a part of the great riddle of sex" (Freud, 1937c, p. 252). (This repudiation was seen to afflict men as well: femininity, along with male homosexuality, were proxies for passivity and subjugation.) These dicta have remained mystifying and troubling to psychoanalysts of every generation and every school of thought (see, e.g., Aron & Starr, 2013).

While it is true that not everyone can have a vagina, we all can and must claim its symbolic space, the vaginal symbolic. It is not a symbol of invisibility or inferiority; in naming it we bring space into presence. Its receptivity and responsiveness open the possibility for mystery *and* for knowledge. We may dread naming and knowing, but we also desire them. That desire is itself dependent on naming and knowing what lies at the brink of what cannot be fully known—what thus remains in the mysterious realm of Lacan's "Real," of Bion's "O." Desire is born not out of lack *qua* lack; it is not erected on Freud's imagined bedrock of envy and shame and repudiation. Desire is actually born in our very need to claim it, to experience and sustain receptivity, to sustain a reverberant gap. A (feminine) space births desire.

The truth is not that we, women *or* men, have some fundamental psychological need to repudiate femininity. It is that claiming femininity and its metaphors is so threatening to some that it must be repudiated, as it was by Freud—who nonetheless bestowed upon psychoanalysis the status of "lady."[3] As metaphor, and as that which stands at the frontier of reality, feminine law is the originary metaphor of our space between, a space between telepathy and touch that refutes dichotomy. A principle of opening space, it symbolizes the "gap" whose bridging is the motive and condition for language, for agency, and for knowledge. The vaginal, then, is the real, if paradoxical, "bedrock"— the bedrock that is space—insofar as we discover that the very foundation of all that is erected in cultural and shared life requires (eternally open *and* bounded) space for curiosity, desire, creation, procreation, meaning, discourse, intercourse; for phallic penetration, for erotic life, for free speech, for democracy.

As we claim this metaphor, perhaps we come closer to tapping into the animating pulse of Lacan's specifically feminine jouissance, "beyond the phallus." By situating ourselves on the paradoxical terra firma—the space—of speech, we gain inspiration from this ineffable and mystical jouissance, an antidote to the signifying baggage threatening to lull us into the social conformity that patriarchy markets. Standing in the spaces between (Bromberg, 1998), we gain our capacity and courage for free association and free speech, just as we gain confidence that our rights to gather and give voice are safeguarded and secure. Attachment figures, like courts and governments, are rarely reliable guarantors of free speech, and so we are reminded that the price of liberty is eternal vigilance.

On this account, free association and its correlate free speech have the potential to bring psychoanalysis and attachment theory together in a way that is mutually enriching. They might also bring psycho-analysis and constitutional democracy together as mutually resonant traditions dedicated to a shared goal. These freedoms are expressions of personal and, ultimately, political agency. We, "the people," claim our (inalienable) right to freedom of speech—a right that while "granted" to us, still requires our active ownership. We must actively participate in constituting our sovereignty, lest we remain alienated. We embody our democracy as we constitute (embody) ourselves.

Although free association and free speech are derived from *within*—from an opening of space, where we can initiate our desire—they seek an outlet. They seek to have impact on someone who is a familiar attachment figure, but who also lies beyond our possession and con-trol, in some terrain between repression and memory. Discovering "that one's own mind matters to other people" (Slavin, 2014, p. 33) requires wrestling with matter (with what is real), with what matters, and with those that matter(ed) to us (Gentile, 2014, p. 39). The etymology of "matter" reveals a chain of derivations (and psychoanalytically rich associations) ranging from "material of thought, speech, or expression" to the "hard inner wood of a tree," but also, perhaps most essentially, to *mater*, "origin, source, mother." The word *matter* also came to stand for "grounds, reason, or cause for something," foreshadowing the verb meaning "to be of importance or consequence." Freud grounded his theory not only in his *faith* in free association to guide us to transference but to how transference would illuminate the material, *scientific*, foun-dation to psychoanalysis, but also the reality—the physical reality—of the body, which spoke in lieu of the speaking subject.

We discover that, in sharing, we expose our desires in a relation-ship that matters to us, located between the familiar and the unknown, between our points of origin and our longings for freedom (and its evocative links with maternal reunion), between our hysterical repression and our physical body's telling of our memory and forbidden knowledge. As we communicate intent and desire in a relationship of central importance to us, we give ourselves a chance to want and be wanted. By doing so, we achieve greater attachment security *and* mutual recognition—and we engage in speech that matters. In this dance with desire, we create a home for unconscious, irruptive factors that release new, dislocating energy and knowledge. We evolve even if this dance, with its challenge of sustaining an open space, requires that our felt security is never complete, but always linked with the space that marks the entry of the stranger, the frontier to mystery, to the unknown.

Derrida believed that one must "do everything one can to keep the space open for unknown friends of democratic desire to come" (Glendinning, 2011, p. 95). In sustaining this orientation we make powerful inroads towards the hard-won, but ever elusive and unrealized, "victory" of free association *and* freedom *of* association. These inroads require detours along our journey home. Derrida suggests what is at stake: the dialectic between the familiar and the strange pivots on the third of equality. Democracy requires that we stand as equals in both our radical singularity and in our essential shared humanity (Derrida, 2005, p. 22). Psychoanalysis takes patients to the brink of this aporia, facing the futility of repetition compulsions that leave us without a path (*a-poros*), and so to the brink of a third space, a new path, one between authority and subjection, one both familiar and strange. Tocqueville admiringly observed (or imagined) democracy's (and we would add, psychoanalysis's) possibilities: When "plain citizens ... get together in free associations they have something of nobility in their souls" (Mansfield, 2010, pp. 81–82).

As we find our way along that long and winding road, let's veer one last time into associations of the word "free." We've seen that freedom is tied to (maternal) reunion and to frank, outspoken speech, and thus to the democratic dream of enfranchisement. But perhaps the most alluring association of all is one left unspoken (*infans*), one linked to Freud's deepest insights into the curative power of speech and of psychoanalysis. "Free" dates to the Old English *freogan*, meaning "to free, liberate" but also "to love, to think lovingly, honor"; and to the Old Saxon *fiohan*, meaning "to court, woo"; and to the German *befreien* "to free," or *freien*, meaning "to woo"; to the Old Norse *frja* "to love"; and to the Gothic *frijon* "to love."

Freud retreated to skepticism late in his career, dismissing as naïve any notions of innate sociability and of the transformative powers of love. In a famous passage from *Civilization and its Discontents*, he asserts that human aggressiveness will oppose "the programme of civilization." But he betrays his ambivalence. Musing about Eros, he concludes that it functions to "combine single human individuals, and after that families, then races, peoples and nations, into one great unity, the unity of mankind." Civilization, he says, "is in the service of Eros" (Freud, 1930a, p. 122), and as Winnicott came to conclude, destruction is "the backcloth" to the discovery of the Other, to joy, and to love.

These inroads to love, to freedom, involve not only self-revelation in the context of real relationships and communities but also eternal vigilance and remarkable courage. They require that we actively pursue free association and free speech, a quixotic quest of possible impossibility, akin to democracy's pursuit of "indefinite perfectibility" (Tocqueville, 1835, p. 426) and inevitably also of indefinite *imperfectibility*. These inroads to love, to freedom, to democracy, are also—as President Obama reminded us in commemorating the fiftieth anniversary of the Civil Rights' protest marches from Selma to Montgomery, Alabama— the inroads whereby, in directly confronting fear and prejudice, we arrive at the triumph of "the idea of a just America, and a fair America, an inclusive America, and a generous America" (Obama, 2015). We are reminded that (as Freud might have said) "to be afraid of ideas, any idea, is to be unfit for self-government" (Meiklejohn, 1960, p. 28). We are reminded that Freud recognized the imprisonment of his patients by what Justice Brandeis called "the bondage of irrational fears." And we are reminded that if, as Brandeis compellingly wrote, "the greatest menace to freedom is an inert people," then First Amendment doctrine and psychoanalysis have shared lessons to offer in advancing the personal and the political, self and community, liberty and sovereignty. Even Freud, that avowed anti-American, might have (under some other circumstances) marveled at what Floyd Abrams (2013, p. 397) calls "the passion, the voluptuousness with which we embrace the Constitution." Or we might say, true free speech is erotic free speech—it is always the expression of Eros itself.

NOTES

Introduction

1. Recent data paint a sobering portrait of the devastation: Twenty-five per cent of Americans (about 61.5 million people) experience mental illness in a given year; and twenty per cent of youths (ages thirteen to eighteen) experience severe mental illness in a given year (National Alliance on Mental Illness, 2013).

2. Richard Chessick (2000) reports significant growth of psychoanalysis in France, Germany, Italy, Brazil, Argentina, Japan, Russia.

3. Cited by Zaretsky, 2004, p. 223. Wulff was in this instance addressing the question of whether psychoanalysis can be acceptable to Marxism.

4. Throughout this book, I will be referring to "relational" and "intersubjective" schools of psychoanalysis. Painting in very broad strokes, Tony Bass (2014, p. 663) depicts relational theory as offering a "big tent," a "capacious theoretical home base" for "developments associated with American Interpersonal Psychoanalysis, Kleinian and Bionian thought, British Independent School thinking, self psychology, intersubjectivity theory, attachment theory, and more."

5. Earlier references to "feminine law" (Fitzpatrick, 2003, p. 47; and implied in Ramshaw, 2003) draw inspiration from Cixous and trace

it to an originary feminine dimension of law. Though I learned of this use only at the copyediting stage of this text, it resonates in interesting ways with my conception, also indirectly influenced by Cixous (see Chapter Fourteen, fn1). These resonances will become clearer as I elaborate my thesis (see especially Chapters Twelve to Fifteen).

Chapter One

1. In a letter to Wilhelm Fliess, 15 October 1895, cited by Makari, 2008, p. 90.
2. Freud's writings on the occult span twenty-seven years, from 1905 through 1932. On telepathy in particular, see 1941d (written in 1921); 1922a; and 1933a, Lecture XXX, pp. 31–56.

Chapter Two

1. This is Mahony's translation of the German term whose standard English translation would be "free association."

Chapter Three

1. Mahony, 1987, p. 130. Mahony references Freud's assertion that there is a point, a navel, in every dream that remains undecipherable. Mahony recognizes this navel in terms of the uterine relationship that establishes both contiguity and similarity but also separation. The act of birth launches linguistic and physiological consequences that sustain a dialectic between contiguity and separation.
2. Supreme Court decisions are cited from the United States Reports in the standard form of volume, page number, and year. In this instance, we're citing page 48 of U.S. Reports volume 249, for a case decided in 1919. These reports are published and reprinted on a regular basis by the U.S. Government Printing Office. Searchable versions of U.S. Reports may be found online at www.law.cornell.edu/supremecourt/text/home.
3. It would take almost fifty years for the court to advance beyond its reasoning in *Abrams* and to propose a stronger test for permissible censorship. In its 1968 decision in *Brandenburg* vs. *Ohio*, the majority held that

speech could not be prohibited only because it was likely to cause harm; it also had to demonstrably incite "imminent lawless action."

4. See the list of cases on Cornell University's Legal Information Institute website at www.law.cornell.edu/supct/cases/topics/tog_freedom_of_ speech.html.

5. *Citizens United* vs. *Federal Election Commission* (2010). In this case, the Court held that the First Amendment prohibits the government from restricting political independent expenditures by corporations, associations, or labor unions.

Chapter Five

1. A recent check of the Psychoanalytic Electronic Publishing archives (www.pep-web.org) revealed not a single citation.

2. It is worth noting that Freud was referring not to the female's discovery of her vagina but to the discovery of her clitoris. Further, Freud clearly recognized the excitability of the clitoris, seeing this stimulation as marking girls' retreat to a "fresh wave of *repression*" (1905d, p. 220). See also D'Ercole, 2011, p. 405.

Chapter Six

1. Let us mark at this point, as does Paul Verhaeghe (1997, p. 39), that Freud had discovered that "the traumatic Real, for which there is no signifier in the Symbolic, is femininity" but leave open the question of whether this is essential to the symbolic realm.

Chapter Eight

1. If including more voices in the public conversation is necessary to fulfill the promise of the First Amendment, perhaps then a full recognition of the facilitating power of psychotherapy for silenced, excluded voices might provide a constitutional argument for universal psychotherapy insurance benefits. This would be a public recognition that in its pursuit of "cure," analysis provides a foothold for speech to the silenced and disenfranchised, and thus promotes equality and freedom.

Chapter Nine

1. Freud did not use the term "Thanatos." His acolyte Wilhelm Stekel did, at one of Freud's regular gatherings, years before the master wrote *Beyond the Pleasure Principle*. See Makari, 2008, pp. 158–159.

Chapter Ten

1. Of course, the patient's free associations, in Freud's originary conception, always implicated the analyst and the transference. But contemporary theorists make a stronger claim: the analyst's subjectivity is fundamental to the patient's organization of experience and of any purportedly free (singular) expression.
2. These include false and deceptive advertising, fraud, insider trading, copyright, trademarks, and perjury among others. See O'Brien, 2010, p. 81.

Chapter Eleven

1. Bion employed the letter "O" to signify that which cannot otherwise be named ("thoughts without a thinker"). O represents Absolute Truth or Ultimate Reality, which is forever unknowable, ineffable. He contrasted "O" with "K"—the latter representing that which can be symbolized and, therefore, apprehensible, known.
2. Phrased this way by Ogden, 2003, p. 596, with reference to Bion, 1963. The aphorism is sometimes expressed as "It takes two people to think the unthinkable thought."
3. What the French call *jouissance* is a concept central to Lacan's thought. Briefly put, he defined jouissance as excitement "that is excessive, leading to a sense of being overwhelmed or disgusted, yet simultaneously providing a source of fascination" (Fink, 1995, p. xii). Lacan associated jouissance with the unmediated (mother-infant) relationship.
4. The dynamics of giving and withholding in psychoanalysis, and with respect to the patient's silence in the treatment, has often been interpreted in terms of oral and anal-erotic transference and resistance. See, for example, Bergler, 1939; and Fliess, 1949. And, in terms of the dynamics of shame, see Coltart, 1991.
5. There are several other places in Shakespeare where "nothing" is associated with the female genitalia, for example in the "play within

the play" scene of *Hamlet* (where he puns with Ophelia), and in *Much Ado about Nothing,* where the key word of the title has three separate meanings: nothing, female sexuality, and noting (remarking upon, noticing).

Chapter Twelve

1. Further elaborating on the symbolism of the female genital, Freud also mentions tables, books, snails, mussels, the mouth, churches, and a panoply of objects animate and inanimate (1916, p. 156).
2. Projective identification was a concept introduced by Melanie Klein. In her original usage, it referred to an unconscious omnipotent phantasy. Bion's recognition of it as normal communication between mother and infant is what makes it, for our purposes, centrally relevant as a precursor to the capacity for free association.

Chapter Thirteen

1. This term was coined by Ernest Jones. See Jones, 1927, p. 459.
2. On the presumed need to control reproduction as an excuse for controlling women's bodies, Katie Gentile (2013, pp. 165) observes that female bodies gain visibility "only by virtue of their temporal relationship to a fetus … [and so are cast as embodying] risk and danger to the fetus. The biomedical system and the state, in proximity to the fetus, emerge as invulnerable, heroic rescuers."
3. Psychoanalyst Leon Hoffman (1999) describes how psychoanalysis has diverted sustained attention away from the once "hotly debated" clitoris and wonders whether this is because its sole purpose is pleasure. See Balsam, 2012, p. 82.

Chapter Fourteen

1. In the Introduction, I noted precedents for the term "feminine law," inspired by Cixous and used by Fitzpatrick (2003), and implied by Ramshaw (2003), to refer to an originary dimension of law. According to Fitzpatrick, feminine law opens to an "illimitable wildness" and offers a challenge to a "closedly masculine" rendering of law and its phallic authority.

Chapter Fifteen

1. Reflecting on her character Lonzi (and on his name) in her celebrated novel, the *Flamethrowers*, Kushner observes (Owens, 2013): "He's a fictionalized futurist of sorts. ... I named him after the radical and great Italian feminist, Carla Lonzi, who wrote *We Spit on Hegel*. He has contempt for women but he invokes a really cool one every time someone says his name." Though in the novel Carla herself is just a cool hidden historical reference, it is she who—*her name* that—underwrites Lonzi's strength. In this meta-story of naming, the fictional macho Lonzi doesn't just silently and enigmatically etch the name of a celebrated feminist, evocatively naming *her*; he also boldly and explicitly names what defies naming.

2. Percy's and Peirce's use of the term *sign* is at odds with how it is commonly used in contemporary semiotics, which derives more directly from the work of the linguist Ferdinand Saussure, via Roland Barthes. In short, what Saussure called a *sign* is what Percy will call a *symbol*.

3. All etymologies are from the Online Etymology Dictionary unless otherwise noted.

4. I will use the words female/feminine and woman interchangeably, even though for Lacan these had different applications and even though my thinking draws from and plays with Lacan's. Furthermore, in my discussion of signification and symbolization, I draw mostly but not exclusively from Peirce's terminology, even though Lacan drew mostly from Saussure's. In order to maintain some consistency in discussing Lacan's ideas, I will therefore sometimes use a term such as "signifier" rather than, say, Percy's "name." I do hope the meanings of these terms will be evident from the context, where I don't explicitly define them.

5. Patrick Mahony (2001, p. 148) describes his scholarly aims in deciphering Freud's writing as "apocalyptic in the etymological sense of that word: *apo kalyptein*, 'to uncover.'"

Chapter Seventeen

1. Wachtel cites, among those seeking to integrate attachment theory with contemporary psychoanalysis, Beebe & Lachmann, 2002, and Wallin, 2007.

2. I will use "mother" here, as it is conventionally used in psychoanalytic texts, to signify a child's primary caregiver, who might be the mother, but who might be the father or someone else.

Chapter Eighteen

1. All etymologies, unless otherwise noted, are from the Online Etymology Dictionary www.etymonline.com/index, last accessed 20 October 2015.
2. That free speech is both priceless and free is an important and under recognized aspect of its power. We currently spend $$$$$$$$ on national security and the Defense Department budget. The percentage that is directed to building a natural resource (free speech) through genuine dialogue and education that fosters semiotic competence is not obvious.
3. In a correspondence with Jung, Freud writes, "[Y]ou represent the lady's future and I her past" (Mahony, 1987, p. 181, quoting McGuire, 1974, p. 292).

REFERENCES

Abat i Ninet, A. (2013). *Constitutional Violence: Legitimacy, Democracy, and Human Rights.* Edinburgh: Edinburgh University Press.

Abrams, F. (2013). *Friend of the Court: On the Front Lines with the First Amendment.* New Haven, CT: Yale University Press.

Abrams, S. (1974). A note on "nothing." *Psychoanalytic Quarterly, 43*: 115.

Adler, E., & Bachant, J. (1996). Free association and analytic neutrality: The basic structure of the psychoanalytic situation. *Journal of the American Psychoanalytic Association, 44*: 1021–1046.

Adorno, T. (1951). *Minima Moralia: Reflections from Damaged Life.* E. F. N. Jephcott (trans.). London: Verso, 1985.

Al-Kassim, D. (2010). *On Pain of Speech: Fantasies of the First Order and the Literary Rant.* Berkeley, CA: University of California Press.

Alexander, F., & French, T. M. (1946). *Psychoanalytic Therapy: Principles and Application.* Lincoln, NE: University of Nebraska Press, 1980.

Amar, A. R. (1998). *The Bill of Rights.* New Haven, CT: Yale University Press.

Arendt, H. (1958). *The Human Condition.* Chicago, IL: University of Chicago Press.

Arlow, J. A. (1961). Silence and the theory of technique. *Journal of the American Psychoanalytic Association, 9*: 44–55.

Arlow, J. A. (1979). The genesis of interpretation. In: H. P. Blum (Ed.), *Psychoanalytic Explorations of Technique: Discourse on the Theory of Therapy* (pp. 193–206). New York, NY: International Universities Press, 1980.

Aron, L. (1990). Free association and changing models of mind. *The Journal of the American Academy of Psychoanalysis, 18*: 439–459.

Aron, L. (1991). The patient's experience of the analyst's subjectivity. *Psychoanalytic Dialogues, 1*: 29–51.

Aron, L., & Starr, K. (2013). *A Psychotherapy for the People: Toward a Progressive Psychoanalysis*. New York, NY: Routledge.

Atlas, G. (2012). Sex and the kitchen: Thoughts on culture and forbidden desire. *Psychoanalytic Perspectives, 9*: 220–232.

Badiou, A., & Tarby, F. (2010). *Philosophy and the Event*. L. Burchill (trans.). Cambridge: Polity Press.

Balint, M. (1958). The three areas of the mind—theoretical considerations. *International Journal of Psycho-Analysis, 39*: 328–340.

Balsam, R. (2012). *Women's Bodies in Pyschoanalysis*. New York, NY: Routledge.

Barnett, M. (1966). Vaginal awareness in the infancy and childhood of girls. *Journal of the American Psychoanalytic Association, 14*: 129–141.

Barthes, R. (1978). *A Lover's Discourse: Fragments*. R. Howard (trans.). New York, NY: Farrar, Strauss and Giroux.

Bass, A. (2014). Three pleas for a measure of uncertainty, reverie, and private contemplation in the chaotic, interactive, nonlinear dynamic field of interpersonal/intersubjective relational psychoanalysis. *Psychoanalytic Dialogues, 24*: 663–675.

Bassin, D. (1982). Woman's images of inner space: data towards expanded interpretive categories. *International Review of Psycho-Analysis, 9*: 191–203.

Bazelon, E. (2014). Do online threats count as free speech? *New York Times Magazine*, 24 November 2014. www.nytimes.com/2014/11/30/magazine/do-online-death-threats-count-as-free-speech.html, last accessed 31 December 2014.

Beebe, B., & Lachmann, F. (2002). *Infant Research and Adult Treatment*. Hillsdale, NJ: Analytic Press.

Benjamin, J. (1988). *The Bonds of Love: Psychoanalysis, Feminism, and the Problem of Domination*. New York, NY: Pantheon.

Benjamin, J. (1994). What angel would hear me? The erotics of transference. In: *Like Subjects, Love Objects: Essays on Recognition and Sexual Difference* (pp. 143–174). New Haven, CT: Yale Univeristy Press, 1995.

Benjamin, J. (1995). *Like Subjects, Love Objects: Essays on Recognition and Sexual Difference*. New Haven, CT: Yale University Press.

Benjamin, J. (2001). The primal leap of psychoanalysis from body to speech: Freud, feminism, and the vicissitudes of the transference. In: M. Dimen & A. Harris (Eds.), *Storms in Her Head: Freud and the Construction of Hysteria* (pp. 31–63). New York, NY: Other Press.

Benjamin, W. (1916). On language as such and on the language of man. In: M. Bullock & M. W. Jennings, (Eds.), *Selected Writings, Vol. 1: 1913–1926* (pp. 65–71). Cambridge, MA: Belknap Press, 1996.

Benveniste, É. (1969). The semiology of language. In: R. E. Innis (Ed.), *Semiotics: An Introductory Reader* (pp. 226–246). London: Hutchinson, 1986.

Bergler, E. (1938). On the resistance situation: The patient is silent. *Psychoanalytic Review, 25*: 170–186.

Bergler, E. (1939). On the psychoanalysis of the ability to wait and of impatience. *Psychoanalytic Review, 26*: 11–32.

Bernardi, R., & Bernardi, B. (2012). The concepts of *vínculo* and dialectical spiral: A bridge between intra- and intersubjectivity. *Psychoanalytic Quarterly, 81*: 531–564.

Bernstein, D. (1990). Female genital anxieties, conflicts and typical mastery modes. *International Journal of Psycho-Analysis, 71*: 151–165.

Bion, W. R. (1959). Attacks on linking. In: *Second Thoughts: Selected Papers on Psychoanalysis* (pp. 93–109). Northvale, NJ: Jason Aronson, 1967.

Bion, W. R. (1962a). A theory of thinking. In: *Second Thoughts: Selected Papers on Psychoanalysis* (pp. 110–119). Northvale, NJ: Jason Aronson, 1967.

Bion, W. R. (1962b). *Learning from Experience.* New York, NY: Basic Books.

Bion, W. R. (1963). *Elements of Psycho-Analysis.* London: Heinemann.

Bion, W. R. (1967). *Second Thoughts: Selected Papers on Psychoanalysis.* Northvale, NJ: Jason Aronson.

Bion, W. R. (1977). *Seven Servants.* New York, NY: Jason Aronson.

Bion, W. R. (1991). *Cogitations.* London: Karnac.

Birksted-Breen, D. (1996). Phallus, penis, and mental space. *International Journal of Psychoanalysis, 77*: 649–657.

Birksted-Breen, D. (2004). *The Gender Conundrum.* New York, NY: Routledge.

Blasi, V. (2002). Free speech and good character: From Milton to Brandeis to the present. In: L. C. Bollinger & G. R. Stone (Eds.), *Eternally Vigilant: Free Speech in the Modern Era* (pp. 60–95). Chicago, IL: University of Chicago Press.

Blasi, V. (2004). Holmes and the marketplace of ideas. *The Supreme Court Review, 2004*: 1–46.

Blos, P. Jr. (1972). Silence: A clinical exploration. *Psychoanalytic Quarterly, 41*: 348–363.

Blum, H. P. (2011). Introduction. *Psychoanalytic Review, 98*: 597–612.

Bohleber, W. (2007). Remembrance, trauma, and collective memory: The battle for memory in psychoanalysis. *International Journal of Psycho-Analysis, 88*: 329–352.

Bollas, C. (1987). *The Shadow of the Object: Psychoanalysis of the Unthought Known*. New York, NY: Columbia University Press.

Bollas, C. (1989). *Forces of Destiny: Psychoanalysis and Human Idiom*. Northvale, NJ: Jason Aronson.

Bollas, C. (2002). *Free Association*. Cambridge: Totem.

Bollas, C. (2009). *The Infinite Question*. New York, NY: Routledge.

Bollas, C. (2013). *Catch Them Before They Fall: The Psychoanalysis of Breakdown*. New York, NY: Routledge.

Bornstein, R. (2001). The impending death of psychoanalysis. *Psychoanalytic Psychology, 18*: 3–20.

Botticelli, S. (2004). The politics of relational psychoanalysis. *Psychoanalytic Dialogues, 14*: 635–651.

Bowlby, J. (1969). *Attachment and Loss, Vol. 1: Attachment*. London: The Hogarth Press and the Institute of Psycho-Analysis.

Brann, E. T. H. (1999). *What, Then, Is Time?* Lanham, MD: Rowman & Littlefield.

Bromberg, P. (1994). "Speak! that I may see you": Some reflections on dissociation, reality, and psychoanalytic listening. *Psychoanalytic Dialogues, 4*: 517–547.

Bromberg, P. (1998). *Standing in the Spaces: Essays on Clinical Process, Trauma, and Dissociation*. Hillsdale, NJ: Analytic Press.

Busch, F. (1994). Some ambiguities in the method of free association and their implications for technique. *Journal of the American Psychoanalytic Association, 42*: 363–384.

Butler, J. (1997). *Excitable Speech: A Politics of the Performative*. London: Routledge.

Butler, J. (1999). *Gender Trouble: Feminism and the Subversion of Identity* (2nd edn, revised). New York, NY: Routledge.

Calvino, I. (1988). *Six Memos for the Next Millennium*. Cambridge, MA: Harvard University Press.

Cantarella, E. (1987). *Pandora's Daughters: The Role and Status of Women in Greek and Roman Antiquity*. Baltimore, MD: Johns Hopkins University Press.

Cassidy, J., & Shaver, P. R. (Eds.) (1999). *Handbook of Attachment: Theory, Research, and Clinical Applications*. New York, NY: Guilford Press.

Celenza, A. (2010). The analyst's need and desire. *Psychoanalytic Dialogues, 20*: 60–69.

Chafee, Z. (1919). Freedom of speech in war time. *Harvard Law Review, 32*: 932–973.

Chandler, D. (2002). *Semiotics: The Basics* (2nd edn). New York, NY: Routledge.

Chandra Raj, K. B. (Ed.) (2012). *Your Sense of Humor: Don't Leave Home Without It.* Bloomington, IN: Trafford Publishing.

Chessick, R. D. (2000). What is psychoanalysis? *Journal of the American Academy of Psychoanalysis, 28:* 1–23.

Cixous, H. (1991). *"Coming to Writing" and Other Essays.* D. Jenson (Ed.). Cambridge, MA: Harvard University Press.

Coburn, W. (2010). Passion and gratitude in psychoanalysis. *International Journal of Psychoanalytic Self Psychology, 5:* 369–372.

Coltart, N. (1991). The silent patient. *Psychoanalytic Dialogues, 1:* 439–453.

Cornell, D. L. (1991). Gender hierarchy, equality, and the possibility of democracy. *American Imago, 48:* 247–263.

D'Ercole, A. (2001). "I'll have what she's having": Commentary on paper by Starr and Aron. *Psychoanalytic Dialogues, 21:* 398–405.

Davies, J. M. (1998). Multiple perspectives on multiplicity. *Psychoanalytic Dialogues, 8:* 195–206.

Demaske, C. (2009). *Modern Power and Free Speech.* Lanham, MD: Lexington.

Derrida, J. (1978). *Writing and Difference.* Alan Bass (trans.). Chicago, IL: University of Chicago Press.

Derrida, J. (1992). Force of law: The "mystical foundation of authority." Mary Quaintance (trans.). In: D. Cornell, M. Rosenfeld, & D. G. Carlson (Eds.), *Deconstruction and the Possibility of Justice* (pp. 3–67). London: Routledge.

Derrida, J. (2005). *Politics of Friendship.* New York, NY: Verso.

Dershowitz, A. (2013). Speaking freely: Thomas Healy's "Great Dissent." *New York Times* Book Review, 22 August 2013, www.nytimes. com/2013/08/25/books/review/thomas-healys-great-dissent.html, last accessed 23 December 2014.

Dimen, M., & Harris, A. (2001). Introduction. In: M. Dimen & A. Harris (Eds.), *Storms in Her Head: Freud and the Construction of Hysteria* (pp. 1–30). New York, NY: Other Press.

Donnet, J.-L. (2001). From the fundamental rule to the analysing situation. In: D. Birksted-Breen, S. Flanders, & A. Gibeault (Eds.), *Reading French Psychoanalysis* (pp. 155–172). New York, NY: Routledge, 2010.

Doolittle, H. (1956). *Tribute to Freud.* Oxford: Carcanet Press, 1971.

Dor, J. (1998). *Introduction to the Reading of Lacan.* New York, NY: Other Press.

Douthat, R. (2015). The blasphemy we need. *New York Times,* 7 January 2015 www.douthat.blogs.nytimes.com/2015/01/07/the-blasphemy-we-need/, last accessed 14 January 2015.

Dunn, J. (Ed.) (1993). *Democracy: The Unfinished Journey: 508BC to AD1993.* New York, NY: Oxford University Press.

Dunn, J. (2005). *Democracy: A History.* New York, NY: Atlantic Monthly Press.

Dunn, J. (2014). *Breaking Democracy's Spell.* New Haven, CT: Yale University Press.

Eagleton, T. (2011). *Why Marx Was Right.* New Haven, CT: Yale University Press.

Eigen, M. (1981). The area of faith in Winnicott, Lacan and Bion. *International Journal of Psycho-Analysis, 62:* 413–433.

Eigen, M. (2014). *Faith.* London: Karnac.

Elise, D. (1998). The absence of the paternal penis. *Journal of the American Psychoanalytic Association, 46:* 413–442.

Elise, D. (2000). Woman and desire: Why women may not want to want. *Studies in Gender and Sexuality, 1:* 125–145.

Emerson, T. I. (1984). The state of the First Amendment as we enter "1984." In: R. O. Curry (Ed.), *Freedom at Risk: Secrecy, Censorship, and Repression in the 1980s* (pp. 31–44). Philadelphia, PA: Temple University Press.

Erikson, E. H. (1963). Womanhood and the inner space. In: J. Strouse (Ed.), *Women & Analysis: Dialogues on Psychoanalytic Views of Femininity* (pp. 291–319). New York, NY: Grossman, 1974.

Evans, D. (1996). *An Introductory Dictionary of Lacanian Psychoanalysis.* New York, NY: Routledge.

Falzeder, E., & Brabant, E. (Eds.) (1993). *The Correspondence of Sigmund Freud and Sándor Ferenczi, Volume 1: 1908–1914.* Cambridge, MA: Belknap Press.

Fanon, F. (1961). *The Wretched of the Earth.* New York, NY: Grove Press, 2007.

Farrar, C. (1992). Ancient Greek political theory as a response to democracy. In: J. Dunn (Ed.), *Democracy: The Unfinished Journey, 508 BC to AD 1993* (pp. 17–39). Oxford: Oxford University Press.

Feldt, G. (2009). Beyond Roe. *Democracy: A Journal of Ideas, 11:* 78–85.

Fenichel, O. (1939). Problems of psychoanalytic technique. *Psychoanalytic Quarterly, 8:* 303–324.

Ferris, T. (2010). *The Science of Liberty: Democracy, Reason, and the Laws of Nature.* New York, NY: HarperCollins.

Fink, B. (1995). *The Lacanian Subject: Between Language and Jouissance.* Princeton, NJ: Princeton University Press.

Fish, S. (1994). *There's No Such Thing as Free Speech, and It's a Good Thing Too.* Oxford: Oxford University Press.

Fitzpatrick, P. (2003). Breaking the unity of the world: Savage sources and feminine law. *Australian Feminist Law Journal, 19:* 47.

Fliess, R. (1949). Silence and verbalization: A supplement to the theory of the "analytic rule." *International Journal of Psycho-Analysis, 30*: 21–30.

Fonagy, P., Gergely, G., Jurist, E. L., & Target, M. (2002). *Affect Regulation, Mentalization and the Development of the Self.* New York, NY: Other Press.

Fosshage, J. (2010). Implicit and explicit dimensions of Oedipal phenomenology: A reassessment. *Psychoanalytic Inquiry, 30*: 520–534.

Foucault, M. (2001). *Power: Essential Works of Foucault, 1954–1984, Vol. III*, R. Hurley, J. Faubion, & Y. P. Rabinow (Eds). New York, NY: The New Press.

Freud, S. (1890a). Psychical (or mental) treatment. *S. E., 7*: 283–302.

Freud, S. (1893a). On the psychical mechanism of hysterical phenomena. *S. E., 3*: 25–39.

Freud, S. (1900a). *The Interpretation of Dreams. S. E., 4*: 1–338; *S. E., 5*: 339–627.

Freud, S. (1905a). On psychotherapy. *S. E., 7*: 257–268.

Freud, S. (1905c). *Jokes and Their Relation to the Unconscious. S. E., 8*: 9–236.

Freud, S. (1905d). *Three Essays on the Theory of Sexuality. S. E., 7*: 123–246.

Freud, S. (1905e). *Fragment of an Analysis of a Case of Hysteria. S. E., 7*: 1–122.

Freud, S. (1906c). Psycho-analysis and the establishment of the facts in legal proceedings. *S. E., 9*: 97–114.

Freud, S. (1908d). "Civilized" sexual morality and modern nervous illness. *S. E., 9*: 179–204.

Freud, S. (1909d). *Notes Upon a Case of Obsessional Neurosis. S. E., 10*: 151–318.

Freud, S. (1910a). *Five Lectures in Psycho-analysis, Fourth lecture. S. E., 11*: 40–48.

Freud, S. (1910c). *Leonardo Da Vinci and a Memory of His Childhood. S. E., 11*: 63–137.

Freud, S. (1910i). *The Psycho-Analytic View of Psychogenic Disturbance of Vision. S. E., 11*: 209–218.

Freud, S. (1912–1913). *Totem and Taboo. S. E., 13*: 1–161.

Freud, S. (1912b). The dynamics of transference. *S. E., 12*: 97–108.

Freud, S. (1912d). On the universal tendency to debasement in the sphere of love. *S. E., 11*: 179–190.

Freud, S. (1912e). Recommendations to physicians practising psycho-analysis. *S. E., 12*: 109–120.

Freud, S. (1913c). On beginning the treatment. *S. E., 12*: 123–144.

Freud, S. (1913f). The theme of the three caskets. *S. E., 12*: 291–301.

Freud, S. (1914g). Remembering, repeating and working-through (Further recommendations on the technique of psycho-analysis II). *S. E., 12*: 145–156.

Freud, S. (1915a). Observations on transference love (Further recommendations on the technique of psychoanalysis III). *S. E., 12*: 157–171.

Freud, S. (1915b). Thoughts for the times on war and death *S. E., 14*: 273–300.

Freud, S. (1915e). *The Unconscious. S. E., 14*: 161–215.

Freud, S. (1916–1917). *Introductory Lectures on Psycho-Analysis. S. E., 15*: 1–240; *S. E., 16*: 241–463.

Freud, S. (1919a). Lines of advance in psycho-analytic therapy. *S. E., 17*: 159–168.

Freud, S. (1919h). The uncanny. *S. E., 17*: 219–256.

Freud, S. (1920g). *Beyond the Pleasure Principle. S. E., 18*: 1–64.

Freud, S. (1921c). *Group Psychology and the Analysis of the Ego. S. E., 18*: 65–144.

Freud, S. (1922a). Dreams and telepathy. *S. E., 18*: 200–220.

Freud, S. (1923b). *The Ego and the Id. S. E., 19*: 12–66.

Freud, S. (1923e). The infantile genital organization (An interpolation into the theory of sexuality). *S. E., 19*: 139–146.

Freud, S. (1924f). A short account of psycho-analysis. *S. E., 19*: 191–209.

Freud, S. (1925d). *An Autobiographical Study. S. E., 20*: 1–74.

Freud, S. (1925h). *Negation. S. E., 19*: 233–240.

Freud, S. (1926d). *Inhibitions, Symptoms, and Anxiety. S. E., 20*: 77–174.

Freud, S. (1926e). The question of lay analysis. *S. E., 20*, 179–258.

Freud, S. (1927c). *The Future of an Illusion. S. E., 21*: 5–56.

Freud, S. (1927e). *Fetishism. S. E., 21*: 147–158.

Freud, S. (1930a). *Civilization and Its Discontents. S. E., 21*: 64–145.

Freud, S. (1931b). Female sexuality. *S. E., 21*: 221–244.

Freud, S. (1933a). *New Introductory Lectures on Psycho-Analysis. S. E., 22*: 1–182.

Freud, S. (1937c). Analysis terminable and interminable. *S. E., 23*: 211–253.

Freud, S. (1941d). Psychoanalysis and telepathy. *S. E., 18*: 181–195.

Freud, S. (1950a). Extracts from the Fliess Papers. *S. E., 1*: 175–199.

Freud, S., & Breuer, J. (1895d). Studies on hysteria. *S. E., 2*: 1–305.

Gay, P. (1987). *A Godless Jew: Freud, Atheism, and the Making of Psychoanalysis.* New Haven, CT: Yale University Press.

Gay, P. (1988). *Freud: A Life for Our Time.* New York, NY: W. W. Norton.

Gaztambide, D. J. (2012). "A psychotherapy for the people": Freud, Ferenczi, and psychoanalytic work with the underprivileged. *Contemporary Psychoanalysis, 48*: 141–165.

Gentile, J. (2001). Close but no cigar: The perversion of agency and the absence of thirdness. *Contemporary Psychoanalysis, 37*: 623–654.

Gentile, J. (2007). Wrestling with matter: Origins of intersubjectivity. *Psychoanalytic Quarterly, 76*: 547–582.

Gentile, J. (2008). Between private and public: Towards a conception of the transitional subject. *International Journal of Psycho-Analysis, 89*: 959–976.

Gentile, J. (2010). Weeds on the ruins: Agency, compromise formation, and the quest for intersubjective truth. *Psychoanalytic Dialogues, 20*: 88–109.

Gentile, J. (2013). From truth or dare to show and tell: Reflections on childhood ritual, play, and the evolution of symbolic life. *Psychoanalytic Dialogues, 23*: 150–169.

Gentile, J. (2014). On mattering, materiality, and "transitional memory": A discussion of Jonathan H. Slavin's essay. *Psychoanalytic Perspectives, 11*: 35–43.

Gentile, K. (2013). Biopolitics, trauma and the public fetus: An analysis of preconception care. *Subjectivity, 6*: 153–172.

Ghent, E. (1990). Masochism, submission, and surrender. *Contemporary Psychoanalysis, 24*: 108–136.

Gilligan, C., & Richards, D. A. J. (2008). *The Deepening Darkness: Patriarchy, Resistance, and Democracy's Future*. Cambridge: Cambridge University Press.

Gilman, S. L. (1993). *Freud, Race, and Gender*. Princeton, NJ: Princeton University Press.

Glendinning, S. (2011). *Derrida: A Very Short Introduction*. New York, NY: Oxford University Press.

Green, A. (1995). The psychotherapy of hysteria. In: M. Dimen & A. Harris (Eds.), *Storms in Her Head: Freud and the Construction of Hysteria* (pp. 65–90). New York, NY: Other Press.

Grotstein, J. S. (2007). *A Beam of Intense Darkness: Wilfred Bion's Legacy to Psychoanalysis*. London: Karnac.

Grunbaum, A. (1984). *The Foundations of Psychoanalysis: A Philosophical Critique*. Berkeley, CA: University of California Press.

Harris, A. (2014). Curative speech: Symbol, body, dialogue. *Journal of the American Psychoanalytic Association, 62*: 1029–1045.

Harvey, D. (2005). *A Brief History of Neoliberalism*. New York, NY: Oxford University Press.

Harvey, D. (2014). *Seventeen Contradictions and the End of Capitalism*. New York, NY: Oxford University Press.

Hayner, P. (2011). *Unspeakable Truths: Transitional Justice and the Challenge of Truth Commissions* (2nd edn). New York, NY: Routledge.

Hentoff, N. (1992). *Free Speech for Me but Not for Thee*. New York, NY: HarperCollins.

Heyman, S. J. (2008). *Free Speech and Human Dignity*. New Haven, CT: Yale University Press.

Himes, M. (2012). The weight of the proper name (review of C. Masson & G. Wolkowicz (Eds.), *La force du nom: Leur nom, ils l'ont changé.*). *Division/Review, 4*: 15–18.

Hoffman, I. Z. (1998). *Ritual and Spontaneity in the Psychoanalytic Process: A Dialectical-Constructivist View.* Hillsdale, NJ: The Analytic Press.

Hoffman, L. (1999). Passion in girls and women: Toward a bridge between critical relational theory of gender and modern conflict theory. *Journal of the American Psychoanalytic Association, 47*: 1145–1168.

Horkheimer, M., & Adorno, T. (1947). *Dialectic of Enlightenment: Philosophical Fragments.* E. F. N. Jephcott (trans.). Stanford, CA: Stanford University Press, 2002.

Horney, K. (1924). On the genesis of the castration complex in women. *International Journal of Psycho-Analysis, 5*: 50–65.

Isbister, J. N. (1985). *Freud: An Introduction to his Life and Works.* Cambridge: Polity Press.

Jakobson, R. (1971). *Selected Writings: Word and Language, Volume 2.* Berlin: Walter de Gruyter.

James, H. (Ed.) (1920). *The Letters of William James, Vol. II.* Boston, MA: The Atlantic Monthly Press.

James, W. (1902). *The Varieties of Religious Experience.* New York, NY: Modern Library, 1929.

Jensen, R., & Arriola, E. (1995). Feminism and free expression. In: D. S. Allen & R. Jensen (Eds.), *Freeing the First Amendment: Critical Perspectives on Freedom of Expression* (pp. 195–223). New York, NY: New York University Press.

Jones, E. (1927). The early development of female sexuality. *International Journal of Psycho-Analysis, 8*: 459–472.

Jones, E. (1953). *Sigmund Freud: Life and Work, Volume One: The Young Freud 1856–1900.* London: Hogarth Press, 1972.

Jones, E. (1955). *Sigmund Freud: Life and Work, Volume Two: Years of Maturity 1901–1919.* London: Hogarth Press.

Jurist, E. L. (2010). Elliot Jurist interviews Peter Fonagy. *Psychoanalytic Psychology, 27*: 2–7.

Kalinich, L. J. (1993). On the sense of absence: A perspective on womanly issues. *Psychoanalytic Quarterly, 62*: 206–228.

Kalinich, L. J. (2007). The concept "superego": Another look (up to par or a hole in one?). In: J. P. Muller & J. G. Tillman (Eds.), *The Embodied Subject: Minding The Body In Psychoanalysis* (pp. 29–54). Lanham, MD: Jason Aronson.

Kanzer, M. (1972). Superego aspects of free association and the fundamental rule. *Journal of the American Psychoanalytic Association, 20*: 246–266.

Kirsh, I. (2010). *The Emperor's New Drugs.* New York, NY: Basic Books.

Kirsner, D. (2000). *Unfree Associations: Inside Psychoanalytic Institutes.* London: Process Press.

Klein, M. (1932). The effects of early anxiety-situations on the sexual development of the boy. In: *The Psychoanalysis of Children* (pp. 240–278). London: Hogarth Press, 1980.

Knight, R. P. (1953). The present status of organized psychoanalysis in the United States. *Journal of the American Psychoanalytic Association, 1*: 197–221.

Kris, A. O. (1996). *Free Association: Method and Process.* Hillsdale, NJ: Analytic Press.

Kristeva, J. (2000). *Crisis of the European Subject.* New York, NY: Other Press.

Kristeva, J. (2001). *The Sense and Non-Sense of Revolt: The Powers and Limits of Psychoanalysis.* J. Herman (trans.). New York, NY: Columbia University Press.

Kristeva, J. (2007). "Speech in psychoanalysis": From symbols to the flesh and back. In: D. Birksted-Breen, S. Flanders, & A. Gibeault (Eds.), *Reading French Psychoanalysis* (pp. 421–448). New York, NY: Routledge, 2010.

Kubie, L. S. (1950). *Practical and Theoretical Aspects of Psychoanalysis.* New York, NY: International Universities Press.

Kushner, R. (2013). *The Flamethrowers.* New York, NY: Scribner.

Lacan, J. (1954–1955). *The Seminar of Jacques Lacan, Book II: The Ego in Freud's Theory and in the Technique of Psychoanalysis, 1954–1955,* J.-A. Miller (Ed.). New York, NY: W. W. Norton, 1988.

Lacan, J. (1956–1957). *Le Séminaire, livre IV: La relation d'objet, 1956–1957,* J.-A. Miller (Ed.). Paris: Seuil, 1994.

Lacan, J. (1957). The agency of the letter in the unconscious, or reason since Freud. In A. Sheridan (trans.), *Écrits: A Selection* (pp. 146–178). London: Tavistock, 1977.

Lacan, J. (1959–1960). *The Seminar of Jacques Lacan, Book VII: The Ethics of Psychoanalysis, 1959–1960.* J.-A. Miller (Ed.), D. Porter (trans.). New York, NY: W. W. Norton, 1992.

Lacan, J. (1969–1970). *Le séminaire, livre XVII: L'envers de la psychanalyse, 1969–1970,* J.-A. Miller (Ed.). Paris: Seuil, 1991.

Lacan, J. (1972–1973). *The Seminar of Jacques Lacan, Book XX: Encore, 1972–1973.* J.-A. Miller (Ed.), B. Fink (trans.). New York, NY: W. W. Norton, 1998.

Langlieb, A., & Kahn, J. (2005). How much does quality mental health care profit employers? *Journal of Occupational and Environmental Medicine, 47*: 1099–1109.

Laplanche, J. (1989). *New Foundations for Psychoanalysis.* Cambridge, MA: Basil Blackwell.

Laplanche, J., & Pontalis, J.-B. (1973). *The Language of Psycho-Analysis.* D. Nicholson-Smith (trans.). New York, NY: W. W. Norton.

Lear, J. (1998). *Open Minded: Working Out the Logic of the Soul*. Cambridge, MA: Harvard University Press.

Lear, J. (2005). *Freud*. New York, NY: Routledge.

LeClaire, S. (1998). *Psychoanalyzing: On the Order of the Unconscious and the Practice of the Letter*. Peggy Kamuf (trans.). Stanford, CA: Stanford University Press.

Lefebvre, H. (1991). *The Production of Space*. D. Nicholson-Smith (trans.). Maiden, MA: Blackwell.

Lepore, J. (2011). The commandments: The Constitution and its worshippers. *The New Yorker*, 17: 70–76.

Lévinas, E. (1982). The pact. In: S. Hand (Ed.), *The Lévinas Reader* (pp. 211–226). Oxford: Basic Blackwell, 1989.

Lewin, B. (1948). The nature of reality, the meaning of nothing, with an addendum on concentration. *Psychoanalytic Quarterly, 17*: 524–526.

Lewis, A. (2008). *Freedom for the Thought That We Hate*. New York, NY: Basic Books.

Lewis, J. D. (1971). Isegoria at Athens: When did it begin? *Historia: Zeitschrift für Alte Geschichte, 20*: 129–140.

Lichtenstein, D. (1993). The rhetoric of improvisation: Spontaneous discourse in jazz and psychoanalysis. *American Imago, 50*: 227–252.

Litowitz, B. (2006). Where does nothing come from? Commentary on Wilson. *Journal of the American Psychoanalytic Association, 54*: 435–456.

Loewald, H. (1960). On the therapeutic action of psychoanalysis. *International Journal of Psycho-Analysis, 41*: 16–33.

Lombardi, R. (2010). The body emerging from the "neverland" of nothingness. *Psychoanalytic Quarterly, 79*: 879–909.

Mahony, P. (1979). The boundaries of free association. *Psychoanalysis and Contemporary Thought, 2*: 151–198.

Mahony, P. (1987). *Psychoanalysis and Discourse*. New York, NY: Brunner/Mazel: 2001.

Makari, G. (2008). *Revolution in Mind: The Creation of Psychoanalysis*. New York, NY: HarperCollins.

Makari, G., & Shapiro, T. (1993). On psychoanalytic listening: Language and unconscious communication. *Journal of the American Psychoanalytic Association, 41*: 991–1020.

Malater, E. (2014a). Personal communication, 30 May 2014.

Malater, E. (2014b). Personal communication, 1 June 2014.

Mannoni, O. (1968). *Freud*. R. Bruce (trans.). New York, NY: Pantheon, 1971.

Mansfield, H. C. (2010). *Tocqueville: A Very Short Introduction*. New York, NY: Oxford University Press.

Masling, J. (2000). Empirical evidence and the health of psychoanalysis. *Journal of the American Academy of Psychoanalysis, 28*: 665–685.

Masson, J. M. (1984). *The Assault on Truth: Freud's Suppression of the Seduction Theory*. New York, NY: Farrar, Straus and Giroux.

McConnell, M. W. (2012). You can't say that (review of J. Waldron, *The Harm in Hate Speech*). *The New York Times Sunday* Book Review, 22 June 2012. www.nytimes.com/2012/06/24/books/review/the-harm-in-hate-speech-by-jeremy-waldron.html?pagewanted=all, last accessed 14 January 2015.

McGuire, W. (Ed.) (1974). *The Freud/Jung Letters*. Princeton, NJ: Princeton University Press.

McNulty, T. (2014). *Wrestling with the Angel: Experiments in Symbolic Life*. New York, NY: Columbia University Press.

Meaney, T., & Yascha Mounk, Y. (2014). What was democracy? *The Nation*, 2 June 2014, www.thenation.com/article/179851/what-was-democracy, last accessed 7 January 2015.

Meerloo, J. A. (1952). Free association, silence, and multiple function of speech. *Psychiatric Quarterly, 26*: 21–32.

Meerloo, J. A. (1959). Psychoanalysis as an experiment in communication. *Psychoanalytic Review, 46*: 75–89.

Meiklejohn, A. (1960). *Political Freedom: The Constitutional Powers of the People*. New York, NY: Harper & Row.

Mieli, P. (2001). On trauma: A Freudian perspective. In: M. Dimen & A. Harris (Eds.), *Storms in Her Head: Freud and the Construction of Hysteria* (pp. 265–280). New York, NY: Other Press.

Mill, J. S. (1859). *On Liberty* (2nd edn). London: Savill and Edwards.

Miller, A. R. (1982). *Miller's Court*. New York, NY: Houghton Mifflin.

Mitchell, S. (1997). *Influence and Autonomy in Psychoanalysis*. Hillsdale, NJ: Analytic Press.

Moi, T. (1981). Representation of patriarchy: Sexuality and epistemology in Freud's "Dora." In: C. Bernheimer & C. Kahane (Eds.), *In Dora's Case: Freud-Hysteria-Feminism* (pp. 191–199). New York, NY: Columbia University Press, 1985.

Monoson, S. S. (2000). *Plato's Democratic Entanglements: Athenian Politics and the Practice of Philosophy*. Princeton, NJ: Princeton University Press.

Muller, J. P. (1996). *Beyond the Psychoanalytic Dyad: Developmental Semiotics in Freud, Peirce and Lacan*. New York, NY: Routledge.

Nacht, S. (1964). Silence as an integrative factor. *International Journal of Psycho-Analysis, 45*: 299–303.

Nancy, J.-L. (1988). *The Experience of Freedom*. B. McDonald (trans.). Stanford, CA: Stanford University Press, 1993.

National Alliance on Mental Illness (2013). Mental illness facts and numbers. www.nami.org/factsheets/mentalillness_factsheet.pdf, last accessed 19 December 2014.

New York Times Editorial Board (2014). What is a true threat on Facebook? *New York Times*, 1 December 2014, www.nytimes.com/2014/12/02/opinion/what-is-a-true-threat-on-facebook.html, last accessed 31 December 2014.

Neuborne, B. (2015). *Madison's Music: On Reading the First Amendment*. New York, NY: The New Press.

Nocera, J. (2014). Big money wins in a romp. *The New York Times*, 7 November 2014, www.nytimes.com/2014/11/08/opinion/joe-nocera-big-money-wins-again-in-a-romp.html, last accessed 23 December 2014.

Nunberg, H., & Federn, E. (Eds.) (1962). *Minutes of the Vienna Psychoanalytic Society, Volume 1: 1906–1908*. New York, NY: International Universities Press.

Obama, B. (2015). Remarks by the President in eulogy for the Honorable Reverend Clementa Pinckney, 26 June 2015, www.whitehouse.gov/the-press-office/2015/06/26/remarks-president-eulogy-honorable-reverend-clementa-pinckney, last accessed 20 October 2015.

O'Brien, D. M. (2010). *Congress Shall Make No Law: The First Amendment, Unprotected Expression, and the U.S. Supreme Court*. Lanham, MD: Rowman & Littlefield.

Ogden, T. (1989). *The Primitive Edge of Experience*. Northvale, NJ: Jason Aronson.

Ogden, T. (1994). *Subjects of Analysis*. London: Karnac.

Ogden, T. (2003). What's true and whose idea was it? *International Journal of Psychoanalysis, 84*: 593–606.

Ogden, T. (2004a). The analytic third: Implications for psychoanalytic theory and technique. *Psychoanalytic Quarterly, 73*: 167–195.

Ogden, T. (2004b). On holding and containing, being and dreaming. *International Journal of Psychoanalysis, 85*: 1349–1364.

Ogden, T. (2005). *This Art of Psychoanalysis*. New York, NY: Routledge.

Oppenheimer, D. B. (2009). Bill of Rights Series editor's preface. In: V. D. Amar (Ed.), *The First Amendment: Freedom of Speech: Its Constitutional History and the Contemporary Debate* (pp. 9–12). New York, NY: Prometheus Books.

Owens, L. (2013). "It's spelled motherfuckers." An interview with Rachel Kushner. *The Believer Logger*, 23 May 2013, http://logger.believermag.com/post/51246163032, last accessed 9 November 2015.

Pasquino, P. (2013). Opening remarks, Freud and Free Speech, New York University Postdoctoral Program in Psychotherapy and Psychoanalysis, Independent Track colloquium, 26 October 2013.

Percy, W. (1975). *The Message in the Bottle*. New York, NY: Farrar, Straus and Giroux.

Perelberg, R. J. (2013). Paternal function and thirdness in psychoanalysis: Has the future been foretold? *Psychoanalytic Quarterly, 82*: 557–585.

Peters, J. D. (1999). *Speaking into the Air: A History of the Idea of Communication*. Chicago, IL: University of Chicago Press.

Phillips, A. (1993). *On Kissing, Tickling, and Being Bored*. Cambridge, MA: Harvard University Press.

Phillips, A. (2014). *Becoming Freud: The Making of a Psychoanalyst*. New Haven, CT: Yale University Press.

Pizer, S. (1992). The negotiation of conflict in the analytic process. *Psychoanalytic Dialogues, 2*: 215–240.

Plath, S. (1963). *The Bell Jar* (as Victoria Lucas). London: Heinemann.

Pollock, G. (2006). Femininity: Aporia or sexual difference? Introduction. In: B. Ettinger, *The Matriaxial Borderspace*, B. Mussumi (Ed.) (pp. 1–40). Minneapolis: University of Minnesota Press.

Polanyi, K. (1944). *The Great Transformation*. Boston, MA: Beacon Press, 1954.

Post, R. (2002). Reconciling theory and practice in First Amendment Jurisprudence. In: L. C. Bollinger & G. R. Stone (Eds.), *Eternally Vigilant: Free Speech in the Modern Era* (pp. 152–173). Chicago, IL: University of Chicago Press.

Quinodoz, J.-M. (1977). Transitions in psychic structures in the light of deterministic chaos theory. *International Journal of Psycho-Analysis, 78*: 699–718.

Ramshaw, S. (2003). Nearing the "wild heart": the Cixiousian "feminine" and the quest for law's origins. *Australian Feminist Law Journal, 19*: 11–27.

Reik, T. (1968). The psychological meaning of silence [Wie man Psychologe wird] (1927). K. M. Altman (trans.). *Psychoanalytic Review, 55*: 172–186.

Rieff, R. (1959). *Freud: The Mind of the Moralist*. New York, NY: Viking Press.

Roazen, P. (1992). *Freud and his Followers*. New York, NY: DeCapo Press (original publication, 1975, Knopf).

Rohde, S. (2014). Flip-flopping on free speech (Review of T. Healy, *The Great Dissent*). *The Los Angeles Review of Books*, 9 January 2014, www.lareviewofbooks.org/review/flip-flopping-free-speech, last accessed 23 December 2014.

Rose, F. (2014). *The Tyranny of Silence*. Washington, DC: The Cato Institute.

Rose, J. (1982). Introduction. In: J. Mitchell & J. Rose (Eds.), *Feminine Sexuality: Jacques Lacan and the École Freudienne* (pp. 27–58). New York, NY: Pantheon Books.

Ross, A. (2008). Why is "speaking the truth" fearless? "Danger" and "Truth" in Foucault's discussion of parrhesia. *Parrhesia, 4*: 62–75.

Rushdie, S. (1990). In good faith. In: *Imaginary Homelands* (pp. 393–414). London: Granta, 1991.

Ruti, M. (2008). The fall of fantasies: A Lacanian reading of lack. *Journal of the American Psychoanalytic Association, 56*: 483–508.

Ruti, M. (2012). *The Singularity of Being: Lacan and the Immortal Within.* New York, NY: Fordham University Press.

Rutland, R. A., & Mason, T. A. (Eds.) (1983). *The Papers of James Madison, Vol. 14.* Charlottesville, VA: University Press of Virginia.

Schafer, R. (1968). *Aspects of Internalization.* Madison, CT: International Universities Press.

Schafer, R. (1976). *A New Language for Psychoanalysis.* New Haven, CT : Yale University Press.

Schauer, F. (1983). Must speech be special? *Northwestern University Law Review, 78*: 1284–1306.

Schauer, F. (1995). The First Amendment as ideology. In: D. S. Allen & R. Jensen (Eds.), *Freeing the First Amendment: Critical Perspectives on Freedom of Expression* (pp. 10–30). New York, NY: New York University Press.

Schauer, F. (2002). First Amendment opportunism. In: L. C. Bollinger & G. R. Stone (Eds.), *Eternally Vigilant: Free Speech in the Modern Era* (pp. 174–197). Chicago, IL: University of Chicago Press.

Shakespeare, W. (1972). *King Lear.* Kenneth Muir (Ed.). London: Methuen.

Shedler, J. (2010). The efficacy of psychodynamic psychotherapy. *American Psychologist, 65*: 98–109.

Shengold, L. (1989). Further thoughts about "nothing." *Psychoanalytic Quarterly, 58*: 227–235.

Shiffrin, S. (2014). *Speech Matters: On Lying, Morality and the Law.* Princeton, NJ: Princeton University Press.

Slavin, J. H. (2007). The imprisonment and liberation of love: The dangers and possibilities of love in the psychoanalytic relationship. *Psychoanalytic Inquiry, 27*: 197–218.

Slavin, J. H. (2010). Becoming an individual: Technically subversive thoughts on the role of the analyst's influence. *Psychoanalytic Dialogues, 20*: 308–324.

Slavin, J. H. (2014). "If someone is there": On finding and having one's own mind. *Psychoanalytic Perspectives, 11*: 23–34.

Slavin, M. O., & Kriegman, D. (1992). *The Adaptive Design of the Human Psyche: Psychoanalysis, Evolutionary Biology, and the Therapeutic Process.* New York, NY: Guilford Press.

Sokolowski, R. (1978). *Presence and Absence: A Philosophical Investigation of Language and Being.* Bloomington, IN: Indiana University Press.

Spitz, R. A. (1957). *No and Yes: On the Genesis of Human Communication.* Madison, CT: International Universities Press.

Starr, K., & Aron, L. (2011). Women on the couch: Genital stimulation and the birth of psychoanalysis. *Psychoanalytic Dialogues, 21*: 373–392.

Stern, D. B. (1997). *Unformulated Experience: from Dissociation to Imagination In Clinical Process.* Hillsdale, NJ: Analytic Press.

Stevens, J. P. (2012). Should hate speech be outlawed? (Review of J. Waldron, *The Harm in Hate Speech*). *The New York Review of Books*, 7 June 2012, www. nybooks.com/articles/archives/2012/jun/07/should-hate-speech-be-outlawed/, last accessed 12 January 2015.

Strauss, D. A. (2002). Freedom of speech and the common-law Constitution. In: L. C. Bollinger & G. R. Stone (Eds.), *Eternally Vigilant: Free Speech in the Modern Era* (pp. 32–59). Chicago, IL: University of Chicago Press.

Strenger, S. (2010). Review of P. E. Stepansky, *Psychoanalysis at the Margins*. *Psychoanalytic Psychology*, 27: 376–388.

Sullivan, H. S. (1953). *Conceptions of Modern Psychiatry*. New York, NY: W. W. Norton.

Summers, F. (2013). The expressivist turn in psychoanalytic theory and therapy. Bernard Kalinkowitz Memorial Lecture, NYU Postdoctoral Program in Psychotherapy and Psychoanalysis, 28 September 2013.

Sunstein, C. (1995). A new deal for speech. In: R. Jensen & D. S. Allen (Eds.), *Freeing the First Amendment: Critical Perspectives on Freedom of Expression* (pp. 54–78). New York, NY: New York University Press.

Tagg, J. (1988). *The Burden of Representation: Essays on Photographies and Histories*. Basingstoke: Macmillan.

Tauber, A. I. (2010). *Freud: The Reluctant Philosopher*. Princeton, NJ: Princeton University Press.

Thompson, M. G. (2000). "Free association": A technical principle or model for psychoanalytic education? *Psychologist–Psychoanalyst, 20*: 34–39.

Thompson, M. G. (2001). The enigma of honesty: The fundamental rule of psychoanalysis. *Free Associations, 8*: 390–434.

Thompson, M. G. (2004). *The Ethic of Honesty: The Fundamental Rule of Psychoanalysis*. Amsterdam: Editions Rodopi.

Time (1993). Is Freud dead? (cover illustration). *Time,* 29 November 1993, http://content.time.com/time/covers/0,16641,19931129,00.html, last accessed 19 October 2015.

Tocqueville, A. D. (1835). *Democracy in America*. H. C. Mansfield & D. Wintrhop (Ed. & trans.). Chicago, IL: University of Chicago Press, 2000.

Torsti, M. (1994). The feminine self and penis envy. *International Journal of Psycho-Analysis, 75*: 469–478.

Verhaeghe, P. (1997). *Does the Woman Exist: From Freud's Hysteric to Lacan's Feminine* (2nd edn). M. du Ry (trans.). London: Rebus Press.

Verhaeghe, P. (2009). *New Studies of Old Villains: A Radical Reconsideration of the Oedipus Complex*. New York, NY: Other Press.

Vivona, J. (2014). Introduction: How does talking cure? *Journal of the American Psychoanalytic Association, 62*: 1025–1027.

Wachtel, P. (2002). Psychoanalysis and the disenfranchised: From therapy to justice. *Psychoanalytic Psychology, 19*: 199–215.

Wachtel, P. (2010). One-person and two-person conceptions of attachment and their implications for psychoanalytic thought. *International Journal of Psychoanalysis, 91*: 561–581.

Waldron, J. (2012). *The Harm in Hate Speech.* Cambridge, MA: Harvard University Press.

Wallin, D. J. (2007). *Attachment and Psychotherapy.* New York, NY: Guilford.

Warburton, N. (2009). *Free Speech: A Very Short Introduction.* Oxford: Oxford University Press.

West Publishing (Eds.) (1983). *The Guide to American Law, Vol. 5.* St. Paul, MN: West Publishing.

Whitebook, J. (2008). Hans Loewald, psychoanalysis, and the project of autonomy. *Journal of the American Psychoanalytic Association, 56*: 1161–1187.

Wilson, F. (2014). Review of J. Rose, *Women in Dark Times. The Telegraph,* 26 August 2014, www.telegraph.co.uk/culture/books/bookreviews/11047876/Women-in-Dark-Times-by-Jacqueline-Rose-review-rigorously-argued.html, last accessed 5 October 2014.

Winnicott, D. W. (1945). Primitive emotional development. In: *Through Paediatrics to Psycho-analysis: Collected Papers* (pp. 145–156). New York, NY: Brunner/Mazel, 1992.

Winnicott, D. W. (1947). Hate in the countertransference. In: *Through Paediatrics to Psycho-Analysis: Collected Papers* (pp. 194–203). New York, NY: Brunner/Mazel, 1992.

Winnicott, D. W. (1949). Mind and its relation to the psyche-soma. In: *Through Paediatrics to Psycho-analysis: Collected Papers* (pp. 243–254). New York, NY: Brunner/Mazel, 1992.

Winnicott, D. W. (1950). Some thoughts on the meaning of the word "democracy." In: *Home Is Where We Start From* (pp. 239–259). New York, NY: W. W. Norton, 1986.

Winnicott, D. W. (1953). Transitional objects and transitional phenomena. In: *Playing and Reality* (pp. 1–25). New York, NY: Tavistock, 1971.

Winnicott, D. W. (1956). Primary maternal preoccupation. In: *Through Paediatrics to Psycho-analysis: Collected Papers* (pp. 300–305). New York, NY: Brunner/Mazel, 1992.

Winnicott, D. W. (1958a). Psycho-analysis and the sense of guilt. In: *The Maturational Processes and the Facilitating Environment* (pp. 15–28). New York, NY: International Universities Press, 1965.

Winnicott, D. W. (1958b). The capacity to be alone. In: *The Maturational Processes and the Facilitating Environment* (pp. 29–36). New York, NY: International Universities Press, 1965.

Winnicott, D. W. (1960). The theory of the parent-infant relationship. In: *The Maturational Processes and the Facilitating Environment* (pp. 37–55). New York, NY: International Universities Press, 1965.

Winnicott, D. W. (1963a). The development of the capacity for concern. In: *The Maturational Processes and the Facilitating Environment* (pp. 73–82). New York, NY: International Universities Press, 1965.

Winnicott, D. W. (1963b). Communicating and not communicating leading to a study of certain opposites. In: *The Maturational Processes and the Facilitating Environment* (pp. 179–192). New York, NY: International Universities Press, 1965.

Winnicott, D. W. (1964). This feminism (draft of a talk given to the Progressive League, 20 November 1964). In: *Home Is Where We Start From* (pp. 183–194). New York, NY: W. W. Norton, 1986.

Winnicott, D. W. (1965). *The Maturational Processes and the Facilitating Environment: Studies in the Theory of Emotional Development.* New York, NY: International Universities Press.

Winnicott, D. W. (1969a). The use of an object. *International Journal of Psycho-Analysis, 50*: 711–716.

Winnicott, D. W. (1969b). Freedom. In: *Home is Where We Start From* (pp. 228–238). New York, NY: W. W. Norton, 1986.

Winnicott, D. W. (1970). Creativity and its origins. In: *Playing and Reality* (pp. 65–85). New York, NY: Tavistock, 1971.

Winnicott, D. W. (1971a). Playing: A theoretical statement. In: *Playing and Reality* (pp. 38–52). New York, NY: Tavistock.

Winnicott, D. W. (1971b). Playing: The search for the self. In: *Playing and Reality* (pp. 53–64). New York, NY: Tavistock.

Winnicott, D. W. (1971c). The place where we live. In: *Playing and Reality* (pp. 104–110). New York, NY: Tavistock.

Winnicott, D. W. (1974). Fear of breakdown. *International Review of Psycho-Analysis, 1*: 103–107.

Wood, G. (1969). *The Creation of the American Republic, 1776–1787.* Chapel Hill, NC: University of North Carolina Press.

Wordsworth, W. (1818). Two addresses to the freeholders of Westmorland. In: A. B. Grosart (Ed.), *The Prose Works of William Wordsworh, Vol. 1: Political and Ethical* (pp. 212–259). London: Edward Moxon, 1876.

Wu, T. (2013). The right to evade regulation, remain unaccountable, and mock democracy: how corporations hijacked the first amendment. *The New Republic*, 10 June 2013: 34–39.

Young-Bruehl, E. (2011). Psychoanalysis and Social Democracy: A tale of two developments. *Contemporary Psychoanalysis, 47*: 179–203.

Yovel, Y. (1989). *Spinoza and Other Heretics, Volume 2: The Adventures of Immanence.* Princeton, NJ: Princeton University Press.

Zaretsky, E. (2004). *Secrets of the Soul: A Social and Cultural History of Psychoanalysis.* New York, NY: Random House.

Zinn, H. (1980). *The People's History of the United States.* New York, NY: HarperCollins, 2010.

INDEX

Is psychoanalysis a science, an art or a vagina metaphor?

—*Evan Malater*
Das Unbehagen *listserv, 5/29/14*